Tomislav Perko
1000 Days of Summer

How I traveled the world with almost no money

Author
Tomislav Perko

Title
1000 Days of Summer

Subtitle
How I traveled the world with almost no money

Editor
Maja Klarić

Translator
Ana Irena Hudi

Proofreader
Edward Alexander

Graphic design
Ivan Osman

Cover design
Goran Jokić, Norma Nardi

Cover photo
Antonio Oliveira

Photography editor
Caroline Perrier

Publisher
Tomislav Perko Ltd.

Printing studio
Kerschoffset Zagreb Ltd.

Place and year of publication
Zagreb, 2017.

A CIP catalogue record for this book is available in the Online Catalogue of the National and University Library in Zagreb as
000958721
ISBN 978-953-58752-4-6

Day 1000

"My last reason for traveling was to learn new things," I said. "It's true that I graduated from university and had a lot of theoretical knowledge, but contact with other travelers made me realize that I needed more practice. I lacked life experience, like a drop-out from the school of life. I needed to demonstrate more resourcefulness in different situations, more adaptability and more independence. I needed more freedom."

I would often wonder whether I would have gone to college in the first place if my mindset had been like this right after high school. I studied economics, which didn't interest me. It took me eight years to graduate, and I still can't say that I learned that much. With a few exceptions, managing a passing grade in every class was far more important than really mastering the subject.

Actually, truth be told, I probably wouldn't have gone to college at all. But now, looking back at it, I wouldn't change those years for anything in this world. Who knows if any of this would have happened in my life if I hadn't met some truly amazing people during my student years, who directly or indirectly contributed to the way I live my life now.

"Of course, as soon as I started to seriously consider traveling, I started to run into obstacles," I continued. "The first obstacle I had to face was fear. I'm not the bravest person in the world, and no matter how many times my Couchsurfing friends tried to convince me that the world is a wonderful and safe place, I was still skeptical. It wasn't easy to leave the comfort zone and go into the unknown by myself."

"And that's why I tried to overcome my fear in the most logical way possible - I invited my friends to join me. It would be safer, more fun, that sort of thing. However, if you've ever planned anything with your friends, then you know how it usually ends up."

I expected a reaction from my audience, and it duly followed. Most people laughed, and a few of them gave the person sitting next to them the evil eye. It was good to know that I wasn't the only one who got screwed over by their friends.

"In the last few days before our scheduled departure, they started canceling the trip, one after another," I explained. "They thought *traveling has taught me. If I hadn't learned this lesson then all the kilometers and countries I crossed, people I met and experiences I had would have been in vain.*

Best of all, traveling is totally beside the point here. There are a gazillion ways for you to grow (up), to be happier, and to be everything you always wanted to be. Traveling is my way to do it. It's no better nor worse than any other way.

But, this way is my way.

actually having a clue? How many conversations do we have just to prove we're right, even though we've never really thought about the other side of the story? How many times do we start fighting with others just because we can't agree to disagree? How many times do we focus on the differences between people rather than their similarities? This happens way too often.

And there's one more reason for me to travel. Because I'd decided that I didn't know anything. Because I'd decided I wanted to start over. Because I wanted to hear all sides of the story, not just one. I had decided I wanted to listen, not just to preach. I wanted to see the places, people and customs that at that point I only knew from what other people had told me.

While traveling, I realized that those other people had lied. They had done it to hide their ignorance, to cover their asses, to shape us the way they wanted us to be. Well, whoever they were, they managed it.

As I was leaving Croatia, everybody was telling me to be careful in Serbia. In Serbia, they were scaring me about Bulgarians. When I got to Bulgaria, I was told to watch my back in Turkey. Turkish people warned me about the Kurds, and the Kurds told me to watch out for Iranians. Iranians told me that Pakistanis were not to be trusted. And on and on it went. Did I get into any kind of trouble? Not in the slightest. In fact, over the past few years, the only trouble I had was at the main railway station in Zagreb, when I was attacked by Dinamo Zagreb soccer hooligans after they mistook me for being a member of Hajduk Split's fan group. Meanwhile, I'd traveled across thirty countries, hitchhiked, slept by the road, stayed at complete strangers' homes, crossed dangerous countries and gotten ill in some of the dirtiest places in the world, eaten in restaurants that would probably fail to meet basic hygiene standards in the Western world.

But here I am, alive and kicking. I'm happy. Sometimes I'm sad. I'm surrounded by good people. I get lonely from time to time. But, I am FREE. I'm free to do what I want, to follow my dreams, no matter how meaningless or pointless they might seem to others. And that's despite all those people who think I'm wasting my life away just because I'm not doing a regular job, because I don't have an apartment with a mortgage that I need to pay off over the next thirty years, because I don't care about somebody's country of origin, their looks, their religious beliefs or who they're sleeping with. This is what

Day 217

I opened my little black notebook and wrote down the thoughts that were running through my head.

More than ten days have passed since I went vegetarian. I feel fine, I don't miss meat at all, and I also watched some vegetarian documentaries focusing on health. Even though I'm not a fan of extremes and limitations, going vegetarian definitely makes sense.

All of this reminded me of the start of this way of life that I now practise and my first years at college. One day I woke up and told myself that I would defy all my attitudes, forget about everything I'd ever learned at home, at school, in church or from the media and start over from scratch. I wanted to question everything, take nothing for granted, readily changing all of the attitudes that had become engrained in me over the years. I wanted to be prejudice-free. I wanted to learn. I wanted to listen.

It was an eye-opening experience. I realized how wrong I had been about so many things, how my environment shaped me. Croatia is the best country in the world. You can't survive without eating meat. Believe what you read in the newspapers and see on television. Listen to your teachers and professors and don't challenge the facts you read in the textbooks.

That's bullshit. It's astonishing how many people know it all but actually have no idea about anything. They've either heard it somewhere or they don't know anybody who does things differently, so this is just how it should be. And being vegetarian is just one of a whole series of examples. I grew up eating meat every day, except on Fridays, when you should eat fish. Plus there were those two or three days a year when you had to wait until midnight before you could indulge in all the tasty treats you were forbidden from eating during the day.

When Chloe came for lunch at my parents' home and I told them she was a vegetarian, my dad told me with a smile on his face: "She can have some of the grass from the backyard, that's all we've got for vegetarians."

My father's such a hoot.

But seriously, how many things do we think we know, without

"My third reason was a quest for answers," I went on. "By hosting people from all over the world, I realized that the only reason why some of our attitudes and opinions differed was because we were born and raised in different environments. And I didn't like that. Why should I accept a certain point of view just because I was born in Croatia? I wanted to see things from a different perspective, pick up information from different parts of the world, and find my own answers, *my own truth*. I wanted to question everything I had ever learned. Regardless of my location, I wanted to understand my truth and learn what was right and what was wrong for me."

It's sad that, as we grow up, we are discouraged from exploring and seeing out things for ourselves, whereas taking things for granted is encouraged. They teach us to think uncritically and to accept ready-made facts - starting with our morality, religion and behavior. With the best of intentions, our parents raise us the way they think is right, and the vast majority of them don't seem to understand if we fail to follow their advice or if we don't turn out the way they'd hoped. They have their opinions on who you should hang out with, which school you should go to and what's right and what's wrong. Religion is based on a lack of questioning. You shall not eat from the tree of knowledge to uncover good and evil! Just follow the rules in the holy book, for our religion and its way is the only way! You're required to learn from the textbooks you're given at school, in which they impose on you facts that vary from one country to next, depending on when they were written. If you dare to disagree with what's written then you'll get an F. And they keep asking "when are you graduating, when are you going to get a job, when are you going to get married, when are you going to buy your own house/apartment?" They train us to all be the same, forgetting that we're all unique.

"I knew that staying in places that are completely different than the place where I grew up, and hanging out with people from different cultures would help me do that. And I knew that traveling would get me there."

Most people laughed. It was a good sign. Experience has taught me that people come to my lectures because they want to hear an interesting story about a guy who traveled halfway around the globe almost for free. But, no matter how interesting the story, sitting still for an hour and a half takes a lot of mental effort, and the easiest way to keep the audience engaged is to occasionally make them laugh and smile.

"Likewise, if you're the one who's traveling, you can stay with other people completely free of charge," I went on. "Once I discovered Couchsurfing - or CS as we sometimes call it, I became crazy for it, and in just one year, I hosted over 150 people from all over the world in my small rented apartment in Zagreb. Those people truly inspired me."

"Before I met them, traveling was never really my cup of tea. Clearly, I would daydream about traveling, I wanted to do it, and I'd read the books and watched documentaries, but it all seemed far too distant and unrealistic. I simply couldn't relate to the people playing the starring roles in those stories. I thought you had to be very brave, special, daring, or - in brief - you had to be everything I'm not. I also thought you had to have a lot of money, financial security, parental support - which were all the things I didn't have. But, through Couchsurfing I could host real people in my own living room; they were ordinary people my age, who could tell me first-hand stories about their adventures over a pint of beer or a joint, dropping in that same inevitable sentence: If you want to, you can travel the world too.

This was the first reason why I started to seriously consider traveling."

"The second reason was sheer curiosity on my part," I continued, changing slides. The photo showed the open road in Australia. It looked like a good metaphor for curiosity. "From the moment we're born, we're all curious. We always want to know what's around the corner, we want to explore, and try new things. The stories that my guests were telling me only made me wonder even more. Especially whilst I looked at the map of the world on my living-room wall, I began to realize just how small and barely visible Croatia really was. I wanted to travel, I wanted to explore and see what the big wide world has out there. And I knew that travel would satiate my curiosity."

swer.

Who knows, maybe this lecture would transform somebody else's life too.

"So why did I start traveling in the first place?" I posed a rhetorical question and pressed the button on the remote control.

A photograph of me sitting on a wooden bench somewhere in the South of Australia with a pensive, faraway look appeared on the screen. Every photo I show in my lectures has its own story, which I could retell for hours. And yet I had to rattle through a hundred of them in less than an hour and a half.

"My story started some five or six years ago, when I was leading a completely different lifestyle," I said. "I was working as a stockbroker in a Zagreb-based brokerage firm, wore suits and ties to work and made good money. I excelled at work, my life priorities were set around career progression and fattening up my bank account, going out to fancy places and living in comfort. But then came 2008 and with it the financial crisis and a stock market crash."

"In just a few weeks, I lost everything I'd spent years accumulating: my job, my career, my money. I found myself more than $30.000 in debt. Depressively thinking over and over again about what had brought me to this seemingly hopeless situation, I realized that I'd got my priorities all wrong. If I'd spent years building up something that could collapse like a house of cards in just a few weeks then maybe I'd been building up the wrong thing. Maybe I should have built something a bit more solid. Maybe I should have collected experiences, rather than material stuff. This is how I started to think about traveling."

"The first big step toward all this was discovering Couchsurfing," I moved on to the next slide, showing some ten people in my rented apartment, standing in front of a world map that was prominently displayed on a wall. They were all smiles as they pointed their fingers to their countries of origin on the map. "How many of you have already heard about this website?" I asked the audience. Almost all of them raised their hand.

"For those of you who don't yet know, Couchsurfing is a website and online community that makes it possible for you to open up your home to other travelers for free. They can sleep on your couch, in a guest room, on the floor in your apartment or, who knows, maybe even in your own bed."

Day 1000

"Tomislav Perko, travel writer from Zagreb, has just returned from his 1000-day trip around the world. He crossed five continents on just a few euros a day. He hitchhiked, slept in strangers' homes, busked with a guitar, worked odd jobs, volunteered, and even sailed across the Indian Ocean on a 13-meter sailboat. He spent some time with the police at the Iran-Pakistan border, meditated at a Thai Buddhist temple, ended up in a hippie village in Australia, visited the most beautiful island in the world, lived with Maasai warriors in Africa, pondered the meaning of life in the company of shamans in the Amazon rainforest..."

As I listened to the announcement about my lecture at the city library in Split, on Croatia's coast, I was looking down at the ground, smiling. Whenever somebody sums up everything I did over the past one thousand days in just a few sentences, I still find it too unbelievable to be true. If I didn't know that they were talking about me, I would think that the lecture was going to be given by the most interesting person in the world and that we would hear about adventures requiring incredible courage and willpower. I would think that this person had figured out what life was all about and that I would give everything in the world to make my life just as fulfilling.

But I knew they were talking about me - so all I could do was smile.

"When people hear where I've been and what I've done over the past few years, most of them wish for a similar lifestyle," I began with my well-rehearsed introduction. "Most people think it's something sensational, difficult and almost impossible. They think you need to be very brave and resourceful, and that this is too much for an ordinary person. The purpose of this lecture is to prove you wrong, to show you that it's not so difficult and that most of you can travel this way if you really want to."

I was a little bit nervous, but was enjoying myself. I liked seeing curiosity flare up in people's eyes as I tried to explain to them how it was possible to travel around the world *my way*, almost for free. I remember a few years back when I had that same look in my eyes, searching for the answer to the very same question. And I knew that my life had changed irreversibly for the better once I found the an-to something you do like". It seems that Tomislav wrote this book not so much from an inner drive to write and create the art of the written word, but from a need to sincerely retell his story and hence encouraging the reader, at least one of them, to discover what they like and to dedicate themselves to that, to live their life to the fullest, to find a way in which the world can benefit from them. This book's greatest value lies in this selfless sharing. Just like his first book, this is not a typical travelogue, nor does it pretend to be one. The reader cannot rely on it as they could a map or a travel guide, but here, instead, they will find a number of things that will inspire them to set off traveling, to experience it for themselves, to look at the world through their own eyes, which at the end of the day is more important than any official information. We can get where we want to be without a map, but it's not worth doing it if your heart isn't in it.

Maja Klarić

PREFACE

At the very end of the forward to Tomislav Perko's first book *1000 Days of Spring*, the Croatian travel writer Hrvoje Šalković concluded that it has only one flaw: "You will inevitably want to read the sequel to this warm and interesting story". Two years later, we are holding Tomislav's attempt at finally correcting this "flaw" in our hands - and since he did it in such an honest and witty way (just as was the case with the first book) the reader is undoubtedly set to embark on another fun-filled trip.

If this book was just about that - the hilarious adventures of a former stockbroker who decided to travel around the world, venturing up a creek without a paddle - it would have been quite enough to find its way to those people who yearn for a similar change of lifestyle. It already became clear in his first book that Tomislav's quest was indeed one for freedom. After all, we all want to be free and are in search of a way to make that happen. Traveling was his way, always sticking his thumb out by the side of some road, with no big plans, heading into the unknown, which is surely the most beautiful place to go.

Tom keeps on modestly reminding us that he is not a writer and asks us not to expect too much from his book. He does not want us to resent him because of anything, telling us not to hate the book the way he hated it at the very beginning, until he learned how to put his experiences into words. Anyway, how could we resent a man who just wants to tell his story by writing this book and to encourage readers to bravely start creating their own story, whether it be through travelling, hobbies or something else entirely - what it is exactly is completely beside the point. The only step that truly matters is the first step, the one that gets us up out of our sofas and into the world, after which everything takes care of itself, as attested to by this book that you are about to start reading.

Just like Spring, *1000 Days of Summer* does not list the distances traveled nor ho(s)tels' addresses, it does not serve as a travel guide, but instead shows us what it looks like in real life through the example of an "ordinary" man. It does not tell us which is the right way to freedom and how long it will take, but it tells us where we can find its beginning, directing us to a place from which we can start looking. Even if, sometimes, you have to "do what you don't like to get

for you.

1000 DAYS OF SUMMER

HOW I TRAVELED THE WORLD WITH ALMOST NO MONEY

TOMISLAV PERKO

Tomislav Perko Ltd.
Zagreb, 2017.

they couldn't do it because of the money, university exams, their parents or partners. All of them made some sort of excuse and I soon realized that I couldn't count on them. I came to understand very quickly that, if I were to wait for the perfect moment to do something or for the perfect moment to start travelling, I would never leave Zagreb."

Fear can be useful if we're dealing with our survival instincts, or if it warns us of upcoming situations that we need to avoid - death, injury, or unpleasant social contacts. Nobody's saying that's not the case. But I was afraid of traveling, which was something I've never experienced before. How was that possible? Why was it so? Was fear sticking its nose where it didn't belong? Had it eventually become redundant, useless and harmful? Was it something irrational?

I thought about my life a bit, wondering how many times I hadn't done something exciting just because I was afraid, just because I didn't know what would be the final result of this move. How many times had I regretted simply not trying something, without even knowing what I was getting myself into?

It had happened way too many times.

"Once I realized that I couldn't count on my friends, I had to change tactics," I went on. "The time had come to stop thinking. I told myself that I wasn't going to have negative thoughts about what could go wrong while traveling. I said to myself: get going and try it yourself, see if there's anything to be afraid of. Of course, as soon as I tried it, as soon as I really started traveling for the first time, I realized that living on the road was no scarier than living at home."

A fear of the unknown is an inherent part of our nature, no matter how attractive and interesting it may be. However, besides this innate fear, I think we need to blame our environment and the media for the most part for our irrational fears. No wonder we're afraid to travel when we're constantly bombarded with negative news stories from abroad and when a single negative experience resonates stronger than a hundred positive ones.

There has been just one way to test whether something is true. We should go and try it for ourselves.

Is there a risk? Of course there is. But risk is a part of our everyday lives, whether you're in Africa or just crossing the street in front of the house where you grew up. Your whole life is a huge risk that you need to dare to take. Play with it and live it to the fullest.

Especially since in most cases it turns out that the only risk is the one in our heads.

Day 92

My alarm rang at 5:32. I turned it off.

"Let's sleep some more," I winged to Caro as she woke up next to me in the tent. This was the first time that I had used the tent on this trip, hoping to justify lugging almost five pounds around on my back for the whole three months. Apart from that, this was also the first time on this trip that I'd woken up to the sound of my mobile phone alarm. I hate that sound more than anything else. I'd come up with my definition of quality of life a long time ago: the less often I wake up to the sound of an alarm, the better my life is.

"Get up, you!" she said firmly, or maybe she was just a little less lazy and spoilt. "Let's watch the sunrise. Who knows when you'll get another chance to watch it over the ocean?"

I reluctantly obeyed, washing my face and following her to the beach.

We stayed in a camp a dozen or so miles from Puri, with one of the few active couchsurfers in this part of India. How we decided to come here is another story. While we were still in Nepal, we'd come across a map of India and, of all the places, only one was highlighted - Puri. We didn't know who the map belonged to and we knew even less about what had made them highlight Puri, but we took the hint and bought a ticket to this East Indian city that was about six hundred miles away.

I liked the place right from the outset. It was isolated, uninhabited and quiet, and a fifteen-minute walk would take you to an endless sandy beach where all you would only occasionally see was a stray cow or a dead sea turtle, nothing more. We weren't alone in the camp, with other people from the USA, Italy, Hungary, Sweden, Spain, and of course India keeping us company. They were organizing a surfing festival that would be held in a few months' time.

Not much was going on, the days were passing by as we spent time telling stories over a campfire, with homegrown pot that we'd bought in the government-approved *Bhang shop* in Puri. Weed was legal over there and it was really cheap - you could get fifty grams of dark green bud for little more than six dollars.

All things considered, there were enough reasons for us to like the place.

"Well, your sunrise is really great," I said mockingly once we'd arrived on the beach and were met with a blanket of fog through which we couldn't see a thing.

I didn't want to waste the dawn on the beach, so I stripped down to my underwear and jumped into the sea. It took less than ten seconds before a massive wave crashed into me and cast me back out onto the beach.

"You've obviously never swum in open water before," my companion said with a smile as she changed into her bathing suit.

"You need to treat the ocean and waves with great respect," she started her lecture as we carefully crossed the breakpoint, diving under the coming waves and floating safely some hundred feet from the shore. "Everywhere in the world, the ocean strikes fear into the hearts of people living near it because they know that they're throwing themselves at its mercy every time they go into the water, fully aware that if it ever came to a fight then they couldn't win against the ocean. The ocean will always have the last say."

I liked what I heard - her words could easily apply to life in general. Most people treat life just like that, they don't dare to enter a fight because they fear they'll lose.

"And now I'll teach you how to *bodysurf*," she smiled. "Remember, if a wave gets too big, just catch your breath and relax. It'll eventually let you resurface."

She showed me how waves were formed, explaining how important it was to catch just the right moment, when to start swimming to shore and how to catch a wave right before it broke. She showed me how to make the most out of dangerous waves and turn them to our own advantage, how to collaborate with them.

"Oh yeah, that's it," I thought. There are some people out there, very few of them, who at the same time manage to respect the ocean, but also challenge it. They play with it. They wade out into deep waters, wait for the perfect wave, looking for a way to become one with the ocean and indulge themselves in the pure pleasure of surfing. And they know that plenty of times they're going to fail. The wave might be too big, their timing might be wrong, sometimes they'll react too late, or too early, and the wave will make them pay for this, tossing them into the shallows as if they were mere grains of sand. But they'll try again, until they finally make it.

But even then, after they succeed at it, they should never forget who's the boss, who sets the rules and the tempo. Our task is to understand this, but not to give up, to be flexible and always find a new way to work together, to join forces to achieve our common goal.

This is life. Life is like an ocean.

Anyway, Puri is one of the four most sacred sites for Hindu pilgrims in India, along with Varanasi, Mathuru and Kanyakumari, mostly because of the Jagannath Temple that every committed Hindu is expected to visit at least once in their lifetime. As non-Hindus are banned from entering the temple, Caro and I went to nearby Konark to visit the Sun Temple that was built some 750 years ago.

Just like so many times before, the journey to our next destination was as interesting as the place itself, if not even more interesting.

"Are you alright?" a smiling driver asked us as he pulled his motorcycle up alongside to us. His passenger was smiling too, and then another motorcycle with a passenger stopped behind them.

"We're fine, thanks," we replied. "We're just waiting for our transport to Konark."

We were waiting either for a cheap local bus that was passing every half hour, or a smaller, somewhat more expensive tuk-tuk. We didn't consider hitchhiking as we could afford a ride, and quite frankly, we weren't expecting that somebody would bother to stop anyway.

"You can come with us if you want!" said the smiling guy, cheerfully nodding his head. As we smiled back and gave an affirmative nod, he asked his friend to hop over onto the other motorcycle, and sat us behind himself. With the wind in our hair, this was unparalleled happiness - it was the first time I'd hitched a ride on a motorbike!

The entrance fee to the temple was 10 rupees for locals, and 250 rupees for everybody else. This was standard practice in India and in this part of the world in general. Honestly, I don't know what to make of it. Does it count as a form of discrimination? Is it fair to be charged a lot more if you're rich, i.e. white? What about wealthy Indians and poor foreigners - do they fall within this? What rules apply to them?

Since we knew that the Sun Temple was one of the Seven Wonders of India and a world heritage site, we dug deep into our pockets and paid for the ticket. Let's learn something about the local culture.

The temple didn't leave us disappointed. As its name suggests, the temple is dedicated to the Sun God Surya. Its stone carvings depicted a number of scenes from everyday life, but what immediately caught the attention of a cultural ignoramus like myself were of course the erotic sculptures showing men, women, couples, group sex and the like. It was interesting to see such a direct display of sexual activities in such a conservative country.

Besides the beautiful temple and vivid sexual images, we were the biggest attraction that day. Every couple of minutes locals would ask to take a photo with us. We weren't sure what exactly made us so interesting to them, but we happily pandered to their whims and posed with a smile.

In moments like this, you begin to realize that this is what it must feel like to be a celebrity in the West, when everybody's watching you as you walk down the street, when people make comments about you, sometimes being openly judgemental toward you, or when everyone wants some of your time, always expecting you to be constantly happy and smiling.

Living in a voyeuristic society, where all kinds of celebrities and their private lives are in the public spotlight, traveling to this part of the world just to see what it feels like is something we should all do. Maybe then we would stop caring about those things. Maybe then we would instead focus on more important things, and invest our time and energy into our own lives and those closest to us.

Maybe then we would live our lives, rather than just watch others do it.

Day 1000

"Another obstacle I had to face was being broke," I carried on with my lecture. "How was I going to travel if I didn't have any money, I kept asking myself and the travelers passing through my apartment. All of them were telling me that there were three main expenses while traveling: transportation, accommodation and food/drink, so if you managed to lower those costs to the bare minimum, living on the road could be cheaper than living at home."

The faces in my audience were skeptical. It sounded way too simple. If it was so easy then wouldn't everyone be traveling? Their instincts were telling them that in real life there were also other costs, unexpected problems that may arise while on the road.

I had used this argument on my own guests, but they all had the same answer: there were always unexpected costs and surprises, but these were things you could only think about once they occurred. There was no need to think about them in advance. It was actually better to be unprepared for some things.

"As for transportation, I mostly hitchhiked," I said, pressing the button on the remote control and changing the slide. Not just because it was the cheapest and fastest way of getting around, but also because it meant that you experienced something great - it turned traveling from point A to point B into an adventure before you'd even reached your destination. The adventure didn't start when you got there, but as soon as you left your apartment, while you were still looking for a pickup spot, when you stuck out your thumb. If you opt for hitchhiking, you never know what lies ahead, which route you're going to take, who you're going to meet, what kind of conversations you're going to have, and you don't even know where you'll end up."

"Now I'll show you a short video on hitchhiking, so that you see what it looks like in real life," I said and started the video.

I had a few sips of water, watching the shots I had filmed over the past few years. Hitchhiking can sometimes be boring, you're often very tired, hungry and thirsty - but you've got to keep up a smile. Who would want to pick up a grumpy hitchhiker?

However, everything will be awesome in the end. You might be waiting for hours in the unbearable heat, you might see only a single car after waiting for hours, but when somebody stops and offers you a ride in your direction you forget all that negative stuff and all that matters is that present moment and the road ahead of you.

This is just like life. We grow tired, hungry, thirsty, and sick, it seems like there's no way out. And then something good happens and we forget about our worries. Everything negative from the past becomes unimportant, the present moment and what lies ahead is all that matters. Everything falls into place.

You know the famous saying: *Everything will be okay in the end. If it's not okay, it's not the end*.

Every car that pulls over for you, every mile that you travel, it fills you with a sense of accomplishment. You feel as if you're completing mini projects, several times a day. The feelings may vary from despair to ecstasy, round and around.

"Hitchhiking isn't the only way to save on your transportation costs," I said after we finished the clip. "You can walk or ride a bike, and you can also work in exchange for the transportation, just like I worked my way around the Indian Ocean from Australia to Africa. I didn't have to pay a thing, but I had to raise and lower the sails, keep watch at night, and I was cooking for the first two days, until the captain relieved me of this duty. I wonder why..."

And there it was: the first lie in my lecture.

The captain actually never relieved me of doing the cooking, I had to perform my culinary responsibilities during the whole trip just like the rest of the crew. But I knew that the remark would give people a laugh so I repeated it in all of my talks.

Every time I told that lie, I came to realize again and again how easy it was to cross the invisible line and reshape my story in order to make myself look brave(r), so that I could evoke the amazing things from my travels, elicit a sigh or envy from my audience. How would anyone ever know? After all, in most situations I was the only witness, and even if there were others, would anyone ever manage to find a person X in the middle of nowhere who would reveal the truth to them?

This is a thin line and you need to be careful. The truth is, you can benefit from it, your ego will be boosted, and you'll feel cool. But this feeling doesn't last long. At the end of the day, when you're alone with yourself and you have nobody to boast to, you'll become painfully aware of your lie and your conscience will tell you that you're a liar.

Once you experience this, you'll be even more careful about crossing that line.

It doesn't mean you can't play with it, like I did about cooking duties on the ship. You can tell a little white lie if you make everyone aware by your facial expression that this is a small, sweet, innocent lie. The audience will accept it and laugh. And is there anything more pleasurable than making two hundred people laugh? I don't think so.

Maybe making three hundred people laugh.

"The second largest expense is accommodation," I said, switching the slides. "On my travels I mostly used Couchsurfing, not only because it was free, but also because it made me feel like a local wherever I went, and let me observe it from a totally different perspective. I wasn't limited to ho(s)tel rooms, organized tours, famous landmarks and suggestions from printed guides. I had a local guide in each city in the form of my host. I explored their city with them, I went to the places they normally went to, and spent time with their friends and families. I had a feeling that I was living the local life, no matter how short-lived it was.

The truth was that I didn't really care much about the cities and places where my hosts were taking me: I was more interested in people. The stories I shared with them. I wanted to learn new facts, look at life in a different way, get inspired by them, find the desire to explore further, to learn even more. The inspiration that I gave them was also important. After years of being a host and listening to my guests' stories, I now took on the role of a story-teller and motivator. I enjoyed this role so much. Just like I enjoyed standing in front of the audience and talking about the past one thousand days of my life.

"Of course, there's an alternative for Couchsurfing, too," I said. "Sometimes I would bring a tent and camp, other times I slept in a park on a self-inflating mattress, in a sleeping bag."

I brought this up sporadically because for me these were the alternatives for an alternative - CS. If I had a choice, and this was almost always the case, I would always choose to be with other people, on a warm and cozy couch or in bed.

"Another alternative is to work for a few hours a day in exchange for accommodation, and quite often for a meal too. Volunteering is a brilliant idea when you grow tired of traveling and constant movement, when you need a base or when you want to learn a bit more about a place, culture or language. Or when you fall in love. With a place, of course."

I got to know my favorite places through volunteering and staying there for at least a few weeks. I'm not sure whether I stayed volunteering because I liked the place or whether I liked the place because I was volunteering there and so spent more time there than in some other places.

Often, the point of traveling is not traveling per se, it's not the movement, the changing places - but quite the opposite - it's staying somewhere new, making contacts with the locals and creating the feeling of being at home.

"*House sitting* is yet another alternative," I explained. "Some people don't want to leave their homes empty when they're away for a few days, weeks or months. They do it for different reasons: they're afraid of burglars, they have pets that need feeding or a garden that needs watering, so they place an ad on the Internet looking for someone to look after their house, in other words, they look for a *house sitter* who benefits a lot from this by eliminating accommodation costs."

"Last but not least, *home exchange* is an equally good alternative. Let's say you want to visit a destination, but instead of paying for accommodation, you offer your own home and exchange it with somebody else's for a given period - for a few days, weeks or months - there are no rules."[1]

"The third largest expense while traveling is food and drink costs," I said. "In more expensive countries, I limited myself to food from the supermarket because it was the cheapest option, and I often cooked with my hosts. When you sleep in other people's homes, the advantage is that you can always use a kitchen so you don't have to carry kitchen appliances around with you. Besides, you also have a washing machine at your disposal, so you can wash your clothes every week or once in two weeks and further reduce the amount of clothing that you take on your trip."

After all, traveling on a small budget is the best way to rid yourself of excessive weight. Each day you're on the move, you have no money to waste so you only buy food only when you're hungry (and not when you're just bored) and you don't eat processed junk, but

---

[1] *the biggest website for home exchange is www.homeexchange.com*

meals prepared from fruit, vegetables and other local specialities.

In my first six months of traveling around the world I lost over forty pounds and I've never felt better, even though I didn't really plan to lose so much weight. Nevertheless, I put it all back on again after I returned, thanks to the abundance of food in my mom's kitchen.

"Apart from cooking and buying food in the supermarket, I also tried *dumpster diving*, which means rooting through garbage containers," I changed a slide and looked at the horrified faces in my audience. "Although many feel this is too extreme, you need to realize that nowadays between 40 and 50 percent of the food that gets produced is thrown away on a regular basis. For example, after the supermarket shuts for the day, they all throw away a lot of food that won't be on shelves the following day. Discarded food that is near its expiration date, slightly bruised fruit and vegetables or pieces with small blemishes are often chucked out. This's why people in various places take this food directly from the supermarket or wait until it's discarded in the dumpster and then take it. Most of it is still in its packaging and perfectly edible."

I knew that, no matter how much time I spend talking about dumpster diving, trying to bring the concept closer to the audience, almost nobody would understand it, let alone try something like this. It's strange that in our culture, dumpster diving seems disgusting, but at the same time food waste is considered completely normal and is widely accepted.

"As far as drinking costs go, stay away from the bars and restaurants, and instead hang out at apartments, parks and benches. This is one way to save a load of money". And this was the last trick I had to share with my audience, the last piece of advice I could give them about traveling around the world with almost no money. Everything I said up until this point could be easily reduced to three concepts: common sense, using your logic and being a little bit resourceful.

Sometimes I felt a bit silly giving these pieces of banal advice. On the other hand, a few years back I craved such information, until I decided to take matters into my own hands and try it all out for myself.

"Besides being able to travel cheaply, you can also earn some money while traveling," I changed to the slide showing me playing a guitar in the center of Eskişehir in Turkey. "If you're talented, you can make some money on the street. Playing the guitar, making bracelets, juggling - all of these can be a source of income. I'm not a musician, I can only play a few songs, but I noticed it didn't really matter. You need to have a story and get yourself noticed. This is why I always carried around a cardboard sign with a short text about myself, where I was coming from, what I was doing there, and why I needed money. Because they're curious, people will always take a look at your cardboard sign, maybe relate with you, and perhaps give you a penny or two if they have some spare, a sandwich if you're hungry, a drink if you're thirsty, or offer you a ride to the next city if that's what you're asking for, or something similar. You won't get rich as a street performer, but you can earn enough money for that day in just a few hours.

I thought about this for a moment and realised that taking my guitar and playing on the street in Croatia, in Zagreb, in the city where I was born, had never really crossed my mind. There must be a link between traveling and defeating your fears and the things you normally feel uncomfortable with - trying new things is a lot easier in an unknown environment.

"If you find yourself in a rich country, you can even find a real job", I switched the slide which showed myself standing in the street in Brisbane wearing a reflective vest. "For example, travelling across Australia, I worked as a professional traffic diverter..."

Day 286

"Get in, lad," cheerfully said a hefty, tattooed guy in a pick-up truck full of all manner of tools. "But, I can only take you to the city exit."

"That's just what I need!" I replied smiling and jumped in. "It's never easy to find a way out of big cities."

"Where are you going?" He began with the standard question.

"I'm heading north!" I said vaguely.

"What's going on up there?" he carried on cheerfully.

"I've no idea, to be honest," I replied with equal good cheer. "But it's warmer than in the south, and I also think I could go for a long hitchhiking ride across the country."

"Be careful," he said a bit less cheerfully. "You must have heard of Ivan Milat."

That name had been haunting me ever since I got to Australia, and almost every conversation I had about hitchhiking ended with this serial killer of hitchhikers who was — as chance would have it — of Croatian origins.

The guy killed at least seven backpackers in the early 1990s - some of them were shot in the head, some of them were stabbed, and some of them decapitated. He buried all of them in the forest between Sydney and Canberra. And he may have been involved in more murders, but since the bodies have never been found, no further cases have been brought against him, but it's not as if this was decisive in reaching the verdict. He is serving seven consecutive life sentences.

A horror film *Wolf Creek* was partially based on this terrible story.

"Yeah, I've heard of him," I replied, with a deep sigh, not giving away that the serial killer is actually my compatriot. "But I was told all kinds of stories while hitchhiking through Iraq, Iran and Pakistan... A story about a serial killer won't scare me off."

"You're kidding me!" my driver exclaimed, making me jump! "You hitchhiked through all those countries?"

"I did," I replied. "It's not as scary as it seems."

"But what do you do for living, if you don't mind me asking?" He was curious.

"I travel," I replied. "First of all, I travel on a budget, living on a few dollars a day, so I don't need a lot of money. Secondly, I write and publish my stories, I also have some sponsors, and I earn some money doing all kinds of jobs while traveling."

"It sounds fucking amazing!" My cheerful driver was thrilled.

"But it's not always so easy. Ever since I came to Australia I've been trying to find a job but without any luck."

"A job?" He threw a glance at me. "What kind of a job?"

My heart started beating faster. I was sending subtle hints to almost every person I met in Australia about looking for a job, hoping that one of these conversations would get me somewhere. None of those conversations yielded any success. As a rule, the people I spoke with either said that nowadays it was hard to find a job in their country or changed the subject and started talking about something else.

This was the first time that I felt the conversation could lead somewhere after I brought it up. Maybe it would even yield results.

"Any job," I replied, trying to stay cool and not to reveal my growing hope that he might help me in some way. "I have a Master's degree in economics, but I doubt it would be any use over here. I did all kinds of jobs while traveling, from working in a restaurant in Turkey to hoeing fields in Bangladesh. I'm hard-working, I learn quickly, but it's not worth much when I don't have an Australian work permit."

I went quiet for a moment and looked at him through the corner of my eye. He didn't say anything either. He focused on the road, thinking.

"Are you afraid of heights?" he asked me after a while.

"I jumped out of a plane a few days ago," I replied, wisely avoiding a direct answer. "Why?"

"You're not heading north, mate!" He just laughed. "Tomorrow you're starting to work for me!"

"You must be kidding!" I exclaimed. "But I don't have a work permit?"

"I won't tell anyone if you don't," he winked at me, turned up the volume on the radio and turned left at a traffic light.

I kept quiet, looked out the window and smiled.

We picked his son up from school, went to the supermarket, where he bought a trolley full of groceries, and he told me about the accommodation and food that would be provided. He then dropped me off at his house in the suburbs of Brisbane, which had wallabies, the smaller relatives of the most famous Australian wild animal, the kangaroo, bouncing around his backyard. He helped me bring my stuff into one of the rooms, gave me clean linen, made us all a huge dinner and just told me: "Set your alarm for 6 a.m."

I was overjoyed. I had no idea what he did. I didn't have a clue about my position, what kind of a job I'd just landed or what my potential fear of heights had to do with anything. But I really didn't care. I didn't dare to ask him anything, because I didn't want to screw something up.

Day 1000

I was proud of this job, and even named it myself. A professional traffic diverter. PTD. It sounded like one of those pointless government departments that were there for dropping buckets into empty wells.

"My job mainly consisted of telling people to turn right rather than left," I explained. "Just in case they were blind and couldn't see the signs."

My job wasn't only to divert the traffic, I actually did anything that was necessary. Duane, my employer, was a decorator. He was painting the façade of a large hotel in the middle of Brisbane. I held the ladder for him, helped him paint the wall, and here and there had to climb the scaffold and work a few feet up there. I realized that I was still afraid of heights, but I didn't sweat it. I managed to ignore my fear.

"I was making twenty dollars an hour on this job," I said. "And on top of that my accommodation and food costs were covered."

This caused quite a stir, and it happens every time I mention this sum during my lectures. Unfortunately, in Croatia, a country in which most people work for peanuts, earning twenty dollars A DAY for doing a full-time job and can consider themselves lucky if they get paid on time, this stir is to be expected. This is the minimum wage in Australia.

"It took me just thirteen days working on that job to pay off eight months of traveling. So, I traveled for eight months, arrived to Australia, worked for 13 days and managed to break even."

If my talk had ended at this point, I would consider my mission accomplished. I had told people something about myself, showed them I was just like them and that traveling didn't have to be expensive. I had proved to them that traveling didn't need to be just traveling, but that they could fit their job into it, stay somewhere random and live there from day to day.

"Besides being a street performer and searching for a job, you can also write," I carried on. "Today everybody has a laptop and internet connection, so you just need to find a way to tell your unique story - through blogs, photographs, videos... I became a travel writer by accident, and it all started with a Facebook profile. After seeing the photos from my first travels, my friends advised me to make something out of it because they liked it and felt as if they were traveling with me. This is how my Facebook page, blog, YouTube channel, and website came to life, and my book has recently been published. You can make a living as a writer, find sponsors if your blog is popular and stuff like that."

I changed the slide. The introduction was over and it was time to tell them what it was like to travel around the world. Time for the practical part.

"Let me tell you something about my trip around the world. I've just returned from it," I pointed at the map of the world which had a route marked on it. "I've called it *A Thousand Days of Summer*, and my main idea was to travel around the world for three years, following the summer. I crossed five continents, about thirty countries and one ocean, and it all started on a summer day at a tollbooth on the eastern edge of Zagreb. I had only two things on my mind - the east, which was the direction I wanted to go, and visas for Iran, Pakistan and India. Everything else was pure improvisation.

"I stuck my thumb out and set out for Belgrade."

Day 1

I was awake even before the alarm went off at 6:04.

I didn't feel great. I was hangover from all the beers I'd had the night before, my right hand hurt, and my heart was filled with an excruciating pain. Even though I was setting off on a long-anticipated trip, I felt like I was betraying those who loved me the most. I had a feeling that my quest for freedom was going to bring sadness to everyone but myself.

There's a thin line between being selfish and deciding to follow your dreams. Sometimes this line can even be invisible. If you had to make a choice between two things, and you know that the choice will have the opposite effect for the two sides, which way would you go? Should you please yourself, not give a fuck about anybody else, or should you try to please others at your own expense?

By embarking on this trip, I had decided to please myself and pursue my own desires. It wasn't that I didn't care about anybody else, but because I really believed that I had no other option. I could have stayed, but it would have left a bad taste in my mouth forever. I would have always wondered what would have happened if I had gone. I would have blamed myself if I'd stayed. I would have blamed my parents for talking me into that. I would have blamed everybody around me for constraining me.

As selfishness was my conscious choice, there was still hope that everything would fall into place someday. There was still hope that I would meet my needs, find what I was looking for, create what I wanted to create, and, finally, please other people, especially my parents, by either coming back or living a more peaceful life.

If my kid told me one day that he or she was going to hitchhike around the world, how would I feel? I'd be sad, worried, scared and frustrated. I would feel helpless. But would I want someone to forget about the happiness, challenges, and freedom that they wanted so badly?

No. I'd never be able to forgive myself for that, no matter how bad my child's decision made me feel.

And that's why I decided to leave. I had a theory that in the long run everything was going to be okay, both for me and my parents. I believed in a positive outcome.

I turned on my laptop. An email was waiting for me. It was from Tanja.

Tick-tock, my luv.
It's time for you to go and change the world.
As you hum 'Here I go again on my own', remember you're not alone.
Keep your eyes and heart wide open, everything else will fall into place.

Luv, T.

I also read another email, one that I had received the night before.

I turned off my laptop and went back to bed. I closed my eyes, trying to put my thoughts and feelings in order. To no avail.

I went over to my backpack, put it on my back, still nervous. It was too heavy. I took everything out of it, thinking about what I could ditch. I got rid of a couple of t-shirts and some underwear and socks. I decided to only keep one long-sleeved shirt - after all, I'd be following the summer, so I wouldn't really need them.

Filip and Gabi woke up, we had breakfast in silence and got into the car. We headed east, toward the rising sun, and this would be my last chance to see the streets of Zagreb for a very long time. Sljeme, the peak that stands above Zagreb, was there. How would I find my way in the big wide world without Sljeme showing me which way was north? I wondered if I was going to miss all this. Would I find what I was looking for? Would this travel around the world make sense in the end?

We were getting to the tollbooths, hugging and saying goodbye. I took my backpack, walking to the very same place where my first hitchhiking trip to Sofia began two years ago. Things had changed, but they'd also still stayed the same. I was standing by the road, sticking my right thumb out, trying to smile and waiting for someone to pull over. It had never happened to me that I would be waiting in vain.

Ten minutes later, an elderly man pulled in for me since he was going to Slavonski Brod, a town that was in my direction. I jumped into the car, fastened my seatbelt, took a deep breath of the Zagreb air, and didn't turn back.

Now there was no turning back.

Day 1000

"The first country I visited was Serbia," I carried on with my presentation.

I looked across the lecture hall, trying to decipher the facial expressions among my audience. Although twenty years had elapsed since the war, the mention of Serbia made many feel uncomfortable.

I could never completely get it, which was understandable in a way. My memories of the war were very vague, I had just started elementary school at the time, I lived in Zagreb, a city that wasn't too affected by the wartime atrocities, and to this day, the mention of war always makes me think of the basement shelters where we happily went because it meant that we didn't have to go to school that day.

It's true, I spent my youth listening to patriotic songs, but the reason I related to them so easily was because my environment motivated me to do so. I didn't have my own opinions, I just copied the opinions of adults, who tried to explain the war to the kid, telling them who was good, and who was bad. Croatian president Tuđman was good, his Serbian equivalent Milošević was bad. Croatian singer Thompson was good, Serbian singer Balašević was bad. Croats were good, Serbs were bad.

Many years later, as I thought through it myself, I realized that things were not black and white, that Tuđman had his flaws, that I could relate to Balašević's songs way easier than I could to Thompson's songs and that while there are good Croats and bad Serbs, there are also bad Croats and good Serbs.

On the other hand, who knows what I would think about the war if I were just a little bit older. What if I'd been on the front line? What if somebody dear to me had been killed in the war? What if I'd witnessed my family being killed?

As it was, I grew into a person who was happy to say he came from Croatia, but who, at the same time, didn't see it as a special honor, pride or achievement, since I couldn't take the credit for that. Anyway, what's the point of being proud of something you didn't achieve yourself or didn't work hard to get it? I'm not proud of being a man, right-handed and straight, so why should I be proud to be Croatian?

"Even though I'd heard a lot of warnings as I was heading to Serbia," I continued, "all of my memories of this country are lovely. I liked the people I met, the people who hosted me in their homes, the people who offered me a ride in their car, with whom I even discussed the war. All of this marked a wonderful start of my trip."

I could have told them a story about my host in Belgrade, Miroslav, who was talking for hours about how he perceived the 1990s as lost years, since he, along with many like-minded people, fought for justice and to bring down Milošević's regime. He told me about the sanctions and the bombings, and that also on that side of the border it was those who had done nothing wrong that suffered the most.

I could have told them a story about the truck driver who had lost way too many Croatian friends because of *stupid politicians and their interests*.

I could have done so, but I didn't - because I didn't have enough time. There was still an hour left, but with too many slides, photos and stories lying ahead.

"The second country I visited was Bulgaria," I said, changing the slide. "And this is the only photo I'll be showing of this country."

The photograph showed a woman wearing a backpack, with a puppy in her arms. I could have shown them a photo of my friends in Sofia, the photo that I took on the first night in paid accommodation in Veliko Tarnovo, playing the guitar on the street to earn money to cover this unexpected cost, or I could have told them that in Burgas I had a beer with my new Polish friends, trying to prove to one of them that the red sphere hanging over the Black Sea wasn't Mars but the Moon.

"Look at the Moon, it's so big," I told my CS host Alexandra and her Polish friend, whose name I forget. The Moon had just come out and shone over the Black Sea, large and bright red. I couldn't remember seeing the Moon this beautiful before.

"That's not the Moon," the Polish guy said. "That's Mars."

Aleksandra kept quiet as I looked at him in disbelief, presuming he was kidding. After a few seconds of observing his face and looking for any sign of potential irony, sarcasm, humor or anything, I asked him whether he was kidding me.

He remained serious, and so I burst into laughter and told him I was pretty sure that it was the Moon, since Mars is only occasionally visible to the naked eye as a small dot on a starry sky.

The Pole persisted with his theory, based on the information that the Moon was either white or yellow, whereas Mars was red.

"Okay," I said gently, realizing that I couldn't prove the opposite. "I think that it's the Moon, and you think that it's Mars. There's obviously no way to convince you to change your mind, and as I'm 99.9% sure it's the Moon (I lowered my degree of certainty by 0.1% because you never know), I suggest we just agree to disagree."

Of course, half an hour later the Moon rose up in the sky and turned yellow, and my Polish pal admitted he was wrong. And we carried on drinking beer and laughing. We'd learned a lesson - you should neither want to be right at all costs nor try to prove it to everybody around you.

I could have told them this story, but instead I decided to tell them another, more important one.

"This is Tanja," I began, showing them her photo. "She's been traveling for years too, hitchhiking, couchsurfing, and her dog Nina always comes along."

"So why do I find Tanja's story so important?" I asked them. "When they hear my story, most people think *it's easier if you're a man*. Or *it's easier if you're young*, and things like that. Tanja is a perfect example that you don't need to have ideal circumstances to follow your dreams. Tanja is a lady over the age of forty and this hasn't stopped her from traveling. She even decided to take her dog with her."

This gave the people in the room something to think about for a moment. I guessed that all of them wanted to travel at some point. And that almost all of them had found a reason or an excuse not to do so. What will the others say, what if something happens to me, what will I do when I come back - all of those reasons keep popping up when people start considering something that could change their lives dramatically.

"As with Serbia, I only stayed in Bulgaria for a few days, after which I entered Turkey," I continued my story. "After a few days in the chaos of Istanbul, I headed southward..."

Day 22

"Where am I?" This was my first thought after a loud rooster's cock-a-doodle-doo woke me up before the break of dawn. This is the standard question you ask yourself when you wake up in a different place almost every day.

I was in a small bungalow with two beds and a mosquito net hanging over them. I took a quick stroll down the memory lane to recall how I had ended up there.

After spending time in Istanbul and partying with old acquaintances, I hitchhiked to Eskişehir where I'd played guitar on the street for the second time on this trip, earning me a few Turkish lira. Later on I ended up in Denizli, from where I took a walk to Pamukkale, a very popular tourist destination. After that, I reached here: Kabak valley.

After an hour of hiking, completely sweaty, I threw myself into the warm sea. I witnessed one of the most beautiful sunsets ever, made friends with some hippies on the beach, learned that the owner of a local restaurant was looking for a volunteer - and ended up in this bungalow. In a few hours I would start my first day at work. The deal was that I'd work for 7-8 hours a day in exchange for free accommodation, three meals a day and one free beer a day. But a 0,33l can! I realized that I would have to stay for at least ten days, putting the beers aside, and then get properly wasted on the last day!

Besides, my cousin Ivana, with whom I'd been in contact for a while, was supposed to pay me a visit, and had decided to join me for a few days.

Given that it was still too early to start working, and that I could no longer sleep, I went to the beach where I planned to wait for the sunrise. All village's inhabitants were still sound asleep. Except for the roosters.

Three weeks had already passed since I'd embarked on my one thousand day-long trip around the world.

It was so cool. I was traveling, meeting new people, exploring, visiting new places. However, every once in a while I would ask myself: why am I really here? What exactly am I doing? Would this trip need to have a purpose - beyond the obvious one - traveling for the sake of traveling? Should I be looking for something that would give me an answer to all my questions and help me figure out what to do with my life?

Or should I just let myself go and give myself enough time for the answers to find their way to me?

After an hour of bathing in shallow waters, I returned to the bungalow, put my work uniform on and started helping in the kitchen, putting away the dishes after the occasional guests left, serving drinks and doing other things like that.

"My cousin will be visiting today, do you mind if she sleeps in my bungalow?" I asked my boss during the break.

"No problem," he answered with a smile.

He was cool, relaxed, patient. He showed me how the restaurant worked, where I could find things, and how to serve the guests. He told me that he'd visited this small village as a young man, fallen in love with it and decided to open a restaurant...

"Somewhere over the rainbow..." I was startled by a well-known tune at the end of the shift. I knew that song! I had heard this voice before!

I looked up to see an elderly, grey-haired man standing at the entrance to the restaurant. He had long hair and a reassuring smile, radiating an amazing energy. He was carrying a guitar on his back, but the famous tune didn't come from him.

A split second later, a girl with a small instrument in her hand, a glow in her eyes and a familiar smile made her way into the restaurant. I put away the plate, ran to the door and gave her a passionate kiss.

"How, what, where?" I stuttered.

Out of the corner of my eye, I could see the utmost shock on the face of my boss, with a question mark hanging over his head.

"Don't worry, this isn't my cousin," I explained.

It was my Tanja, with whom I'd spent half a year before embarking on this trip, with whom I'd traveled across Portugal and bought a small *cavaquinho* and played on the streets of Sintra, with whom I'd lived in London for two months and whom I was seeing for the first time after the sad goodbye, when she had almost joined me on this trip.

"I missed you," she replied, smiling like only she could.

"How did you find me?" I was still astonished.

"Ivana helped me with my little secret operation," she wouldn't stop smiling. "My biggest problem was talking the Iranian embassy staff in London into granting me a visa as soon as possible..."

"The Iranian embassy?" I repeated, completely astonished.

"Yes, Iran," she said triumphantly. "I'm flying back in three weeks, hopefully there would be enough time to rush our way through Turkey and Iran before I fly back to London..."

"So who's your friend?" I asked after giving her another tight hug. I was so astonished that I'd completely forgotten about the grey-haired man that I'd seen a minute earlier and who was calmly standing next to us, smiling mysteriously.

"Ištvan, pleased to meet you," he presented himself, not taking the smile off of his face.

"I met him in a bus that was taking us from the airport, he didn't have a plan so he joined me," Tanja explained. "He has been traveling over the past thirty years, out of which he spent fifteen years in India. Best of all, he's only got his guitar, passport and a toothbrush with him - no extra clothes or anything. His travel motto is 'essentials only'."

I looked at him. There was something beautiful in his serenity, his sky-blue eyes and the smile upon his face. The guy had been traveling for thirty years, and it showed. Abundant life experience was apparent on his face - he looked self-confident and relaxed. He looked obstinate, but also modest and humble at the same time, I would really like to look that way when I reach his age.

At the end of my shift, I quit my job so that Tanja and I could get to Iran within three weeks, I showed the two of them all around Kabak, and then we watched a beautiful sunset together, listening to Ištvan play and sing in English, Hindu and Tibetan.

We spent the night on an abandoned mattress on the edge of the bay, under the countless stars.

Tanja and me alone, without Ištvan.

Day 25

We sneaked out of our tiny room so as not to wake up our host and witnessed a beautiful scene - about twenty or so large balloons were flying over the beautiful landscape, providing us with a spectacular view.

Although without a plan, we knew as soon as we left Kabak that we simply couldn't miss what was according to so many people the most beautiful part of Turkey - Cappadocia. We ignored the trucks and other slow means of transport and instead focused on cars, which is only possible in a country like Turkey where hitchhiking is a piece of cake. This way, you could cover a decent 350 miles each day, sometimes even more, which is quite the achievement on the not-always-so-great Turkish roads.

After two days of hitchhiking, we ended up in Göreme, in the heart of Cappadocia. Right after we got out of the car that had taken us to our destination, we noticed a local beckoning us to be his guests from his six-story stone house. We told him we were a bit short of money, but it seemed as though he didn't really mind and would give us a small room in exchange for our company and the chance to practice his English.

Fair enough!

Only later, after we returned from an evening stroll, did we realize that there was a catch - our host entered our room without asking, offered us all kinds of food and booze, and became increasingly weird and too attentive. The conversation revolved around sex and he claimed that in principle he was *up for anything*. He told us that he'd been wild in his youth and had experimented with other couples.

This was a clear enough signal for us to come up with an excuse and go to bed early.

Tanja and me alone, without him.

Looking at the giant balloons on that sunny Cappadocian morning, we went to explore the village. Given that our budget didn't allow a balloon flight, we had to explore it from the usual perspective, using our feet and thumbs as our means of transportation.

We climbed through abandoned caves and got lost in a valley formed through erosion, after millions of years of volcanic eruptions, which had created beautiful, unusual formations resembling minarets and what were known as fairy chimneys. The secret of those unusual forms lies in the non-erodible rocks at the top, while the sides, susceptible to wind and weather conditions, have got thinner over time. People built their settlements there for thousands of years, from the times of the ancient Christians who were considered pagans back then. Nowadays, this is a sensational tourist attraction. Some of the settlements have been turned into mini 5-star hotels, where you can stay at a cost of several thousand euros per night.

Throughout Cappadocia, you can explore underground towns that used to once have a population numbering thousands of people, who were trying to find a shelter from Arab invaders.

Since it was really hot, and we didn't feel like walking, we decided to hitchhike a little into the surrounding villages, which brought about an immediate result in the form of one of the most unique means of transportation in my entire hitchhiking career - the guy who stopped for us offered us a ride on his horse-drawn cart.

Lazy hitchhiking had soon turned into three-hours of sightseeing and a private tour across the nearby valleys. We tried local fruit, explored abandoned temples and churches, bargained with souvenir sellers, chilled out and took photos from the mountain tops, enjoying the amazing views.

"Tanja, do you want to ride a horse?" Hasan, our private chauffeur, asked at the end of the tour.

"Well, I don't know," she said reluctantly, looking at me. "The three of us can't all fit on the horse's back, can we?"

"I can wait for you here," I replied.

We stopped the horse, unfastened the cart and Tanja and Hasan slowly rode away into the sunset.

It took me ten seconds before I got a weird feeling in my stomach, making me wonder: what the fuck have I just done? I let my girlfriend ride off with a random Turkish guy, in the middle of nowhere and without anybody around. What if...

Before I had finished my thought I started to run as fast as possible, trying to find them. I was following the hoof prints, looking into the distance, trying to pick out a cloud of dust behind the horse.

I was quite exhausted by the time I finally noticed them from a far. They had stopped riding, got off the horse and begun talking. I didn't waste any time approaching them, but as I didn't want them to notice that I was worried and out of breath, I took my camera out and started taking photographs, slowly approaching so that Hasan wouldn't think that I'd joined them because I was suspicious.

Once they noticed me, I realised that I had done the right thing - their facial expressions were diametrically opposite. Tanja was beaming with joy to see me, while Hasan was irritated and angry.

"Is everything alright?" I asked her with a smile on my face, trying not to reveal what I was saying to the person that stood next to us. Even if he couldn't speak our language, he could easily work out what we were talking about just by observing our body language.

"Well, so-so," she replied, smiling, as she understood the rules of our new game. "He started talking about watching the sunset together and cracking jokes about not going back to pick you up..."

"Haha," I was still playing my part. "Let's get outta here as soon as possible. We're still in the middle of nowhere."

I was holding a camera the whole time, taking photos, just like any other tourist. I also took a photo of Hasan and his horse, praising its beauty. Despite all this, he still gave the impression of a totally different person from the one we had a chance to meet over the past few hours. He was withdrawn and moody. He was feeding his pet with an apple, cutting it in half with a hunter's knife that he was holding in his right hand.

"Wanna try some?" He suddenly asked me when he noticed that I was watching him. He reached out his hand to just a few inches from my face, with a piece of the fruit jabbed into the knife's blade.

"No, thanks," I replied, pulling a sour smile and spontaneously stepping backwards. "We need to get going, our friends are waiting for us," I murmured.

Tanja and I headed slowly to the cart, and he sat on the horse, once again offering Tanja a ride, his attempt falling flat this time.

"Oh, Tom," she threw herself into my arms once he was far enough away. "How come you came and found us so quickly?"

"I just imagined myself explaining to your mother that the last time I saw you was when you rode off into the sunset with some Turkish guy, and that I'd said that this was OK," I replied. "That was enough for me to panic and chase after you."

We said goodbye to Hasan and hitchhiked back to our little stone house.

We paid for our stay by playing the guitar and Tanja singing, got up early in the morning and headed further east.

Day 1000

"Turkey is beautiful and huge," I carried on, changing slides that show Istanbul, Pamukkale, and Cappadocia. "However, despite its beauties, this is my favorite photo from Turkey and actually one of my favorite photos in general."

I changed the slide to show a photo of myself together with a Turkish family that had picked Tanja and me up as we were hitchhiking eastbound from Cappadocia. My face was showing pure delight at the various Turkish dishes being laid on a table.

"This is the family that picked us up as we were hitchhiking," I continued. "Even though they didn't speak a word of English, we managed to communicate with body language and accepted their persistent invitation to join them for tea. The invitation for tea turned into an invitation for dinner, dinner turned into our performance in the living room with me playing the guitar and Tanja playing a *cavaquinho* and singing, and our concert eventually turned into an overnight stay. The next day, they dropped us off about ten miles further along so that we could continue our journey more conveniently and that was it. Even though they didn't know us and we all knew that the chances of us seeing each other again were quite slim, they treated us like their best friends, as though we had known each other for the whole of our lives.

"This is the most important part of traveling. The people. It's nice to see a foreign country, the wonders of nature, learn something about the history and another culture, but the times spent with people and talking to them are the most precious moments. The moments of letting yourself indulge in a complete stranger's hospitality. Seeing that people's generosity is universal, that we're all the same, no matter how hard we try to emphasize the differences between nations and cultures."

People used to ask me whether I felt guilty taking things from people while traveling. I asked them for a ride, I slept on their couches, sometimes I even ate their food - did I feel like I was using them?

My answer to that question was always a very concise and decisive no.

I had been having people in my apartment for years, I would take them sightseeing, to Sunday lunch at my parent's house, I would invite them to join my friends when we went out, I would often treat them to food and drink, I always tried to be a good host. Also, whenever I travel, I try my hardest to be a good guest. I try not to abuse other people's kindness and I always give something back, whether it was an interesting story, a shoulder to cry on, making bracelets, cooking a Croatian meal, playing guitar, anything. It's all about giving and taking.

The beauty of this exchange is that it doesn't necessarily need to be financial. Kindness doesn't cost a thing and this is why it should not be viewed through a financial prism.

Of course, you should pay for the things that have to be paid for and shouldn't take bread out of someone's mouth, but sometimes we can fearlessly and shamelessly enjoy the beauty of life and somebody's kindness.

"After visiting Turkey, we went to Iraq," I said.

Day 29

"Son, are you out of your mind?" I got my mother's message while I was waiting at the border between Turkey and Iraq. "What are you going to do in Iraq?"

I sent my mother a message or an email every day just to let her know about my whereabouts and that I was alive and kicking. This was our deal and, according to her, the only way she could survive my wandering around the world. It didn't matter what I wrote, a single word each day was enough to set her mind at ease, at least for that day.

I should, however, have considered my tactics and kept some things to myself, such as this brief visit to Iraq. Just like in the beginning (when mothers still didn't have Facebook profiles), when I would bend the truth and lie about traveling by train and bus, without mentioning hitchhiking.

"Don't worry, Mom," I replied, trying to reassure her, knowing full well that this was almost mission impossible. "We've heard that it was safe over here."

We ended up at the Iraqi border by accident, hitchhiking eastbound from Diyabakir and left ourselves to fate and our drivers to take us wherever they wanted, either south-east to Iraq or east to Iran. After shunning the taxi drivers who stopped for us, having misinterpreted our thumbs up, with a simple Turkish expression *para yok*[2], a van going toward the border with Iraq stopped for us. There was a couple sat inside - an Armenian girl and an Iraqi guy. They had lived in Germany for the last 12 years, and were now heading to Dohuk, a city which, by all accounts, was about to become our next destination.

We waited for hours at the border, while kind customs officials kept offering us tea that was far too sweet and ran around to find out what Croatia was like. We got a ten-day visa at last, which was supposed to be more than enough for our stay in northern Iraq, known as Iraqi Kurdistan.

As we drove along disastrously bad, dusty roads to Dohuk, we realized that this was only Iraq on paper. Most of the population in this part of the country were Kurds, with their own autonomy, military, government, red, white and green flag, and their own traditional

---

[2] *Turkish: we've got no money.*

clothing.

The Kurds generally live in the eastern part of Turkey, northern Iraq and Syria and the north-western part of Iran. They are about 30 million strong, and their situation in those states isn't ideal, meaning that lately there have been frequent clashes between the PKK (the Kurdistan Workers' Party) and members of the police and armed forces of the states that they live in. This is with the exception of Iraq, where they have been left to their own devices since 1970.

We settled in a cheap hotel and took a walk into the city center. Everybody observed us with curiosity, some people stopping here and there, and the bravest among them smiling and politely saying a few words of basic English. We had just stepped from the more or less touristy Turkey into the untouristy Iraq and all of a sudden we were constantly the center of attention.

"What's that, then?" I asked Tanja as we walked down the town's main street and noticed a man with a glass box containing a load of money. Euros, dollars and local currency.

"What's this?" I asked the moustachioed man, since Tanja had no idea either.

"It's an exchange office!" He said. "Do you need to change some money?"

"Well, not exactly," I was confused, exchanging looks with my travel companion. "Are you not afraid to stand out here in the middle of the street with so much money? Even in my country it would be dangerous, someone would rob you, let alone here in Iraq."

"No way!" The moustachioed man chortled. "This is Iraqi Kurdistan, the safest country in the world!"

The puzzled expression and disbelief that had been visible on my face soon turned into thoughtfulness. What if this man was right? What did I really know about Iraq? All I knew about it was what I read in the newspapers or on the Internet. Just what I heard on television, from someone else's perspective. I knew it was relatively safe from what I'd discovered in neighboring Turkey, talking to people living in this area and those who had first-hand information about the security situation in Iraq, but obviously that hadn't been enough for me to completely overcome my prejudices.

But this situation and this experience could change my attitude and opinion.

Walking through the streets where we felt quite safe, especially after the currency exchange experience, we reached an amusement park for which we'd been told was a very popular gathering place. And indeed it was - the ladies were wearing their best dresses, jewelry and scarves, the men were all dressed up to the nines with hair to match, enjoying the rides altogether.

In the morning, we visited the local bazaar and then headed on to the east. Tanja's return flight was getting closer so we had to hurry up.

The first car dropped us off at one of the many military barricades. Although we didn't feel especially comfortable among the military personnel and police officers, everybody turned out to be cheerful, smiling and willing to help. We got the impression that they were constantly asking to check our passports just to be able to have a little chat and proudly speak a few words of English.

As we were the only ones at the checkpoints with no means of transportation, they were happy to lend us a hand. They asked every vehicle that they stopped what direction it was going, and asked the driver of the first vehicle going in our direction, with enough room for the pair of us, to give us a lift.

Our driver was an elderly man in traditional Kurdish garb. Since he didn't speak a word of English, we drove in silence and took a lunch break at a roadside restaurant. Within seconds, no more, no less than twenty-two plates were lined up in front of us, with various specialties of the house.

"We shouldn't have eaten in the morning," Tanja said, observing the mountains of food.

"Definitely," I agreed. "But at least we learned a lesson."

"Which one?" She asked.

"If you hitchhike in this part of the world, start your journey on an empty stomach."

After stuffing ourselves, our offer to pay for lunch was refused in disgust and our driver drove us further on to Erbil. He showed us photos of his wife and his other wife and eleven children, inviting us to stay at his place. We thanked him, but had to refuse. If we had accepted every invitation, Tanja would have probably missed her flight, and winter would have eventually caught up with us.

We changed several vehicles since it was gradually getting dark and we ended up seventy kilometers from the border with Iran.

"Are we allowed to camp here?" We asked the owner of a nearby restaurant. In nature, away from people, we wouldn't need to ask anyone's permission, we just had to make sure that there were no wild animals around. But it's always safer in unknown places to ask and make sure you are allowed to stay - so that Mom wouldn't be without her a message or e-mail the following morning.

"Camping 10 dollars, room 40!" The owner said firmly.

Of course, we opted for a tent, but first we sat down to have some tea, which turned out to be a wise thing to do. Every now and then the owner looked in our direction, but didn't look at us, but at the guitar and its little brother, the *cavaquinho*. We made eye contact, sending him a question across the restaurant using our body language as to whether he wanted us to play something for him, and the glimmer in his eyes and the smile on his face told us that he would indeed love that.

Our line-up was the same - I played the guitar, Tanja played the *cavaquinho* and imaginary microphone. We knew a couple of songs, some Croatian, some English, but people around us didn't seem to mind as they slowly gathered, jigging along with our every song.

It's an interesting phenomenon - in some cities, you need a license and a lot of skill to play music on the street, but even that is often not enough to attract the attention of passersby. Somewhere else, even a basic repertoire and limited knowledge will make you a real star.

At the end of our performance, the owner took us by the hand and led us into a small room, pointing a finger at the blankets that could be used as a bed and alluded that we should spend the night here, and not outside in the freezing cold. When asked about the price, he just waved his hand.

We hugged him and went down to finish our concert that had by now gathered quite an audience. Soldiers. My instincts told me to be careful. You never know, these young soldiers were on leave, and here was a pretty girl with a pale complexion and a guy who could be easily restrained... In the end, they turned out to be the perfect audience, and the only inconvenience was the fact that we had to take at least thirty pictures with them. With each of them. Iraqi Facebook must be full of photos and video clips of us.

Once our fingers and vocal cords had grown tired, we retired to our quiet corner to sleep.

Seeing a kalashnikov on the chair in the hall perked us up for a bit, but we comforted ourselves by telling each other that nobody would do us any harm, then locked the door, barricaded it with a desk and slept like a log.

Day 1000

"We spent only two nights in Iraq," I continued my talk. "But it was more than enough to fully confirm my assumption that you don't need to fear those countries that have a bad reputation. Of course, you should always be careful, but the main sources of information about the dangers in particular countries should be people living there, those who experience the pluses and minuses first-hand. Just like sometimes we laugh at people who are reluctant to come to Croatia because they think the war is still raging, we also need to get informed about the situation in other countries."

Those stupid foreigners don't know where Croatia is, tut. Haha, they still think Yugoslavia exists. They don't even know the capital of Croatia, what the heck are they teaching them in schools...

I'd heard those statements hundreds times before, initially from other people and in the media, but then over time I started saying those things myself and adopted this way of thinking.

How is it possible that they don't know that the war is over, that Yugoslavia broke up a full quarter of a century ago, and what kind of fool believes that Dubrovnik is Croatia's capital?

Years later, I caught myself without a clue about the exact location of Gambia, Swaziland or the State of Maine. Let alone their capitals. Should the citizens of those countries be offended and make fun of us because we don't know the exact locations of their countries, we don't know about their history and we haven't got a clue about the capitals?

When we put things this way, it makes you think. It's easy to know a lot about your immediate surroundings and mock those who don't know everything you do, without thinking about your own ignorance. Double standards result from a lack of education and experience, and an excess of prejudice and arrogance.

"Also, we've learned new lessons about hitchhiking," I continued. After a night spent on blankets in the barricaded hotel room, we headed for the border. First, the owner, who obviously liked us, drove us some thirty kilometers to the next town. There the taxi drivers who had never heard of hitchhiking started to annoy us, and when we finally thought we'd managed to explain the point of hitchhiking to them, we got in the car and noticed that some local guy gave the driver a couple of notes so that he could drive us to the border. It made us sad because other people paying for our ride was not the point, but rather we wanted to get lifts from people if our destination was on their way.

"We faced a similar situation after crossing the Iranian border. After Tanja got herself sorted out, covered her hair with a scarf and put on a long sleeve shirt, and after border guards cheerfully remembered Croatian football coach Ćiro Blažević and star striker Davor Šuker, we found ourselves at a roundabout, looking for transport to Tehran. The first thing every hitchhiker will tell you if you're going to Iran is that you mustn't hitchhike with a thumb stuck out, as in Iran it means the same as a raised middle finger in our culture."

"With a little effort, we found a guy who spoke perfect English and who was happy to write/draw 'Tehran' on a cardboard sign in their alphabet. Within five minutes, a mass of people had gathered at the roundabout, half of them directing us with a smile to the bus terminal and the other half advising us to take a taxi. One of them even told us that it didn't make any sense to hold a cardboard sign for Tehran since they had perfectly good tin signs by the road so everybody knew which way to go to get to Tehran. "Your country might not have road signs, but Iran is a developed country…"

"We remembered what had happened just a few hours earlier when others had paid for our ride just to help us out, looked at each other, and walked to the bus terminal. And then we realized why no one got the point of hitchhiking in this part of the world. Fuel and bus tickets are so ridiculously cheap that there is no need for hitchhiking. The ticket for Tehran, that was almost 600 miles away, only cost us about 10 dollars each."

"Apart from the odd bus ride in a city, this was the first time that I paid for transport on this trip. But even we, travelers with a limited budget, can sometimes afford conventional means of transport."

Day 31

"Taxi! Taxi! Taxi!" Barely had we collected our backpacks from the trunk, and we were already surrounded by a dozen taxi drivers just before sunrise, offering us their services at the Tehran station, constantly shouting and shoving each other. After a thirteen hour-ride, we were only half awake, and it was the last thing we wanted to experience, so we kindly rejected their offers about twenty times over and, with a lot of patience, finally managed to rid ourselves of them.

Maybe it was just because of this initial stress, but probably because Tehran is a huge city and we hadn't arranged any accommodation and didn't feel like wandering around the city, we just caught the next bus to Esfahan, which was five hours away and about which we'd already heard a lot of nice things. The local taxi drivers there must have been given the heads up by their colleagues in Tehran and so, believe it or not, left us in peace.

We caught a bus to the city center, politely entering the bus through the front door. Like a true gentleman, I got on first, with Tanja coming behind me. Whilst I was trying to buy a ticket, the driver and the passengers on the bus looked at us weirdly, trying to explain something to us.

"Women, back!" The driver managed to stutter.

We took a more careful look inside the bus and it all became clear to us. Just like in the first half of twentieth century America, *the Land of the free*, buses were the scene of segregation, seating men in the front and women in the back.

"If your name was Rosa Parks then perhaps we could change things," I told Tanja, who just smiled, fixed her *hijab*, stepped back and entered through the rear door with the other women. There was a physical barrier in the middle of the bus, so we wouldn't mix or touch accidentally in the crowd. I covertly looked toward the part of the bus where the second-class citizens were and noticed that all the eyes of veiled women, dressed in black, were riveted on Tanja's colorful clothes. She was talking to the young Iranian women, smiling... I didn't look in the forbidden direction for long though since I really didn't want to break any of the rules.

It looked like we would need some time to get used to Iran, its laws and its customs.

In the city center, we did what we always do when we get somewhere and don't have anywhere to sleep. We found an internet café and sent two or three CS requests, hoping that the quality of our witty e-mails would yield more success than sending a bunch of copy-paste requests to all couchsurfers in Esfahan. At the same time, we wanted to check good old Facebook too, but it turned out that it was... blocked.

I could understand it if websites with adult content were blocked, like in Turkey (at least this was what my Turkish friends were saying), but hello, how can you block Facebook? It's my life, my job, my friends are there, even my parents... everything. Luckily enough, every internet café has a hacker who with just a few clicks lifts the blockade imposed by the state against any social network with the Western world, allowing us to access the miracle of the Internet. It comes as no surprise that Iran is home to some of the most notorious hacker groups, that were created in response to the blockade, media censorship and attacks on freedom of communication.

We let our families know by email that we had safely arrived in the heart of Iran and were then off to explore the famous Esfahan, Iran's third largest city.

We wandered the streets carrying our backpacks in the hot weather. I didn't even want to imagine how Tanja felt, covered in all those scarves and covers. We looked at passersby, although we were the ones that were being observed. Passing by, with a beaming smile, they kept asking us questions. Where are you from? Do you like Iran? Would you like a cup of tea? Or more specifically, they only addressed me, clearly avoiding any conversation with Tanja. After all, she's only a woman.

All major streets in Esfahan lead to the impressive Naghsh-e Jahan, the city's main square, which, as some sources suggest, is the second largest square in the world, after Beijing's Tiananmen Square. The whole square is a UNESCO's World Heritage site and is surrounded by the Shah Mosque, Ali Qapu Palace, Sheikh Loft Allah Mosque and the Esfahan Grand Bazaar. At the same time, it's also Esfahan's second largest gathering place, especially in the early evening as the sun sets, and the square takes on completely different colors through the play of light on the colorful façades.

We put our backpacks and instruments down on a grassy area within the square and I took my toothbrush and headed over to a public restroom, while Tanja kept an eye on our belongings.

On my return I had quite something to see - Tanja was surrounded by several women, curiously asking her questions and begging her to play something for them. We asked them if this was allowed since we'd previously been warned that street performing was illegal (unless you played the accordion - Iran's national instrument), but they just waved their hands and said that as foreigners we had nothing to worry about.

We liked their interpretation of the law, so we performed a couple of American songs. We were rewarded with a standing ovation, our burgeoning audience doubled, we were given a few notes (even though we sang *We don't need your money, money, money*), and one girl popped over to a nearby shop and bought us local candy that we tasted and then politely saved for later.

"Would you like to join us for dinner and sleep at our place?" a young couple asked after we had lamented about having nowhere yet to stay.

"Sure thing!" we accepted. Since we were still waiting for answers from the CS, this fit perfectly into our plans.

"Great!" they said timidly and gave each other a look. They left a cell phone number and told us that they'd be in touch later.

As we were saying goodbye, we became aware of another cultural difference. In Iran, just like in most Islamic countries, men shake hands with men, and women shake hands with women. People of the opposite gender do not touch each other. Even the men's looks during the conversations were mainly focused on me, with an occasional, humble, almost smuggled look at Tanja. Here, women talk to women, and men talk to men.

We moved a mere hundred yards from the lawn, and a guy from a nearby workshop invited us in for tea. He showed us his handiwork, relaxedly telling us about the various things that bother him, most of which were political. We didn't expect people to be so open about their criticisms of the current political situation. We touched on the rights of homosexuals in Iran, which of course were non-existent because this was deemed an offense punishable by death. Like for drug dealing, murder and rape.

"We can forget about dinner," I told Tanja during our time with the guy from the workshop. "The couple from earlier in the park just texted to say that they can't put us up for the night."

"What a pity," she said sadly.

"What's the problem?" Our new friend asked us, as disappointment crept onto our faces. I explained to him in English what I'd just told Tanja.

"I can tell that you've never heard of *tarof*," he replied with a smile.

"*Tarof*?" We gave him a quizzical look.

"It's something inherent in us Iranians," he started to explain. "Being kind and hospitable is a cultural thing, but as if this wasn't enough, we have to take it to an even higher level. The unwritten rule says that in some circumstances Person A offers something to a Person B, expecting Person B to politely decline the offer, meaning that neither of them lose face."

"So there was a catch!" Tanja interrupted him. "Do you remember when we bought that bottle of water at the kiosk, and the lady didn't want to charge us?"

"Haha, of course I remember," I replied. It had happened during the ride to Tehran, when we played this *tarof* game without even realising. We'd taken a bottle of water at a kiosk, asked how much it cost, and the lady replied that it was okay, we didn't have to pay. In the end, we did pay for the water, thinking this must have just been mere linguistic misunderstanding.

Maybe Croats are of Iranian origin, as some anthropologists have tried to claim, which means that we can play this game too. I remembered a joke that definitely comes from a real-life situation. Two Croatian families sat around a table in a restaurant. They all ate well and had a good time together, but once the bill arrived, a huge debate was sparked about who should and shouldn't pay. Various arguments were laid out: you paid last time, I invited you, you will pay next time...and goodness knows what else. After a good five minutes, one of the males at the table prevailed and took great pride in paying the bill. Laughter and good spirits continued until they parted ways. On the way home, the one who paid turned angrily to his wife: "I can't believe he let me pay!"

"It takes a lot of skill to master *tarof*," our friend explained. "You know, there are situations around a dinner table, when a host offers his guests more food after they have already eaten, and the guest refuses because he is full, but the host insists because he thinks that the guest is bluffing, *tarofing*, so he piles extra food on the guest's plate, and the guest doesn't want to offend the host, and feels obliged to finish all the food, which eventually leads to the host remaining hungry and guest uncomfortably full."

I burst into laughter because I'd experienced this plenty of times. Every summer, in fact, when I visit my dad's relatives in Herzegovina. Who would have thought that two distant and culturally different countries have so much in common?

"Islam, Islam!" Three policemen walking past us interrupted my thoughts. They were pointing at Tanja's ankle, an inch of which remained uncovered, letting us know that this was the problem. These joints must be covered, that was the law.

Oh, Allah!

We pulled Tanja's dress down and started exploring the city, still waiting for a kind person to reply to us on CS. The Jameh Mosque was one of the major attractions in the city. We entered its impressive courtyard but didn't feel like paying for tickets for a guided tour inside. We turned toward Mecca and enjoyed the silence with a view of the dome. We had hardly sat down, when a local visitor handed us a pomegranate. We devoured it with gusto, not caring too greatly about the historical and artistic sights around us.

I wondered if in Iran there was a penalty for this as well.

Beep beep. Beep beep. Our peace and meditation was interrupted by the well-known text message alert from my Nokia. "We've got a place to stay tonight!" I said to Tanja happily.

Faryad, our new host, picked us up at the Azadi Square and told us that a few months ago he'd been arrested there for taking two foreigners around the city despite not being a tourist guide. This was quite ironic, because Azadi Square in Iranian means Liberty Square. He explained that Couchsurfing was semi-illegal in Iran, so hosts and guests should be beware of the police and have answers ready in case someone asks you a question.

On the way to the southern part of the city, he took us to see the magnificent bridges of Esfahan, which are the city's most famous attractions. The Zayande River dried up about four years ago, so now the bridges connect the two sides of the riverbed, between which runs a non-existent river. Where once flowed a river, there's now a gathering place for young people, who discuss a better life under the bridge, when they will be able to listen to music in the open and talk freely with whoever they want, without fear of being put behind bars. Or worse.

"How do you like Iran?" Faryad asked us after the lavish dinner that he prepared for his two weary travelers.

"I've never met such cheerful, smiling, hospitable people," Tanja replied. "Regardless of your famous *tarof*, people's faces show curiosity and genuine kindness."

"I agree," I said. "But, there are too many rules, there's a lack of personal freedom, the laws are too conservative, you have to be careful about what you say, what you do, what parts of your body are kept covered at all times..."

"Oh, tell me about it," Faryad replied, sitting in a comfortable sofa. "Being liberal in Iran is a nightmare. I spent my whole youth in fear, and so did my friends. You know, we would take some booze to student parties, but if you're caught drinking alcohol then you're sentenced to eighty lashes on the back. Or ten strokes with an eight-tongued whip."

Tanja and I exchanged looks. How lucky we had actually been to have had the opportunity to grow up in the time and country where we grew up, despite the atrocities our country hadn't been spared of either. We took up positions on the living room floor and looked on, wanting to hear more stories about Iran. I remembered the anecdotes from my couchsurfing guests who had been passing through my living room for years, telling me about their adventures, and thought about how it affected me. I remembered that there was a huge difference between hearing about something from the media or reading about it in history textbooks and actually having someone tell you about their first-hand experiences. Such stories take you right to the scene and bring its energy to you, whether that energy is good or bad.

Unfortunately, Iranian stories seemed to give off more bad energy.

"Every mention of Iran in the Western world is always the same old story," he went on. "They talk about our politicians, the strict laws, the religious leaders. But almost nobody is talking about people who don't necessarily endorse those politicians, religious leaders or laws. No one asks us anything. Most women don't want to respect the laws about compulsory coverage of their heads, but they have to obey them. And it starts when they turn nine. Their sleeves have to cover their wrists, with their heads covered, curves must be hidden and things like that. Nine years old is also the legal age for marriage."

"People also used to protest against the government, but they soon gave up when, during these protests, the soldiers got deployed at nearby buildings and snipers took protesters out without a warning, even though their only weapon had been a band-aid over their mouths, by which they wanted to point to the lack of freedom of speech. At the end, you make peace with it, you give up your desires and ideals, just to save your own life and the lives of your family."

Although I couldn't relate to the terrible stories that Faryad told us, I understood the human need to save your own life. After all, this is all we've got. Once your life ends, everything we once knew stops. Suspense, mystery, and fear emerge. On the other hand, the world has always been changed for the better thanks to those people whose beliefs and attitudes mattered more to them than their own lives, who went against the flow, put everything at stake for the ideals in which they believed.

The problem is that for every person who succeeded in their plan, even at the cost of their own life, there were thousands of other people who tried and whose deaths went unnoticed. Nobody ever asked a question, nothing ever changed.

Is it worth the risk? Is it better to rise up, or should we simply give up?

Day 39

"Don't be sad, Tanja," I told her as we were saying goodbye early that morning. "See you soon in India!"

"Well, I will!" she smiled with tears in her eyes, giving me a kiss and getting into the taxi that would take her to the airport.

I knew she would be sad. Over the past three weeks, she'd kept complaining about how London wasn't what she'd dreamed it would be for so many years. She told me that her mind kept wandering through Asian countries, with me, and that she couldn't focus on her new job. She said it was way too rainy, even by London standards, that everything was gray and gloomy, and that she didn't know what to do.

"I wish I could just leave everything and come traveling with you," she told me once. "But at the same time, I still don't think that I can give it all up and run away, chasing an easy way out."

I was also sad. It was wonderful traveling with her smiling all the time, sharing all the mishaps with her, and we understood and complemented each other so well. I would miss her in the evenings, when I lie down on a random couch and wake up the following morning alone. But I was also sad because I knew that a part of me wouldn't miss her. The part of me that liked to be alone, who liked to travel alone, who enjoyed meeting new people, waking up alone every morning and being the only master of my destiny, free to follow my own dreams, whatever they might be. The part of me that, from time to time, would still think back a few years back to another story, which was still hanging there, unfinished.

With those deep, sad thoughts flowing through my mind, I trudged Yazd's dusty streets to my next host. We had arrived in Shiraz yesterday, popping into Persepolis on the way to see the remains of the Persian Empire's main ceremonial center, which dates back to the fifth century BC.

Meanwhile, we'd experienced some interesting rides - first, a trucker who treated us to dried dates (the most popular sweat treat in Iran), water, tea and grapes, and in the midst of the ride even stopped the truck, rearranged our bags, took out a mattress, blanket and pillow and made me a bed. Just to make me feel more comfortable. Or was it so that I would fall asleep and he could make a pass at Tanja?

But when he took out a wig and started to comb it into a women's style, we realized that if he would make a pass at anybody then it would be me.

The second ride was offered by a family of four who had somehow managed to squeeze our backpacks into their trunk, and during the ride taught us how to drink tea in the Iranian-style. You put a sugar cube between your front teeth and, while you drink, the sugar melts and sweetens it. Awkward, but interesting. We also visited a four thousand year-old tree, which is considered to be the second oldest tree in the world.

Some say that Yazd is one of the oldest cities in the world. It's believed that the first inhabitants lived here around five thousand years ago. Yazd is the center of the Zoroastrian religion, which is based on a struggle between good and evil, and people's choices to take sides. These sorts of stories also exist in other religions that emerged later, but Zoroastrians remained optimists - they were convinced that good eventually triumphs over evil and that hell has an expiry date, but this fight will take some time.

All of the buildings in the town are made of mud, clay, water and straw, which is typical for a place that suffers from extremely high temperatures.

We visited the Towers of Silence, Zoroastrian's sacred places where they would leave their dead to be eaten by carrion birds. They did this for religious reasons, but also because of their environmental awareness - they didn't want to bury them so as to avoid contaminating their soil, nor cremate them so as to protect the air. Besides, this way they also fed hungry animals.

I was tired. I'd crossed well over three thousand miles in just a single month. I changed so many countries, towns and even beds, met so many people and learned so much. I needed a break. When I reached my host's apartment, I made a decision - I would head to India as soon as possible. Two people I knew were volunteering on a farm in the foothills of the Himalayas, it sounded like the perfect place to take a break and recharge my batteries (even though I was pretty sure that the place itself didn't have any electricity).

Leaving a place is fairly easy, especially when you're alone and you make all of your own decisions. I'd pack my things into my backpack, haul it up onto my back, say goodbye to my host or leave a message on the kitchen table if he or she wasn't there, and then that was that. There are no complications or overthinking. Deciding which direction to take next is your only decision.

I opted to head towards the east today, toward the Pakistani border. I slept in Kerman but didn't manage to get in touch with Ćiro Blažević, Croatia's most famous soccer coach who at that time was employed by the local team, so kept going. I passed through Balochistan, a province where the locals don't have the best reputation. In 2003, when a terrible earthquake struck Iran, they allegedly stole around 90,000 tents from the Red Cross that were intended for the victims in Bam, a city that had been completely destroyed, leaving more than 40,000 people dead.

After a long night and far too many hours on bad roads in old buses, I finally reached the border crossing early in the morning. This was the only one that connected Iran and Pakistan. Hundreds of locals were waiting for it to open. Just before this happened, an elderly man who spoke a few words of English approached me and asked me to follow him. He took me to the booth where passports were handed in through a side entrance, so that I could be the first one to cross without having to wait several hours with the other mortals.

He asked me a bribe for his help in skipping a queue at passport control - he wanted a pen.

I crossed the border, leaving Iran, and just before I set foot in Pakistan, I sent a message to my Mom that I'd crossed the border without any problems and got on the bus to Quetta, my first stop in Pakistan.

"Problem," the officer at the Pakistani side of the border said after I put the phone in my pocket. "Visa. No good."

He explained to me in his broken English that, while issuing my visa, the consul forgot to put a stamp with his name. Oh. Great. I waited for half an hour. Then I waited for an hour. So much for crossing the border first or getting in the bus to Quetta. Two white guys walked past me and I took the opportunity to exchange a few brief stories with them, only to see them get the stamp in the passport, allowing them to cross the border.

I was still waiting.

"You have to go back to Iran," the officer ruled two hours later.

In short, the procedure looked like this: I had to go back to Zahedan, a city about forty-five miles away, to visit the Pakistani Embassy that would then contact the Embassy in Sarajevo that issued my visa, they in turn would have to send an official letter confirming that my visa was valid, and only then I could return and cross the border. There was a catch though - the Embassy in Zahedan was closed for two days since it didn't work on Thursdays or Fridays (and I'd turned up at the border on a Thursday), and then I would have to wait for another two days for the Embassy in Sarajevo to open (because after Thursday and Friday come Saturday and Sunday, non-working days in the rest of the world) and only then I could come back here.

Nobody cared about what I would do and where I would stay over the next four days.

They sent me back to the Iranian side of the border where they gave my passport an entry stamp and let me wait. I exchanged a number of text messages with Tanja, who had just arrived back in London, asking her to try to get in touch with the Pakistani consul in Sarajevo and ask him what I should do. I soon got her reply - the consul asked me to call him from the Pakistani side of the border and he would take care of everything.

Now I *only* had to explain to the Iranian customs officers that I wanted to go back to their Pakistani counterparts in order to make a phone call to the consul. Hardly anyone spoke English, so they kept passing me over to another person every ten minutes. My passport became the most desirable object on the Iranian-Pakistani border that day. Everybody stared at it, but nobody had any idea what to do with it. In the end, they told me that I would have to go back to Zahedan after all.

They couldn't care less about where I would stay for the next few days in what was, according to many, the most dangerous city in Iran.

At that moment, I decided to apply the *pul nadaram* tactics that I'd picked up while hitchhiking across Iran. *Pul nadaram* means *I don't have any money*. This meant that I had no money for the taxi back to Zahedan, or a hotel where I could stay for a few nights.

I wondered whether this was going to be the first time that I had to spend the night at the police station or in a prison cell. I was asking myself whether this was going to become my own version of a travel story starting with the words: "Oh, once upon a time, when I was in prison..."

I sat on the floor, took out my guitar and started a hunger strike until they let me go to the Pakistani side of the border. The officers approached me and told me to go back to Zahedan, but I kept telling them *pul nadaram* and carried on strumming my guitar, still feeling pretty down.

I was so desperate that I even wrote my first song, *The Border*.

*Pakistani border,
came here early morning, feels like I'm getting older,
it's fucking 4pm.*

*Never liked borders,
they're just giving orders, putting in folders,
for them you're just a number.*

*Should go back to Zahedan,
but no fucking way, I just came from Bam,
pul nadaram.*

I wasn't feeling especially inspired so, after a few hours of waiting and trying to explain that I just wanted to go to the Pakistani side to make a call, they packed me, my backpack and guitar into a car that would take me straight to Zahedan. Or at least I thought so.

In fact, I ended up spending the next three hours driving around from one control point to another, always with different drivers each time, explaining my situation to the soldiers over and over again. I played for them, trying to persuade them to take me back to the border with a smile. But to no avail.

I got to the police station in Zahedan. And there was yet another round of waiting. A couple more phone calls. Two more police officers. Yet another car. Yet another ride. A guy smoking a joint in a little park. The cops found out what the guy was doing. They sat him next to me, in the back seat of the police car. The guy kept asking them to let him go in tears. The police officers completely ignored him.

Yet another police station, at the bus station.

"You. A bus. Tehran," one of the two police officers said.

I was so numb and desperate that I didn't react with surprise that they wanted to put me on a bus and send me to the capital that was 1,000 miles away.

"Oh, yes!" The first optimistic first thought of the day crossed my mind. "The other day I wrote to Ahmad, the CS guy from Zahedan, I still had his phone number, so maybe he could help me." I called him to explain the situation.

"No problem," the voice on the other end of the line was calm. "I'm coming to get you. May I speak to the police officer?"

I handed the cell phone to the police officer, hoping that they were negotiating my handover. The day-long nightmare was coming to an end. The police officers sat me in the car again, we drove through the city and got to the only police station in Zahedan that I hadn't yet visited. My escort left me, which meant that I had to explain over and over again to the curious cops that my friend was on his way and that I would be staying at his place.

"You stay here," they replied strictly. "Not go with friend."

I took a look at the policeman's belt, and all sorts of thoughts sprang to my mind. I could easily imagine the headlines in the Croatian newspapers: *Crazed Croatian hitchhiker takes police hostage in Iran, insisting that they let him go to Pakistan!*

I sat in a corner, waiting for Ahmad. Soldiers and police officers approached me, flicking through my passport, and the younger ones asked me to play something for them on the guitar, but gave up once they saw the expression on my face. Three handcuffed guys were sitting right next to me. They were looking at me, trying to figure out what I had done wrong. What a wonderful feeling it was.

Ahmad finally arrived. I felt so lousy that I could barely shake his hand and I couldn't' even smile at him.

"It'll be okay," he just smiled. "It is not the first time I've had to do this."

He walked around the station, calmly filling in the forms for my release. It took him more than half an hour to write various statements and sign them, giving his passport and cell phone number, trying to assure them that the next day he would bring me back to the station and things like that.

"Welcome to the city of smugglers, weapons and opium!" He proudly said as we drove through the streets of Zahedan. It was all dark.

I told him what I was going through and thanked him for picking me up. He just smiled and said that there was no problem. He took me to the lab where he usually worked, making dentures, and welcomed his guests, away from his wife and child at home.

Just as I was thinking that this was like a scene from a horror movie - the desperate stranger, an overly polite host, a dental lab, a vicious, dark city - Ahmad approached me and asked "Would you like to try some opium?"

In a country where alcohol is banned and strictly controlled, opium is the most common intoxicant. If you take into consideration the fact that we were about thirty miles from the Afghan border, the world's largest poppy producer (and therefore opium too, which is made from the dried milky juice of unripe poppy heads) and that for just a single dollar you could get a couple of grams of high quality stash, it becomes abundantly clear why the Iranian population, along with Afghanistan, has the highest percentage of drug addicts in the world.

Zahedan, the main stop-off point from where opium is sent from east to west, leads the pack in this infamous statistic. That evening, after an exhausting day, I too became part of it. And fell into the deepest sleep ever.

As agreed, Ahmad dropped me off at the police station the next morning, from where the cops would take me to the border so that I could try to cross it again and call the consul in Sarajevo, just before the weekend. I thanked him for everything he had done for me, and he just laughed and told me to feel free to call him if I got stuck.

As I was sitting at the station, soldiers and police officers kept approaching me as usual and I kept telling them that I was waiting for transportation to the border, to which they nodded their heads. After forty-two minutes, a man with a moustache entered the lobby.

"The border is closed," he firmly declared. "Holiday."

"What damned holiday?" I replied quite upset. "Are you trying to say that nobody knew anything about this yesterday when they promised to take me to the border or this morning, while I've been waiting for them to pick me up for the last hour?"

The guy with the moustache gave me a blank look, listened to me indifferently and left.

I took a deep breath.

I decided to call Ahmad and spend another day at his place, far away from all these incompetent guys in uniforms. I turned to the young soldier who spoke a few words of English and politely asked him whether I could borrow his cell phone or a telephone to call my friend.

"No," he replied succinctly.

"Why?" I asked, not believing my ears.

"There's no phone," he replied, looking at me blankly, even though I could hear one ringing in the background.

I opened the door of the first available office and saw the officers talking on their phones and typing text messages. I turned to the fresh faced soldier and told him a few choice words in Croatian, which I'm sure he could presume the meaning of.

It took them a good fifteen minutes to give me a phone so that I could call Ahmad, and even then some of them were saying that it wouldn't be possible for me to go with him, even though we'd gone through all of this the previous day and had exactly the same conversation.

I took another deep breath.

After what felt like a very long hour, Ahmad eventually arrived, again walking around the station, writing and signings statements, leaving his passport at the station again, putting me in his car and taking me to his laboratory while he went home to his wife and child for lunch.

This was yet another day in Zahedan, a city that I hadn't even planned to visit. I sent a text message to my Mom, telling her that I'd safely arrived in Quetta, the first city in Pakistan and that I was just switching buses so we'd be in touch tomorrow. I had to take this into account, after having rejoiced too soon about crossing the border.

I managed to get in touch with Pakistani consul in Sarajevo, told him the whole story and asked him to send me an official statement by email that I could take with me to the border the following day or to the Pakistani embassy, but he assured me that it wasn't necessary. He gave me his private number so that I could call him tomorrow in case of emergency, but this would probably mean waking him up at around 6.00am due to the time difference.

Whatever.

It was now my third morning in Zahedan, and my second morning spent at the police station. After the inevitable waiting, the cops dropped me off to the Pakistani embassy, where I was greeted by a smiling, bearded man who spoke perfect English and looking very capable. This put me at ease after two days of dealing with incompetent cops/army officers. He explained to me that he needed an official memo from Sarajevo confirming that the visa had been issued and that crossing the border wouldn't be a problem after that. He made a call to his fellow consul in Sarajevo and explained to him the same stuff that I'd said the day before and, given that it was Saturday, he urged him to get his ass out of bed, go to the office and send the memo, even if it was the weekend and only seven o'clock in the morning in distant Bosnia.

The bearded man was funny, offering me food and telling me fascinating stories about his country.

"Be sure to visit the north of the country," he enthused, describing the natural beauty of this part of the world. "But be careful, the Taliban is most active there."

Great, man, thanks for the suggestion.

"The border closes at two o'clock in the afternoon," he added anxiously, looking at his watch. The memo still hadn't arrived.

It was already noon, and the ride to the border took almost an hour. Would I make it?

The memo finally arrived, we made a few copies just in case, I said goodbye to the consul and sprinted out of the embassy to take a taxi that, under whatever conditions, would drop me off at the border as soon as possible. The Iranian army again made sure to make matters as convoluted as possible. As I was leaving the Pakistani embassy, they took my passport and told me that I had to wait for a police escort that would accompany me to the border. My police escort arrived no long after, but it only dropped me off at the first checkpoint in the direction of the border, leaving me with the kid who was standing there on duty with an assault rifle over his shoulder.

I tried to explain to the kid that I had no time and that I needed to catch a taxi because the border was about to close, but he didn't get it. He kept saying - *escort, escort*. I was overcome by a mild sense of despair and panic as it became clear to me that I wouldn't make it unless someone came to pick me up soon. I took the passport from the kid's hands and tried to flag down a taxi. He came after me, yelling in Persian; after that, the commander showed up, took my passport and told me to calm down - the escort was on their way. He also told me that the border didn't close at two o'clock, at least not for tourists.

I realized that any effort was a waste of time and so sat down by the side of the road, putting my head in my hands. Thirty-five minutes later, they called out to me, and I saw that my new escort was a clean-shaven, unarmed guy, who was smiling cheerfully as he asked me where I was from. We stopped a taxi, I put things in the trunk and got in, with my head bowed down. The driver asked for money. *Pul nadaram.* He started to shout. I got out of the taxi, my head still bowed, taking my backpack and a guitar back out of the trunk. Since I apparently needed an escort, maybe they could pay for the ride. In the end, the driver let us in the car and took us towards the border.

It was two o'clock in the afternoon. I just prayed that the consul was wrong and that the border was still open for at least a few hours, hoping that there would soon be an end to all of this. Much to my disappointment, the taxi driver kicked us out halfway along, at yet another *check point*, where I had spent a few hours two days earlier, waiting for transport in the opposite direction, back to Zahedan. Once again they passed my passport around like a cheap hooker, then asked me to play something for them and told me that I had to wait for another police escort.

I took another deep breath.

I got another unarmed, clean-shaven officer to accompany me and another car, and got close to the border at around 3.00pm. My escort and I had to get out of the car once more, probably at the last checkpoint before the border. A group of soldiers had a good-old giggle, watching the sulking traveler, poking fun at me, laughing in my face, and confirming my fears - yes, the border was now closed.

"*Go to hotel, wait tomorrow.*"

I couldn't remember the last time I felt so miserable, humiliated and helpless. A tear in my left eye was searching for a way down to the Iranian desert sand, but I raised my chin and looked up to the sky to prevent this. I wanted to get away from it all, I wanted to get to the border, I wanted to illegally enter Pakistan, I wanted to do whatever it would take. I used all of my remaining strength to somehow persuade one of the soldiers to let me go to the border, telling him that it was open and that they were waiting just for me. My despair convinced him, so he stopped a Pakistani truck and went with me to the closed border.

At last, I finally stood outside the border crossing, three and a half hours after leaving Zahedan, while the drive from there onwards should apparently take less than an hour. That was the third day that I tried to cross the border without success. I yelled *heeeelloooo* at the top of my lungs, hoping that someone would come out of the booth, recognize me, take me by the hand and lead me to the other side of the border. But this didn't happen.

We returned to those nasty soldiers, and I sat down on a rock, having no idea what to do. A small car with British number plates turned up. The guy in the car was also late for the crossing, although he didn't look half as desperate as I did. He was Pakistani, living in London, and had decided to visit his family by land. And I thought I was the crazy one. I shared my tale of woe with him, and although he didn't seem particularly sympathetic, he did offer me some water and snacks, which was more than either the Iranian police or army had done for me in the past three days. But now this guy and I came as a set. It was getting dark, they dropped us off at the hotel, and tried to explain to us that we had to spend the night there because staying elsewhere would be dangerous.

So let's try again - *pul nadaram*. We were the only guests, so the hotel staff looked at me in amazement and tried to squeeze some money from me. I had just enough money to cover the room, but I also had principles. And I can be as stubborn as a mule. The Pakistani guy ordered dinner and let me have what he couldn't manage, which I devoured with relish, and eventually the staff reluctantly showed some mercy and allowed me to sleep on an air mattress in my sleeping bag under the awning in front of the hotel.

The next day, it took me two hours to get to the border that was six miles away, and once again I had three different police officers escort me on the way. Following what was now a well-established tradition, I approached the counter in front of which I had been standing three days ago, sad, nervous and feeling empty inside, and proceeded to present them my passport without even saying hello. They browsed through it, but didn't understand why I had two entry and one exit stamp.

Just when I thought things were about to get complicated again, they gave me an Iranian exit stamp and let me go through the gate.

Day 1000

"Iran is a beautiful country," I said, concluding this part of my talk by showing photographs of Esfahan, Shiraz, Yazd and Persepolis. "This is a country with a rich history and heritage, but what definitely stands out are the people."

It was already getting on my nerves how I kept praising people and their kindness, telling the same stories for each country I visited. But I couldn't do it any other way because it was true.

I didn't care so much about the culture, history or other attractions. Whenever I browsed through travel guides or read about the history of a place, I would get bored. Most of all, I got the feeling that I was missing out on something - an interesting conversation, an interesting anecdote about that culture, history or other attraction that a real-life person could be telling me from their first-hand experience. That was the way I learned about a specific place.

There was another reason why I constantly emphasized the kindness of locals, especially in those *dangerous* countries such as Iraq or Iran. The image that the Western world has of these countries is tainted by the negative image of politicians, religious leaders and fanatics. Spreading positive stories about ordinary people is the perfect way to combat this negative image, the prejudice that ordinary people in the West have about these people. It's the perfect way for me to do my bit to changing this image for the better. In a certain respect, it's a traveler's duty to share positive stories of their time somewhere so as to pay the people there back for their tremendous hospitality.

Many travelers feel wary about public disclosure, so they prefer to keep their stories and experiences to themselves. And that's just fine, a story tends to lose its particularity every time you tell it (or write it), so many people want to keep it private. My way is different. I give up part of my privacy in order to educate thousands of people and possibly change the attitudes and mindsets of a certain part of the population - that sounds like a fair deal to me.

My hosts and the people I met during the trip would probably choose this path for me if they had the choice - all those people who asked me so many times whether I liked their country, who would have a sparkle in their eyes when I told them that their country was beautiful and people were friendly and hospitable.

If they were in a position to do so, they too would share uplifting stories about their countries with the world and invite people to visit them. So if I can do this then why wouldn't I?

"After three days at the border of Iran and Pakistan," I carried on, "I entered the sixth country on my trip."

Day 44

I went through the same procedure as on the Iranian side, handing the officer my passport and the memo from Sarajevo without saying a word. The way I was looking at him motivated the officer to stamp the passport immediately and wish me a pleasant stay in Pakistan.

Thank you very much.

I had to fill in a number of forms, from which I learned that tourist wanting to cross the border by land showed up on average once a week. I learned that the only way to get to Quetta was by a bus that was scheduled to depart in four hours' time. They took me to the prison hall that served as a shelter for illegal immigrants, so that I could wait for the bus in good company. They asked me for money for the mandatory armed escort that would accompany me through Balochistan, the province which, just like its Iranian namesake, was known for particularly nasty things - a month ago, two Swiss nationals were abducted and held by terrorists who demanded the release of their mates in prison in exchange for them. Normally I would pay for the escort because I knew it was mandatory, but I still couldn't quite forget how they had treated me for the past three days, so I explained to the police officers that I wouldn't pay because their embassy was responsible for my staying in Iran for three days more than planned. Finally they gave in and granted me a 78-year-old chap as escort, with an old rifle slung over his shoulder. I said to myself that, if things went south, it would be me saving him, not the other way around.

They got me on the bus to Quetta. I felt exhausted, tired and empty. I didn't even want to think about the 14-hour ride that was ahead of me, after which I would have to take another bus to other town. I had no idea which town it would be, though.

The people in the bus were very friendly, but I didn't feel like talking or anything for that matter, especially when I saw what the driver was like and the condition of the road.

We arrived in Quetta early in the morning. I didn't have the slightest idea what I would do next. The town is known as being one of the most dangerous in Pakistan so I decided to leave as quickly as possible. The first bus going towards the east was heading for Islamabad, so I decided that Islamabad would be my next stop. All I had to do was take a stroll into the city and find an ATM or an exchange office since I had stubbornly refused to exchange the little money I had left at the border.

The town was a mirror image of those that I'd visited the previous year in Bangladesh: chaos, filth, too many people, but the food was similar, and the dusty air, the sound of horns on the streets - the same as always. The people on the streets were very friendly and showed me where I could find what I was looking for. At the same time they warned me to watch out for the swindlers who were on the lookout for tourists.

What they didn't know was that I wasn't a tourist but a traveler. I couldn't be tricked that easily.

I finally came across an exchange office; I entered and with their welcome I came to think that I must be dreaming - the owner greeted me, kissed my hand, offered me some tea, with two children standing behind him, the sum of whose ages was about fourteen. It all made me feel suspicious. The exchange rate was very good, so I grew even more suspicious. I exchanged a small number of dollars, checked on my cell phone converter whether I'd received the right amount of Pakistani rupees, I then checked whether the banknotes were genuine and finally asked him to give me some smaller notes - he did it all without a single complaint and everything seemed perfectly above board. I got out, checked once again whether everything was okay, and it was.

Feeling proud of myself because of the fact that nobody had even tried to fool me, I returned to the exchange office to exchange another small amount of money, but this time only the kids were there. The one serving me didn't offer me as good an exchange rate as his father because the banknote was a bit older than the last one. I smiled at him saying that he was a good businessman - I accepted the lower exchange rate. He exchanged the money and handed it over to me. I counted the money once again to make sure everything was okay and tried to put it in my pocket.

"No, sir!" The kid yelled, taking the notes from my hand. "You should put the smaller banknotes on the outside of the wad - that way people will think that you don't have much money."

I listened and observed very carefully; paid the kid a few compliments, took my wad back and headed for the bus station.

I bought my ticket, sat down in the bus and, while I was waiting for the bus to set off, started to count my money. Something was wrong. I recounted it all, searched my pockets - but 1500 rupees were missing. I thought about it and realized that the only place where I could've lost them was in the exchange office. I remembered how the kid showed me how to put the smaller notes on the outside of the wad. That was probably the moment when he pulled some kind of a trick on me and stole the missing amount. After I felt sorry for my hurt ego for a few moments, I laughed and gave the kid some credit - I didn't notice anything suspicious even though I was watching him the whole time.

It served me right for thinking that I was special. A traveler, not a tourist. Yeah, right.

The bus driver found every hole on the bumpy Pakistani roads and unbearable music was playing so I couldn't sleep. I didn't like Pakistan. Since I was known for making rash decisions, I took my little black notebook and made a list of ten objective reasons why Pakistan and I could not be friends:

1. The Pakistan visa was the most expensive of all the visas I had ever had to apply for. I had to go to Sarajevo to get it, write and sign my acceptance of risk and a liability waiver statement in which I took responsibility for everything that might happen to me.

2. Because of the mistake made by their consul and their incapable customs officers I had to wait for 78 hours to cross the border. It was one of the most frustrating experiences in my time traveling.

3. Hitchhiking was forbidden, at least for the first four hundred miles, and right after crossing the border you get a mandatory armed escort.

4. It was the first time I got robbed - by a smiling 10-year-old kid, changing money at the exchange office.

5. Their roads are terrible, and their drivers were even crazier than those in Bangladesh.

6. Pakistan reminded me of Bangladesh, my first non-European love. And we all know that there's only room for one first love.

7. My friends were waiting for me in India, on a farm at the foot of the Himalayas but I wasn't sure how long they would be there so I had to hurry.

8. I'm tired. I've spent a month and a half without a break for more than three days.

9. I had a runny nose, ever since I'd been in Iraq. The main suspect was the poor air quality, which would hopefully get better on an Indian farm at the foot of the Himalayas.

10. Apart from one CSer in Lahore, I had no other contacts in Pakistan.

I was thinking very seriously about skipping Pakistan and letting other people discover its qualities instead. Why had I felt such bad karma for the past few days?

But then I simply stopped whining about my bad luck, stopped thinking about the negative things and focused on the present moment. I started talking to other passengers. I was cracking jokes with the driver. I switched places with the guy standing at the door while the bus was moving and shouting the names of our destination to attract new passengers. I shared lunch with the local people at the stops along the way.

I was missing all of these beautiful moments while I was over-thinking the things that had already happened and that I could no longer change, or the things that were about to happen, which I couldn't influence either.

Day 1000

"I didn't stay in Pakistan for too long," I said, moving through the slides and talking about the kindness of the people that I had met in yet another *dangerous country*.

I told them about a twenty-five hour ride on the bumpy road to the capital - Islamabad. This town was built according to a plan some fifty years ago, it is only the tenth largest city in Pakistan and completely different from the rest of the country. There were no bumps on the roads, the drivers respected the traffic rules, the streets were clean, and there were expensive hotels everywhere, fast food restaurants, big shopping centers and things like that. The only thing that reminded me that I was in Pakistan was the routine police checks here and there around the city.

Even though the name of the country clearly showed that it was an Islamic republic, just like Iran, things were different. They were much more easy-going. You could hear foreign music from the passing cars, women weren't obliged to walk around with their heads covered, there was much more freedom. I even had a few drinks with some people, including a woman. Unbelievable.

But, people in Pakistan were still quite traditional. When I told my new friends about my travels and plans for the future, I saw a glimmer of excitement in their eyes, but also a tinge of disappointment as it dawned on them that their parents would never allow them to do something similar. In their lives, everything was decided in advance - their studies, their profession, and maybe even the person with whom they were going to spend their life. And those were the well-off ones, lucky enough to have some decisions they could make on their own.

"I spent Eid al-Adha in Lahore," I continued. "It's a Muslim holiday on which they celebrate the moment when Abraham, according to God's command, was prepared to sacrifice his own son. Eventually, God changed his mind, but since he was still hungry, he asked for a sheep instead of the child. So now, a couple of thousand years later, Muslims all over the world sacrifice an animal on that day. In Pakistan alone, almost a million animals get sacrificed. The only good thing about this bloodbath is that one third remains with the family and another third goes to relatives and friends, whilst the final third goes to the poor."

Who knows when God decided to relinquish his share.

"As for cultural attractions, I visited the Badshahi mosque that, twenty years ago, was the largest mosque in the world and it seriously reminded of the Taj Mahal, which had also been mostly built by the Pakistanis, just a few years earlier."

I also remembered observing an amazingly enchanting moon that was in a perfect position above the beautiful mosque. It was the ideal way to spend my last day in Pakistan, since the following day I would be heading for India.

Setting off on a trip around the world

Tanja and her dog, Nina

Kabak Valley

Tanja and her thumb

Cappadocia's stone houses

With our overly friendly host

Countless balloons

Göreme

Turkish-Kurdish hospitality

Exchanging money in Iraq

A feast in Iraq

Do not turn right at the crossroads

Artisans

One of Esfahan's many bridges

Jāmeh mosque

Toilet sign

Driving through Iran

A good truck driver

Persepolis

Towers of Silence

Day 51

"Oh my God!" That was the first thing that crossed my mind when I finally made my way through the crowd and boarded the train to the east.

I have traveled a lot, I've passed through a few underdeveloped countries, but nothing could prepare me for the chaos and mess that I experienced on that train. There were at least three times more passengers than the wagon could really take. Five people onto seats that were made for three. Some were sleeping on the luggage racks. Small children were everywhere, and definitely outnumbered adults. Most of the passengers were standing or sitting on the floor, squashed in like sardines.

What was most astonishing, they found it perfectly normal. Every few minutes a different hawker would make his way through this flood of people, carrying containers of food or drinks in his hands. They were selling tea, snacks, bottles of water and mango-flavored juice. I'll never figure out how they didn't lose their balance with all those things in their hands.

I looked around and saw all those poor people everywhere - I didn't know what to think. Should I feel sorry for them? Should I treat everyone to a nice meal?

The noise just wouldn't stop. The kids cried for a bit and would then sleep a little, constantly fidgeting. A young girl who had barely entered puberty was breastfeeding a baby, a five-year old was rocking his two-month old sister.

The train set off.

A colorfully dressed woman entered the wagon. She went from one person to another, clapping her hands and begging for money. She woke up those who were asleep, and although nobody actually spoke to her, some of them gave her five or ten rupees. As she was getting closer, I realized that she was, in fact, a he. I watched, feeling pretty confused, observing the ease with which (s)he got money out of people. Maybe I could try to do the same thing one day.

"What's going on here?" I asked a young man standing next to me, since he was only person who spoke to me and said a few words in English.

"It's *hijra*," he said. "They're neither completely male nor female. You'll see many of them in India, and their story is quite sad. They are rejected by their families and community, they face discrimination in education and employment so they're forced into prostitution or begging, like this one who has just passed by. Also, they're believed to have supernatural powers, so if you give them a rupee or two they will bless you, but if you don't, they may curse you."

It got dark.

The noise and bustle in the wagon calmed down. The train stopped less frequently. The people that were not standing were all asleep. I was thinking about the past fifty days and the upcoming period. I would take a break and slow down in India. Anyway, there were no more visas in my passport, and I had nearly four months to think about my next destination, until my Indian visa expired.

In the middle of the night, at about 3:14 am, I felt something trickling down my left foot. It caught me by surprise and I tried to move my leg, but couldn't because it was way too crowded. The kid who had been breastfed by the young girl earlier was peeing. This firstly filtered through his pajamas, then his mother's dress, and finally over my foot.

In an instant, I saw the whole thing transpire in my mind's eye, and there were two possible versions of the event. The first one was the impulsive one - I would wrestle my foot free in revolt, no matter what, try to wipe it on the first person next to me and give the boy's mother the evil eye. Or maybe just take the kid and throw him to the other side of the wagon.

The second scenario went something like this: calm down, take a deep breath and accept the situation as it is. You're in India, you're a guest in a foreign country. A country where different rules obviously apply. The cute baby boy was sleeping when he peed, I'd done the same thing when I was his age. The only difference was that my parents had enough money to buy me diapers. A teen mom was sound asleep, exhausted by life and the trains, as well as the fact that she was a teen mother. She had also been peed on.

I opted for the second scenario. After all, I'd just been peed on by a sweet baby. It was ninety-five percent water anyway. What was the worst thing that could happen to me because of this? Absolutely nothing.

"Welcome to India!" I said to himself. "The land in which my left foot is half clean, rather than half peed on."

I got off at the stop where I would switch to a train for Kathgodam, but it was a few hours late so I joined a bunch of local people who were sleeping on the floor at the station. There was another guy who was taking the same train as me so I could count on him to wake me up on time. This was my first sleep in India. Before I actually fell asleep, I wrapped my backpack around my leg, and clasped my guitar in my arms - just in case.

A few hours later, I got up off the station floor and got into a bunk bed on my train. I woke up at the last stop, managed another eight miles to Bhimtal with a trucker, from where I start to climb up to the farm.

The first thing I saw after getting off the truck was a group of monkeys that were leaping around a nearby forest and coming right up to the road and the nearby food stands. The locals weren't especially fond of them - almost every person held a slingshot in their hands so that they could chase the monkeys off and goad them back into the woods. Despite their best efforts, the agile monkeys nevertheless succeed in pinching a piece of food at least every couple of minutes. They would mischievously show off and then, seeking sanctuary in the trees, sprint back into the forest.

The locals soon became aware of my existence and, without even asking, they showed me a path that would take me to the farm. With my burdensome backpack on my back, I set off! On my way up, I saw a number of signs indicating that I was on the right track. At one point the path branched in two direction - one was uphill and shorter, while the other was longer, but flatter. Being the damsel that I am, I chose the latter. That was my first mistake.

I crossed a stone bridge, pondering why I hadn't seen any signposts for quite some time. It didn't cross my mind that there was anything suspicious going on, so I carried on. That was my second mistake. But eventually, it didn't seem so difficult to just keep on walking. Maybe it was because of the fresh mountain air or the fact that I was going slightly downhill, I couldn't tell. Taking this way turned out to be my third mistake. I assume that the fundamentals of hiking state that if you're supposed to climb upwards then you shouldn't be going downhill. Maybe this even counts as a fundamental piece of logic.

Feeling completely exhausted from all this wandering, I came upon a courtyard where two ladies gave me a curious look and offered me some tea. One of them, with a huge baby bump, spoke a few words of English. She explained that the local kids were about to come home from school and that they could take me to the farm because they lived nearby. While we were sipping tea I tried to explain what I was doing in their village - we had a good laugh. I was already fairly sure that by the end of this journey I would earn myself a PhD in body language because that was my native tongue wherever I went.

When the kids came back from school they seemed excited to be my guides. I found it funny observing them - there were five of them in total and although all combined their ages barely reached double digits, they showed great ability in climbing up the path. By comparison, I found it difficult to keep up with them. The children took some rest here and there, but I wasn't quite sure whether this was for the sake of the youngest among them, who was only five, or for me. Anyway, after half an hour we arrived at their house where they handed me over to a young man who was supposed to take me all the way up to the farm. He was at least twenty, so I could ask him to help me and carry my guitar without feeling guilty. Before we started walking again I turned around, because I wanted to thank the kids in some way for showing me the way. As I didn't have any candies, I gave them the crayons I used for writing my hitchhiking signs. Anyway, let the kids draw, the candies would only rot their teeth.

We were pretty close to the summit and I suddenly noticed I was no longer able to hear the noise coming from the road below. I was surrounded by forest, vegetation and wildlife. Here and there I could hear the water flowing downstream, but otherwise not a mouse stirred. We came across two workmen who were digging up a huge stone, but they still found some time to say hello, beaming at me. *Namaste*. Our next stop was a *Sadhu*, a Hindu holy man who had been living in a small stone temple for the past twenty years. I greeted him by bringing my hands together and we carried on.

Just before I passed out, I caught sight of a little house, which was to be my final destination. Two familiar faces were there outside of the house - Keveen, the best person I had never met, and Gina, a girl who I had met a couple of years before, in Keveen's camp house in

the middle of woods in the south of France.
I was finally home.

Days 52 - 66

The moment I arrived at the farm at the foot of the Himalayas, a new chapter in my journey was set to start. Since I was tired from two months of wandering from town to town, I was looking for a place that I could call home: a place where I could have some peace and quiet to spend at least part of the remaining nine hundred-and-something days. *The Himalayan Farm Project* seemed like the perfect place for this - an emerging permaculture farm where I would volunteer for a couple of hours each day in exchange for a bed, and my food would set me back 200 rupees per day, which was a reasonable price. Most importantly, Keveen and Gina were there.

In the fall of 2009 I had traveled across Europe and stumbled upon Keveen's CS profile. He was a bearded man who lived in a little caravan in the middle of the forest in the south of France. I sent him an e-mail to which he replied from Mexico, where he was running an alternative school for poor local kids. After studying his website for a while,[3] I noticed that he was working on a couple of other admirable programs and that was why I decided to keep in touch with him. By chance, a couple of weeks later, I came across Gina's CS profile. She was staying in Keveen's caravan, so I decided to stop by. Having spent several days in the middle of the forest, I decided to get more actively involved in this whole story so began sponsoring the school in Mexico and also one in Guatemala the following year. We stayed in touch for two years, but kept missing each other all of the time. Until that time when I found myself in Iran and realised that they were barely thousand or so miles to the east. I sped up a bit and was finally in a position to give them a hug.

Over the following two weeks, life on the farm proceeded at quite a gentle pace, but it was also hugely interesting. I'd been dying for some peace and quiet and some time to rest from the constant journeying. Moreover, I craved the physical labor that I'd successfully managed to avoid throughout my whole life - whether in my parents' garden in the Zagreb suburbs or in Ričice and Dobrkovići, the little villages where I whiled away every summer with my relatives. For some inexplicable reason I wasn't such a lazybones when I was away from home, but I was too lazy to try to get to the bottom of this mystery.

---
[3] www.korakor.org

I was happy here, even though there was no electricity, no hot water and no toilet. We solved the electricity issue by waking up with the first rays of sun and going to sleep when the sun set. We heated water over a fire so we could have improvised showers behind the bushes. If we had to use the toilet then we did it the good old Indian way - you dig a hole and use your left hand as toilet paper. It took me some time to adjust to their way of life, but it was certainly worth trying. If you wanted to charge the battery of your phone or use the Internet, you had to walk down to the not so nearby village, but even this didn't prevent me from contacting my parents every day - battery life on a *dumb* phone lasts much longer than on a *smartphone*.

"Wait a minute, you get in touch with your parents every day?" Keveen couldn't believe his eyes when he saw me trying to find a signal so that I could text my Mom.

"Yeah, yeah," I replied, with a touch of pride in my voice. He wasn't the first nor the last person to be surprised by this. But I was still proud of this ritual. It didn't cost much and it meant a lot to my parents, who were thinking of me twenty-five hours a day.

"Hats off!" He said. "My mom gets worried if I don't call every ten days or so. But I guess it comes with time."

"You mean to say that one day my family will get used to my wandering all over the place?" I asked hopefully.

"Probably," he said after a short pause. "You must understand that your parents only want you to be safe. They'll be fine once they realize that you're capable of looking after yourself, without the help of others. You just need to convince your parents that you can be trusted."

"But how can I do that?" I asked, my interest having been piqued.

"Calling them every day puts you on a right track," he smiled. "And time plays its part, too. My parents couldn't understand my need to keep traveling and living a nomadic lifestyle. It didn't match their perception of what life should be. And they only cared about one thing: *and what happens then?* Once you've traveled the whole world, what happens then?"

"Yeah, they keep asking me that too," I said. "So, have you come up with a good answer?"

"More or less," he replied. "I told them I didn't know what I'd do after I'd traveled the whole world, but that it wasn't so important anyway. I also asked them a question. I wanted to know about their understanding of the meaning of life. The meaning of life for them was being happy. We all agreed about that. But saying that, what happens if their vision and my vision of happiness aren't exactly the same? Do I have to follow their recipe for happiness or I should follow my own vision?"

"What did they say?"

"They didn't know what to say. In the end, I just told them that I love them and care about their happiness, but that even though they have a lot more life experience than me, they need to respect my choices and not judge them. I don't know why some people feel the need to interfere in other people's lives and lecture them about how they should live. Imagine what it would be like if I went from one office to another, from company to company, telling everyone how stupid and pointless it is to stare at a computer for eight hours every day. People would think I'm crazy, and tell me to mind my own business. But they're doing exactly the same thing when they tell me how *I* should live *my* life. We just need to agree to disagree, and that way we can all live our lives whatever way we want to."

"After all, that's the problem with today's schools," he continued shortly afterwards. "Nowadays, kids at school are taught to be good students and leave school with good grades so that they can find a good job and make a lot of money. If you make a lot of money and you're well-off, then you can enjoy your life. In my opinion, education needs to be completely different. We should be learning about how *not* to spend money. How to live life to the fullest and do what you want with very little money. It's simple, really. We've been living like this for the past few years. Instead of spending eight hours a day on a job you don't like just to earn money and enjoy the remaining couple of hours each day, the weekend and the odd holiday, you should spend the time you have available doing what you like, spending as little money as possible."

"People wonder how I've managed to travel for years almost for free," he said. "It's really very simple. I don't waste my money on a new TV, new clothes, and dinners at restaurants. A dinner at the restaurant costs as much as a week of traveling. A shower, a bed, a toothbrush - all of these are luxuries for us. Apart from being able to live on the bare minimum, life teaches us how to appreciate the little things and to never take them for granted."

"It's all about priorities," I confirmed.

"Exactly," he agreed. "Don't get me wrong, I'm not saying that traveling is the solution, and that it's necessarily the best way to spend your time. Some people don't like to travel, especially not the way we travel."

"That's exactly what I've be saying!" I exclaimed. "If we all hitch-hiked, who would pick us up?"

"Precisely," he continued. "For some people, happiness is having a steady job, a career, a house, and three kids. That's fine, there's nothing wrong with people living their life like that, as long as they don't try to tell others how they should live."

"You said you didn't think traveling was a solution," I said while cutting up some potatoes into smaller pieces, "but have you ever come across anyone who has traveled and then regretted this decision?"

"Not a single person," he laughed out loud. "The truth is, you can find all sorts of answers while on the road. When you don't know what to do with your life, just go. It doesn't matter where, left or right, just go. The answers will come. Traveling helps. It makes your life easier, no matter how difficult it may be sometimes. You'll learn a lot about yourself and about others. You'll become more patient, but this is why you have to go all the way. You need to get stuck for days on end in the most dire conditions, or take a ride on a terrible bus along dreadfully bad roads, and develop resilience. Become less picky. This is the life. Life experiences that make you a better, wiser, more experienced person. After a while, you realize that it has nothing to do with being on the road, it doesn't matter how far you travel, what really matters is the inner journey that you take. You can be in a village in the middle of nowhere and travel in your mind. You can be in the middle of a city and learn, grow and share. The important thing is to live your life, not someone else's."

"Lunch is ready!" Gina called out. We all sat down in a circle, thanked the Earth for providing us with another delicious meal and plunged our hands into the freshly prepared food.

The only person living on the farm all year round was Chandan, a local who made sure that everybody there had something to eat, including the cows, bulls and buffaloes. He was absolutely fluent in *Unglish*, so our communication was mostly based on miming and smiles. It worked out just fine.

Indians' use of body language to communicate is something you need to get used to, but once you embrace it you won't let go of it so easily. Besides the well-known customs that you should always keep your right hand clean, and that it's used for eating, handling and making rollies, and that you greet people with folded hands by saying *namaste*, two other traditions caught my attention.

The first thing that impressed me was how people touch the ankles of the elderly and those people who deserve respect. When you meet an elderly person in the village, you walk up to them, bend down and touch their ankle with your right hand to show them respect and attention. The first few times I witnessed this, I was convinced that the greeter was going to grab hold of the other person's ankle, slam him to the ground and that a really nasty fight would ensue.

I was also delighted by another gesture - their head movements. Tilting your head from left to right means "no", just like in the rest of the world. But a quick bobble from side to side means "yes". As if they were stretching the neck or subtly trying to get water out of their ears. But my definite favorite was when they moved their heads in a figure eight, raising their eyebrows at the same time, by which they confirmed what they had just heard or in other situations were saying *"maybe"*.

All of this means that communication with people in India never gets boring or monotonous, even if you couldn't speak the same language.

We went through the same process with several people who lived near the farm. One of them was a boy who helped us carry things. Although he was smaller than us, he would carry loads weighing in excess of 130 pounds up to the farm, using just his neck muscles. The load went into a basket strapped across the forehead like a sweatband, and then you were ready to rock. It was all the more impressive given that his only footwear was flip-flops.

There was a sadhu, a Hindu holy man, who had lived in a nearby temple, or ashram, and hadn't come down from the mountains for the past twenty years. He was supported by food donations from the locals in exchange for his blessing. He dedicated himself to meditation all day and smoking India's famous *charas*, mixed with tobacco into a typical Indian cigarette - the so-called *beedi*. A *beedi* is the Indian version of our *rollie*, wrapped in a brown leaf from a local tree, and *charas* is actually a type of hashish, thriving in this climatic zone where cannabis sativa occurs naturally. If we told the locals that they could get good money for it in the rest of the world, they wouldn't have understood why since there was plenty to go around. The difference between *charas* and hashish is that with *charas* the plant is still alive. So basically, you take the tips of a plant and rub them between your palms. You repeat this a few more times, and after a while your palms turn black because of the plant's resin. Then you just scrape this resin off onto a newspaper, mix it with tobacco and the rest is straight forward.

The rest of the crew there was comprised of people who had heard about the farm and decided to join and help create something new. Still, I was alone most of the time, or in the company of Keveen and Gina. Keveen took up the role of the leader of the farm and he handed out assignments, which were done without any complaint. It was probably like that because he did twice as much work as the rest of us, but also because the way in which he held us together was fascinating - not once did he raise his voice, he only had words of praise and support for every task that was done properly, he made us laugh, all the time keeping the atmosphere thoroughly positive.

When I was with him I was awfully quiet, which wasn't typical for me. I had returned to the days when I was would listen to other people's stories instead of telling them myself. You can learn a lot from a man who has been traveling for as long as he could remember, who had two Master's degrees and who is fluent in three foreign languages. What made him an excellent teacher is the very fact that he wasn't a know-it-all clever clogs who tried to impose his opinion on others but, instead, just looked to set an example.

I only had to wait a couple of hours after we'd left the farm to see him practicing what he preached, at the train station in Lucknow, on our way to Varanasi.

We were waiting for a train that was two hours late, as is usual in India. And then we waited for another hour. It finally turned out that the train would be four hours late. We were just killing time reading books, which was a whole new experience for me on this journey. I don't usually have time for books - it would be awkward if I read them while hitchhiking; when I'm in the car I usually talk to the driver, and when I arrive in a city, CS people tend to meet me so I talk to them. In India, the transportation was so cheap that even I could afford it, so there was no hitchhiking. But there was some reading. This reading, however, was interrupted by someone's moan and the murmuring of people stood some 50 meters from us.

Keveen got up to see what was going on, and I followed him. The scene was terrible - some guy with a huge bamboo stick was yelling at a beggar and beating him in the head, while around 30 people just passed on by, passively observing the whole scene. Even though Keveen had almost got himself injured a couple of years earlier while trying to save a stray dog from a group of local people who wanted to kill it, he intervened once again. He blocked the attacker's blows with his body and gestured for the violence to stop. Instantly, the situation changed dramatically. All those who, moments before, were just observing the situation, took hold of the bamboo stick and stopped the violence. The beggar, with his face covered in blood, pulled himself together quickly, wrapped a piece of cloth around his head and crawled over to our bench, asking us in his perfect English if we could buy him a cup of tea. Handing him a tea, Gina also gave him a painkiller. The man thanked us from the bottom of his heart, telling us his sad life story. When we noticed that the train was approaching the platform, we said our farewells to him and he wished us a safe onwards journey.

Sometimes you just need to get involved, no matter how much it might seem that it's not your job to save the world.

Day 952

I was sitting at a bus stop, not far from the main Zagreb interstate junction. It was dark, and I was waiting for the 164 bus, which would take me to my parents. Bosnian hip-hop group Dubioza kolektiv was blaring through my headphones, getting me in the mood.

There were two other people at the stop, a man and a woman. They were both standing up. I noticed that the man was saying something, and based on his body language I could tell he'd been on the juice. I watched the situation unfold. He kept talking. He was talking to the lady but she obviously didn't know him. The man moved a step closer to her. I took my headphones off.

"Are you deaf?" He raised his voice. She looked at him out of the corner of her eye, and then again stared out into the distance. This made him even more frustrated so he took another step forward.

I got up from the bench, took a deep breath and, standing as tall as I could, I slowly inserted myself between them, looking straight ahead. I had a serious expression, with my shoulders pulled back, and I think I also cracked my knuckles on my right hand. Whatever he had planned, I had obviously distracted him. He muttered something and then walked away.

The bus arrived shortly afterwards, the lady got on first and I entered right behind her.

"I was chatting with a neighbor the other day," my mother told me a few days later.

"Which one?" I asked.

"I'm not sure if you know her," she replied. "She told me that the two of you were waiting for a bus at the same stop the other night and that you stood up for her to protect her from some drunkard."

I didn't know that she was our neighbor, but I remembered Keveen and how he had intervened in that messy situation at the station in the northern India and the lessons I had learned that day.

Sometimes you just need to get involved, no matter how much it might seem that it's not your job to save the world.

Day 69

"I'm sorry," I said to Keveen, Gina and Mario as I went over to a quiet corner in the alley and threw up. A pair of curious locals just looked at me and then continued walking as if they had already got used to seeing this sort of thing.

"Most people get sick in Varanasi," said Mario, our new acquaintance. "It'll pass."

We had met Mario the night before, on our hotel's roof terrace, where we watched the sunset and the countless kites that flew up into the sky every night. His story was an interesting one. He had come to Varanasi planning to buy a few hundreds live fish at the fish market and take them to the river, where he would set them free. Kev, Gina and I exchanged looks and grinned saying that this was one of the noblest things we'd heard in a long time.

"Is there a particular reason why you want to do it?" Gina asked.

"Of course," he replied confidently. "Tomorrow is one of the four days each year when all the good deeds that you do count a thousand times more than if you do them on a *normal* day of the year. That way you buy yourself good karma for the next life."

I didn't get the concept. Doing good deeds and buying good karma for the next life? And it was only possible on certain days of the year? What had happened to good old altruism and doing good deeds without expecting something in return?

I didn't say anything and tried not to judge.

I drifted away from the conversation and continued to watch the kites and the monkeys that were bouncing around the roofs, eating flies around the glowing street lights. One of them even got into an argument with a guy who had come out onto the roof to hang up some wet clothes. The humanoid creature ended up with the short end of the stick.

In the distance you could make out the outlines of the river Ganges, the holiest of the Indian rivers.

Although the competition is fierce, Varanasi ranks as the oldest and the holiest of all Indian cities. Every Hindu wants to die there so that they can be cremated and have their ashes scattered in the Ganges, which is in itself a way of offsetting all earthly sins and guaranteeing that they won't be reincarnated as a cow or a dog. For those who aren't lucky enough to have their ashes scattered in Varanasi, it can also be done in other cities through which the holy river flows. For this reason, but also because a great deal of Indian life being intertwined with the river, the Ganges is one of the most polluted waterways in the world. However, this doesn't stop the locals, and a few brave (let's stick to this word, even if many others spring to mind) tourists from taking a dip, washing their clothes and even having an occasional sip.

Early in the morning, we joined Mario at the fish market to help him carry two trunks with wriggling fish inside all the way down to the docks, or ghats as they're called there, where we loaded the trunks onto a boat. Mario negotiated with some kid to take us out into the middle of the river where we would set the fish free while Mario said a prayer to The One Who Counts Karma. The deal was to give the kid 100 rupees for half an hour, even though the kid had asked for twice as much. We said the prayers, set the fish free and returned to the bank of the river. After we returned from this highly spiritual journey, Mario took a look at his watch and noticed that the kid had brought us back at least four minutes early. He refused to pay the agreed price, after which the two of them ended up arguing about a couple of rupees.

If good karma is worth a thousand times more on that day, then the same ought to be the case for the bad karma. I'm afraid that our dear Mario only just broke even.

At that moment, a nauseous feeling knotted my stomach, forcing me into the small backstreet and leaving me bedridden in a mouldy room in a cheap hotel, which I couldn't leave for the next forty-eight hours, apart from to crawl to a filthy squat toilet every quarter of an hour.

I was sick in India. Even though I'd known this was inevitable, especially since I had been eating in local eateries and drinking the same water as the locals, it didn't ease the pain or suffering I had to endure over the next two days.

So many things crossed my mind those days. I decided to visit Nepal. Not only was I curious and it wasn't very far, I also wanted to see two old friends. And I likewise wanted to take this opportunity to get a visa for Thailand because I was planning to go there sooner or later, and finally I wanted to spend some time alone.

I missed being alone.

I thought about Zagreb, my parents' house, mom's homemade soup, my friends. A place where I felt at home, even if I sometimes didn't like it. I missed it all. Being safe, healthy, full, and sleeping in a clean bed.

For the umpteenth time, I started asking myself what I was doing there. The fact is that I'd been dreaming of this journey for the past three years and everything else had played second fiddle to it. But now, two months after I'd set out, I was lying sick and alone in a dirty bed in an unfamiliar country and I didn't even know why. The same song kept playing in my head: *And I still haven't found what I'm looking for...*

And then it hit me. *The moment*. On the third day my symptoms began to subside so I somehow managed to pull myself together and to drag myself to the *ghats*, sat on the curb and observed the world around me. The people and their ritual bathing, washing their clothes in a dirty river, tourists in rented boats taking photos of them with their big cameras, the city silhouetted in the background. The multiplicity of colors. The hustle and bustle. The people. The energy. Above all, the freedom. I was there because it was my decision. Because I wanted it to be that way. Because I had the courage, even if it hadn't taken a huge amount of courage. And no, I didn't have the slightest idea what I was looking for. But that didn't even matter. I wasn't sure if I was going to find what I was looking for. But I knew I was going to have a great time looking for it. I didn't want any more than that. Not for the time being.

I shed a tear of joy and stood up without feeling dizzy.

It felt great to be healthy again. So great that I even considered getting sick more often. I took a stroll around the city which I was finally able to see in all its *glory* - walking past the cows, bulls, stray dogs and their combined faeces, the filth, beggars, intense odors... Everything finally made sense. Learn, observe, engage your senses. The people you pass look at you more kindly if you walk with your head held high and with a smile on your face. I sat down in one of the tourist restaurants (one of the more expensive ones for that matter) and decided to treat myself to a bowl of soup, a main course and some freshly squeezed fruit juice. I thanked my body for feeling better and made a promise that I would take a better care of it.

Meanwhile, Keveen and Gina were working on their small projects: one day they offered passersby a free morning coffee; another day they repaired the local children's kites; sometimes they gave our fellow hotel guests a free massage on the rooftop. Always with a smile on their faces. We also organized the *Love Carpet*, an activity about spreading love in which you buy colorful chalks and use them to write messages of love, peace and friendship on the pavement. People, children and even animals would join in.

The next morning I was as fit as a fiddle and set off for Nepal.

Day 73

"Stop!" shouted a sleepy customs officer on the India-Nepal border. "Passport control!"

It was pitch black, and we hadn't noticed that we'd crossed the official line separating the two countries. The customs officer was asleep, the border was closed, and only a dozen nervous passengers with rucksacks on their backs were standing there. The odd stray dog wandered by every so often.

It was my first organized mini-trip on this journey and it served its purpose. It reminded me why I liked to organize everything myself. I decided to take a bus from Varanasi to Kathmandu by booking a place with one of the many travel agencies operating in the city. Breakfast, a direct ride to the border in a comfy tourist bus (without driving with the locals or having to stop), accommodation in a hotel at the border and a connecting service in another tourist bus were all included in the price.

I wasn't the only naive one. A dozen of us became suspicious at breakfast. An egg and two slices of old toast didn't help to regain our trust. The bus "unexpectedly broke down", so we had to take a local bus to the border. That bus was literally falling apart, the seats were made of wood, and more than half of the windows simply *weren't there*. On top of that, the locals were pressed up against us and the bus stopped in every village it passed through.

We were five hours late arriving at the border, the hotel which we were booked into was on the Nepalese side, and the border was closed, of course.

"We've booked accommodation on the other side of the border," we begged the customs officer who was merciful enough to let us go through, asking us to come back to his office in the morning so that he could stamp our passports. We did as we were told and entered Nepal legally the next day.

After having been ripped off by the tourist agency from Varanasi, I also learned of some of the ways they rip tourists off in Nepal.

Here's one way. You go into a local restaurant and order food from people that appear to be nice, without asking the price. Then you realize the bill seems to be too high. Just don't give in and ask to see the menu. They won't have one. You go out on the street and ask random passersby how much they would pay for the same meal. Your doubts are confirmed: you paid three times the going price. So, you go back to the restaurant, but they just laugh in your face. For the first time in your life you go to the police and return with a broad-shouldered cop. Suddenly they stop laughing. They give you back the equivalent of two dollars, because that's how much they ripped you off.

Let's talk about a second way. You're walking down the street when, all of a sudden, a guy carrying a load of colorful leaflets offers you a trekking tour. Even though you tell him you're not interested, he keeps trying to convince you but without much success. But then he uses the ace up his sleeve: he nonchalantly mentions that, just a few moments ago, three Swedish girls signed up to take the same tour. You're instantly interested so you pay a couple of hundreds dollars hoping for... But then you find yourself with six German dudes and two French guys who, probably just like you, are looking for the three blondes. I'd definitely fall for this if I was a little more naive, had a bit more money and if I was into blondes.

Now a third way. A guy walks up to you in the street carrying a local string instrument and asks you if you're interested in buying it. Of course you're not but he then starts asking you where you're from, what you're doing there - the usual stuff. Then he generously offers to play something for you with his friends, for free. You get a nice mini concert although you can tell from the look in the band's eyes that they aren't putting their heart and soul into the performance and that they will ask for something in return once they're done. And this is exactly what happens - they also have their CD, which they're selling at a reasonable price, and all the profits, of course, go to the local orphanage. You try to leave, saying that your laptop doesn't have a CD drive, and that's no problem, instead they offer you something else - hashish, pot or whichever other illegal substance you fancy. I never get these sorts of things from people I don't know, so I leave their mini studio with a smile on my face and head back to the safety of the street.

And on and on it goes. Luckily I'm an experienced traveler so nothing can surprise me. Only that kid in the Pakistani exchange office. And the travel agency in Varanasi. And the local restaurant I just mentioned...

During my stay in Kathmandu, I couchsurfed at Taya's place. She was an Australian girl whom I'd met a year before in Bangladesh and was volunteering there for the second year in a row despite being only 19. She taught kids English and was one of the many young travelers I met on the road. Pretty much all of them had the same story - they finished high school, some of them graduated from college, and they weren't sure what to do in life, so they took a *gap year* and traveled the world, to volunteer and to educate both others and themselves. They wanted to try out all sorts of things before reaching the big decision about what they wanted to do in life.

They put aside money from a young age to be able to afford it without their parents' financial assistance. They work at local supermarkets a couple of hours a day from the age of thirteen, before going home to do their homework. From an early age, their parents try to instil in them skills such as resourcefulness and independence.

"Is everything alright with him?" asked Chloe one Sunday lunch at my parent's home in a village near Zagreb regarding my brother Filip, who was twenty-seven at the time. "Why does he still live with his parents?"

I tried in vain to explain that this was perfectly normal in Croatia. You stay with your parents until: a) you get married, b) you find a job and sign up for a 30-year mortgage on your own home, or c) for as long as you want. I tried in vain to explain to her that my family almost disowned me when I told them that I would rent a flat whilst I was a student. She didn't seem to understand being so close to your family, she even found it a bit disturbing.

I, on the other hand, quite liked it. Parents care about their children and want nothing but the best for them. However, getting to know lots of kids who travel around the world, I realized that there was another side of the story. By doing this, these Croatian parents are raising future adults who won't be able to live independently or cope with life's challenges. The parents are raising spoilt little imbeciles.

"When I turned 18, I got a nice present from my parents," she said. "They told me: you either start paying rent and your share of bills or you move out now."

No matter how brutal it may sound, sometimes you have to be cruel to be kind. This is the only way that children can learn to be responsible and experience real life. Parents should let their children go and tell them that they're not kids anymore. Let them find their own way in life.

The road to hell is paved with good intentions.

If I lived according to my parents' good intentions, I would never be where I am now, in Nepal. I wouldn't have found out what the future had in store for me.

"Very sentimental," said a Buddhist priest, a professional palm reader at the foot of Swayambhunath, a popular Monkey Temple. "And non-belligerent."

Even though I was very skeptical when it came to psychics and palm readers, one of my goals was to forget everything I had ever known, tear down prejudices and try new things, so I decided to give him a chance. The price was a decisive factor - you could pay what you wanted.

The first thing he told me was "sentimental and peaceful". I'd say he was spot on. All my life I'd tried to follow my heart and do unto others what I would have them do unto me. Of course, I screwed up here and there, but fortunately it didn't show on my palm. For instance, I got into a fight in elementary school and lost. Maybe that's why I'm not a fighter. If I had won that fight, I might have become a bully.

"Sometimes you believe in God, sometimes not," continued the old man.

Again, he was right. There was a period in my life when I believed in Him, giving religion a lot of attention and showing Him kudos, but as I was got older, I drifted away from religion and found my very own little God to whom I pray secretly. I'd talk to him from time to time, like back in Croatia when I was climbing up that steep hill from the docks at Prizna to the highway. I came to realize that out of all world religions, there was just one you had to stick to - your conscience.

"The business line is blocked, you don't have a steady job," he got it right again, even though that wasn't such a revelation, given that I was a bearded guy visiting a Napalese palm reader.

"There were problems at the age of 8, 13 and 18. Family, school and health problems.

I had to ponder this. The only thing that came to mind was a broken heart at the end of elementary school, when I was thirteen, but didn't we all go through that? At the age of 18, I dumped my high-school sweetheart with whom I'd been in a relationship for three-and-a-half years and I suffered from an injury to my medial collateral ligament whilst playing for a local soccer club. As for 1993, I'll have to ask my parents.

"A very good period in your life from the age 19 to 22," he continued.

Student life, moving away from home, it was great!

"A long journey, changing places, changing jobs from ages 23 to 25."

I was a broker, quit my job, started working in a juice bar, set off on my first trips and started to write. The old man got it all right!

"At 26 and 27, you tried to do something, to learn something, but time passes slowly and you face constant obstacles."

Sitting in front of him, I looked him in the eyes and believed him. I was twenty-six and a half at the time and I had really set off on that trip then to find some answers, to find something. I still didn't know what I was looking for. I kept asking myself, but the only answer I got was: be patient, you'll eventually find what you're looking for.

"At 28 to 32, a long travel, a long journey, changing places, changing jobs, good time to get married," he started projecting my future. "At 33 to 35, good financial situation. At 36, you'll have a bad year. Be careful, pray to God. After the age of 37, things will go very well. A new home, a new country, a happy family."

"The life line is very good, there are some problems with your joints and back; do yoga and meditate."

Hey, show me a person who doesn't have any problem with their joints and back!

"The heart line is very good, you have a good predisposition to be a writer, a painter, a singer, a dancer."

The old man got it right again. I'm not good at drawing, singing or dancing, but here I am, I'm writing...

"The head line is good, you're very smart. The mount of Jupiter is crossed, problems with married life and living together with someone in general. Marriage to a woman of another nationality is good, but a marriage to a woman of the same nationality would be bad. An odd number of children is good. An even number of children is bad. The Sun line is good, you have a good memory. The line of Mercury is crossed so you must stay away from betting and gambling."

Man, where were you when I blew it all on the stock market?! Or when, as a kid, I was hooked on bookmakers and roulette wheels?

"The line of Mars is crossed, your family won't be there for you if you need any help."

Well, he was wide of the mark on that one. The only thing I'm sure about in life is that my family would always be there for me. I know my family loves me and will always be there if I need something, even if I put them through the mill with things like this trip. They'll be there for me even if I don't need anything.

And that was it - all done in four minutes. He did quite a good job, I've got to say.

"May I ask you a question, please," I enquired at the end. "Will I find what I'm looking for, and what it actually is?"

He threw a careful look at my palm, smiled and pursed his lips without saying a word.

Day 81

"Hey, you!" I said to the familiar freckled face that seemed to be aimlessly walking down a dusty street in a suburb of Kathmandu. Much smaller than me, she looked up and leaned her head into my chest.

I met Caro two years ago, on my first big trip across Europe, a few days before I met Gina. We spent two days together in Montpellier; we went rock climbing, which almost didn't end well. I still have a scar on my lower right leg, and it always makes me think of her. On a side note, scars are by far my favorite souvenirs since they're free and they don't take up any space in my backpack.

As was usually the case, we stayed in touch over the years thanks to Facebook, and now here we were, together on the other side of the world.

I wonder how anyone ever travelled before the internet and mobile phones. These two things make it possible for me to do everything I actually do, from finding a host in different cities and checking information about the best place to start hitchhiking to keeping in touch with my parents on a daily basis.

This is also another reason why I tirelessly preach that what I do isn't difficult. Maybe it once was, but today, with an average IQ and a little common sense, almost anybody can travel.

Caro took me by the hand and we got in an overcrowded minibus (with nearly thirty people) and went just a few miles away, to the orphanage where she had been volunteering for a few weeks and practically given new life to the place by helping the two managers there. Since Caro was a teacher, she was also able to give them some advice on how to work with the kids who lived there. But giving advice wasn't the only thing she did. When she noticed that the orphanage needed a refrigerator and an electric stove, she spread the word across France and in just a few days she managed to raise enough money for the much-needed household appliances.

When ten kids aged from 5 to 12 started getting back from school, the fun could really begin. Although it would be normal to expect chaos with so many children in one place, they were probably the quietest and the most polite kids I had ever seen. The short lives of those six girls and four boys were each marked by a sad story. Most of them were abandoned by their parents because they weren't able to take care of them and were, one way or another, brought to the orphanage where they would have a roof over their head, go to school and have a couple of square meals each day. They all spoke broken English: the little ones not so much, the elder ones a bit more.

We helped them with their homework, we had lunch together, watching them sit on the floor and launch themselves at the plates of rice with a bit of sauce. Later, I took my guitar and start playing and singing songs that they'd never heard before. However, that didn't stop them from getting up and showing off their dance moves which reminded me of the dancers in disco clubs. Shortly afterwards, we played a cassette with local hits and even the adults had to let themselves go. I really don't like to dance, but it was a lot of fun to muck about for the kids and pull my best *John Travolta* moves to the Nepal-Indian melody.

Once the sun set and the temperatures dropped, the time had finally come to bring something new to the house - we turned on the electric heater. Minutes after we turned it on, ten kids gathered around it and watched it as if it was the most interesting cartoon in the world.

"Usually I read them bedtime stories," Caro whispered to me. "You can do it this evening if you want."

I took a picture-book *The Wolf and the Three Little Pigs*, turned it into The *Wolf and the Ten Little Pigs*, and made them laugh thanks to a couple of adjustments in the story. Then I sent them to bed. *Good night brother, good night sister, good night Sir, good night Miss*. Like little ducklings, they went off to sleep in their two rooms.

In morning we gave everyone a big hug. They gave us a few presents: a silk scarf and *tikka* on our forehead as a blessing with which they wished us a safe and a happy onward journey.

"Are you sad because we're leaving?" I asked my travel companion as we got on the bus.

"I'm sad, but not because we're leaving," she said. "I have a bad feeling about this orphanage."

"What do you mean?"

"Yesterday I went through the papers and saw that most of these children aren't actually orphans," she said. "They have parents and they all come from the same village as the managers."

"What do you mean?"

"The orphanage has been possibly set up solely to make money from visitor donations. I founded a non-profit organization with my friends from France and besides buying a refrigerator and a heater, I raised some money for the orphanage. When I told the orphanage manager about it, saying that the only condition to get this money was to show the proof of their costs, she started to make all kinds of excuses. She made a mysterious phone call, said that they wouldn't be able to get a receipt for some of the services, that there could always be some unexpected costs - that sort of thing."

"Oh, my God!" I said. "I've heard similar stories about people who set up orphanages, exploiting the kids and the Westerners' kindness for their personal profit."

"I know, I've heard of them too, but I still don't want to believe that we got dragged into a story like this," she added. "And now I'm trying to figure out what it feels like for these kids. Although most of the money doesn't go to them, I wonder whether they are still better off in the orphanage, in those conditions, than at home. This orphanage, which is still far from an honest institution, might be better than their homes."

I was mulling it over, but I still didn't know what to say or even what to think.

After a 10-hour ride in a comfortable bus, we arrived to Lumbini, Buddha's birth place and the place where he spent the first 29 years of his life. The driver tried to help us find an affordable hotel room, but we didn't need any help since we were confident that we were resourceful enough to find the cheapest possible accommodation. We got off the bus in the center where we were met by an interesting sight - hordes of priests bedecked in their red-orange robes were wandering through the city at dusk. Having entered the first guesthouse, we found out that a peace festival had started a day before and that most of the available accommodation had been booked up.

In the end, we ended up in the house of a family that kicked out an old lady out of her room on the ground floor and offered it to us for 500 rupees per night. For the room, not for the old lady. The old lady didn't seem upset about the evacuation, so we assumed that the extra rupees would do her good and we accepted the offer. The room was filled with the old lady's odor and some huge mosquitoes, so we used all the equipment at our disposal to keep the mosquitoes at bay, spread a net above our bed and watched a boring movie on Caro's laptop before going to sleep.

The following day we went sightseeing in Lumbini. A bunch of cheerful kids followed us all the time. They wanted to say hello and take some photos with us. We had fun saying hello back to them and indulging their whims. We also visited a few of the temples built by Buddhists from all over the globe; however, we couldn't help feeling that there was big competition as to who could build biggest and most beautiful monument to Buddha. The path led us to the place where Buddha was believed to have been born, but having realized that we would have to pay 200 rupees for the ticket, we decided to just observe it from outside, sat on a bench, watching the other visitors and taking some shots. I think Buddha would be rather disappointed if he knew that, even in his birthplace, everything revolves around money.

"Look, a map of India!" Caro exclaimed and picked it up from the dirty ground.

"It will come in handy!" I said.

"Well, somebody has circled one of the cities," she showed me the circle on the right side of the map. "Puri."

Day 106

I stayed with a random CSer in Delhi and killed time before Tanja's plane was scheduled to land by reading a book.

During the forty-hour ride from Puri to Delhi, I managed to get through half of the thickest book I'd ever started to read - *Shantaram*.[4] A lot of people travelling across India had read it and were thrilled with it, so I had to get myself a copy. The further I got into it, the more I enjoyed it. As far as my taste in books is concerned, I would say that it maybe goes into a few too many details. The protagonist, going through the same part of the world as I was, seemed to remember more details than I did. This made me question whether I'm actually a good travel writer. Do I manage to absorb the local culture, do I remember the flavors, colors and scents? Am I interested in the local customs, the local food, and the religion of the locals? Considering my knowledge of the countries I had visited, the answer would have to be - no. But I always have the same excuse: I travel because I want to meet new people, not because of the places, customs or everything else.

I shouldn't be making such excuses anyway. I'm not actually a travel writer, I'm just an ordinary guy who travels and writes about his experiences and thoughts, and the people he meets along the way. The point of my journey isn't to write about it, it's to experience it. If I went to the trouble of investigating, following leads and exploring minutiae then it just wouldn't be me. If I adjusted my style of traveling and writing to fit what I think people want to see or read, it just wouldn't make any sense. Everything I do would be shorn of its authenticity.

As I turned the page, an email came through.

Sender: Chloe
Subject: Ummm. So how bout that.
Text: Merry Christmas?
Attachment: plane ticket from London to Kuala Lumpur. Arrival date - 57 days' time.

I rubbed my eyes and read it again.
See you there, I replied briefly.

---

[4] By G. D. Roberts

I put the backpack on, trying to forget about the last half an hour and headed to the airport.

Day 1000

"I visited the can't-miss Taj Mahal," I continued, changing slides to one of Tanja's photos of this beautiful building. The construction project employed some 20,000 artisans and spanned 22 years. It was commissioned by Shah Jahan, the emperor in this part of India, to be built in the memory of his wife Mumtaz Mahal who died giving birth to his fourteenth child. Today it's considered to be the greatest monument to undying love.

I hadn't been especially taken by the Taj Mahal and the whole story surrounding it. The building was amazing, but the energy of the place, the never-ending stream of tourists, the unavoidable romantic story... I remained indifferent. Given how many people are absolutely taken by the Taj Mahal, I'm sure that the problem must be with me. Or maybe the chaos in my head and heart that Christmas. Or the fact that Tanja and I broke up just three weeks after visiting.

"We also went to Jaipur." I showed them a photo of a playful young elephant. "Our CS host there had a place with a farm full of elephants so we spent some time playing with them."

We did some sightseeing in Jaipur, popularly known as the Pink City. We saw Hawa Mahal, where the façade is made of 953 small windows and it reminded me of a beehive from which the women would observe what was going on in the busy streets below, then Jal Mahal, popularly known as the Water Palace, several textile stores with countless rugs, scarves, linen and clothes, and the Amer Fort, the major tourist attraction in this part of India. But the highlight of our visit was definitely staying with our CS host Rahul and his elephants.

He had twenty-four of them, and above all else he valued a professional approach in caring for these wonderful animals. They were treated the way they deserved. Unfortunately, elephants are rarely afforded such treatment at similar farms, where they are often held in terrible conditions. We played a lot with a one-year old baby elephant, tugging its trunk. Tanja then danced and the baby elephant followed her lead in its clumsy moves.

"You see that old elephant over there," Rahul pointed to the other end of the farm, "it cost me my biggest dream in life, and almost cost me my left leg."

"What happened?" We asked.

"Elephants are a family tradition and a family business, I was an elephant-rider in my youth," he began, telling his story. "But besides that, I fell in love with cricket, my biggest love. I was a very good left-handed bowler. Every morning I got up at four, ran ten kilometers and trained until eight, when I went riding with my elephants to the Amer Fort. More than half of the male population in India plays cricket. I was on the cusp of being invited to play for the Rajasthan representative cricket team, but then I witnessed a fight between two elephants, and the older one stepped on my foot several times and smashed it to smithereens.

"Oh, God!" We both exclaimed.

"The doctors somehow managed to save my foot," he told us, looking downcast, "but, I had to forget all about cricket."

"So what did you do?" We asked.

"I did what had to be done," he said with a smile. "I went back to the family business and elephant care. I decided to do my best to create a wonderful place for both the elephants and for tourists who come to see them. I think I'm on the right track."

It's a beautiful, but also sad story. He was so close to fulfilling his boyhood dreams, and then, just like that, they were cruelly ripped away from him. He found the strength to come back, to fight back, and to give his all to a new project - he wouldn't allow himself to be dragged down by misfortune.[5]

Tea with his mother, dinner with his friends (one of whom left early so that he could wait out on the street for an hour to wave to a girl he liked), getting to know Fabio, the only white elephant rider, watching him ride an elephant, navigating through the traffic in the busy Jaipur streets with cars, rickshaws, buses and motorbikes, while talking on a mobile phone and rolling his first joint of the morning... There were just so many memories from Jaipur that I didn't have time to tell.

The photo of the elephant was enough.

"We also visited Goa," I continued. "Goa is a former Portuguese colony and the top destination in India for partying."

Today, Goa is practically a Russian colony - the signs in Russian outnumber those written in local languages, the locals all speak a little bit of Russian and vodka is sold on every street corner. Thanks

---

[5] Today, Rahul's elephant farm Elefantastic is a top tourist attraction in Jaipur.

to cheap flights, the hot climate, low taxes on alcohol and opiates being available everywhere, it really doesn't come as a surprise that Russians are rushing to Goa.

"After Goa, we visited Udupi, where I tried to surf waves for the first time. The result of this was that I was rushed to the hospital and required two stitches to my head," I continued, showing them a new photo. "That's when I realized that I'd probably be better off sticking to couchsurfing. After Udupi, we decided to visit Munnar, with its beautiful tea plantations, Alleppey, exploring its magnificent lagoons by canoe, and then finally ended our Indian tour in Varkala, a charming tourist resort."

"I was pretty shocked while traveling across India," my story about India was coming to an end. "I had no idea that India could be all that. The image of India I had in mind was strongly shaped by *Slumdog Millionaire*: beggars on the streets of cities with huge populations in the millions, dirt, poverty, and crime. Even though all this does exist in India, it is also so vast, so varied, and so beautiful. When I say to people that I spent more than three months in India, everyone thinks that I toured the whole country and saw everything worth seeing. But that wouldn't be possible even if you had three years, let alone three months."

"And then came the first flight on my trip," I continued. "Since it was impossible to head east by land, through Bangladesh and Myanmar, and traveling over the Himalayas was very expensive and complicated, I opted for the simplest solution and bought a cheap plane ticket to Kuala Lumpur."

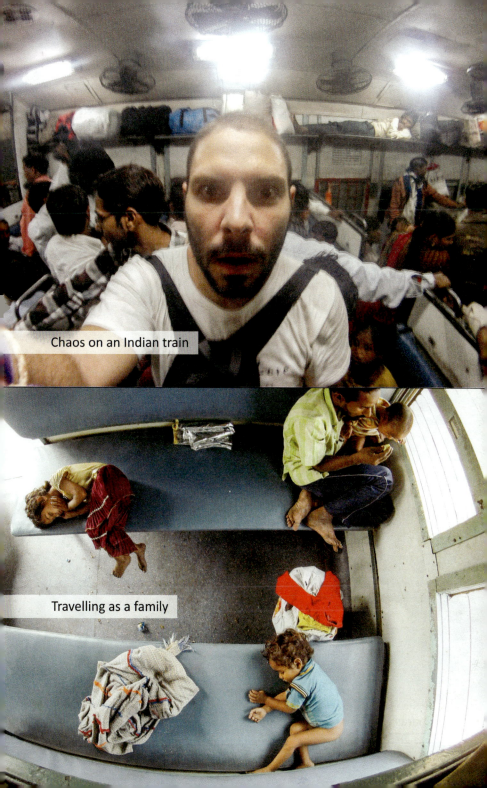
Chaos on an Indian train

Travelling as a family

Keveen and Gina

Charas

With an unavoidable resident of Varanasi

Varanasi from the Ganges

© Caroline Perrier

A cremation
© Caroline Perrier

A moment of healing on a ghat

Manakamana Temple

Swayambhunath

The Hawa Mahal, Jaipur

The Jal Mahal, Jaipur

Elephant love

Sweet kids

An equal participant in the traffic

Goa

A colourful cow

Prayers

Tea plantations in Munnar

Traditional thali served on banana leaves

Sailing the backwaters in Allepey

One of my countless Indian sunsets

Day 163

So there I was, at the airport in Kuala Lumpur, for the second time in three days.

I had been really surprised by what I saw when the plane first touched down: the city was very clean and modern, the cars were new, there weren't any piles of garbage on the streets and everything seemed to work just fine, especially compared to India. Everyone was fluent in English, prices were a lot higher than those I'd been used to, air-conditioning was on wherever I went, and everything just felt unchaotic. At the same time, people were more introverted and more stressed, they didn't say hi and they didn't smile at passing strangers; everything was, in this way, hectic.

I missed India.

My host was Marina - a CSer from Serbia whom I'd met on my trip across Europe. She prepared me some hot dogs, showed me her supply of Vegeta (a Croatian seasoning that's ubiquitous back home) and took me to see the Petronas towers. On the second night of my stay at her place, we went to a party organized by a Slovenian girl who had promised to bring some ćevapi and ajvar, both Balkan specialities. She forgot the ajvar and only started barbecuing around midnight when it was already time for Marina and me to catch a ride home. So, after two nights of *couchsurfing* at Marina's, I went back to the airport.

And there I was, at the airport in Kuala Lumpur, for the second time in three days. I was waiting for a girl whom I hadn't seen for almost two and a half years.

In the summer of 2009 I had been a graduate student at the Faculty of Economics, living in a rented flat in Zagreb, working in a juice bar in Masarykova street and hosting CSers on a daily basis. During that time I had only been on one journey - my first hitchhiking experience, to Sofia and back. I traveled by listening to the stories my guests told me, picking up ideas and plucking up courage so that I might also try something similar one day. Josh hitchhiked from Germany to Iran and back. Christoph cycled from France to China. Steve hadn't been home for the past nine years. Tom had seen half of the world on his motorbike. Chloe had left Australia when she was 18 and had been wandering for the past couple of years, doing random jobs and enjoying life.

She had also been seducing her host in Zagreb. And very successfully for that matter.

So frequently, I had to answer the question: how and why did you decide to start traveling? I always gave the same answer: I blame all of the couchsurfers who I'd hosted over the years. But the truth was a bit different. I started my first serious trip across Europe with just one intention - I wanted to go to Berlin, see the blonde Australian girl and spend a few weeks with her before she headed back to her own country. I set off on the adventure on 10 September 2009. A few days later, I arrived in Berlin, where Chloe broke my heart in a park. I couldn't go back home so forlorn and heartbroken, so I carried on further to the west, hitchhiking and couchsurfing. And that was the beginning of my first two-month trip across Europe.

I returned to Zagreb, carried on with my studies, gave my first talk about Couchsurfing, started my Facebook page, spent 50 days in Spain, came back to Zagreb, took a couple of exams, organized a hitchhiking race to Istanbul, and then returned to Zagreb again. I was doing some selling myself on the TV and in the press back then, so some nice people at MasterCard got in touch and offered me a one-month sponsored trip outside Europe. I chose Bangladesh.

My reason for choosing this country was a wedding in Dhaka to which I had been invited, but there was also the fact that Chloe was in India. There was a possibility we might be able to see each other.

I spent an entire month in Bangladesh; Chloe and I didn't meet up. I returned to Zagreb, did some more exams, met Tanja, went to Portugal with her, did loads of talks all over Croatia, appeared as a guest on radio and television shows, passed my last uni exam, got my diploma, and finally, started planning my lifelong dream: 1000 days of summer traveling around the world. That journey started on 10 September 2011, exactly two years after I set off for Berlin.

While I was in India, Chloe had sent me that email, telling me that she was coming to see me, wherever I was. So we made an appointment to meet in Kuala Lumpur in February. When she heard that I had got an Australian visa, she bought two plane tickets for May, one for me and the other one for her.

And there I was, at the airport in Kuala Lumpur, for the second time in three days. I caught sight of that girl whom I hadn't seen for two and a half years.

I instantly remembered a scene from the film *500 Days of Summer* in which Tom (surely that couldn't be a coincidence?) comes to a party at Summer's place and at that precise moment, the screen splits up in two - one was showing his expectations, the other the reality. Tom was expecting that Summer would welcome him with excitement, give him a big hug, kiss him, introduce him to her friends, and hook up again at the end of the evening. The reality was completely different. She welcomed him as a friend, she was standoffish with him, and it transpired that she had got engaged, so, feeling down, Tom went back to his sad life.

At the airport in Kuala Lumpur, my expectations were diametrically opposed to Tom's. I expected to see Chloe, give her a friendly hug and talk about all the things that had happened over the past few years, thinking I would finally see that the old spark between us was gone, close that whole story, and start a new chapter in my life.

"I told you we'd see each other soon!" A mischievous twinkle came into her blue eyes.

I smiled as much as I could and took another step forward. I didn't feel stable on my feet at all. I gave her a look that revealed everything to her: that I had thought about her every day since we parted, that my heart had never truly healed and that I was completely over the moon to see her again.

"I'm sorry I was a bitch in Berlin," she said frankly, taking a little step forward, standing on her tiptoes and kissing me softly.

Everything around us went quiet. The world stopped turning. Finally it all made sense. All because of a kiss.

I still haven't found what I'm looking for finally stopped playing in my head.

Day 1000

"I spent just a few weeks in Malaysia," I said, continuing my presentation without showing any pictures from that country.

Honestly, I didn't have much to say about the month I spent in Kuala Lumpur and the surrounding area. Two days after we met, Chloe flew back to Australia to visit her family and her ill grandmother whom she hadn't seen for years, and I decided to stay in Kuala Lumpur until she got back so that we could head north together. During that time, I couchsurfed at Henry's place, and this great guy from Nigeria became like a brother to me.

I met many local CSers and visited Batu Caves, one of the most popular Hindu shrines outside India, only a few miles outside Kuala Lumpur. At the foot of the hill where Batu Caves are located, there is also a huge golden statue of the god of war, Murugan. 272 steps lead up to the top where the shrines are situated, but it is totally worth the effort. It reminded me of Zagreb and my favorite 162 steps (or 163, depending which side you go up the famous funicular railway) that lead from the Tomićeva street to the Lotrščak tower.

Batu Caves are the site of the Thaipusam festival, one of the most interesting processions in this part of the world. I missed it, though, by just a few weeks. Some years ago, over a million and a half people gathered there, which made the festival one of the largest events ever. The procession starts early in the morning from the Sri Mahamariamman temple in Kuala Lumpur, and the journey to Batu Caves takes eight hours. The participants carry *kavadi* (a burden) with them, which can be just a cup of milk, but the more *pious* among them choose more radical ways of showing their devotion: using sharp needles, they pierce their cheeks, tongues and sometimes even the skin on their backs, and then pull heavy objects. The greater the sacrifice, the greater the reward, meaning the stronger blessings from the gods.

I also met Patrick, an extremely nice local guy who, one weekend, took me to a permaculture farm a few hours ride to the north of Kuala Lumpur. We spent the night there, enjoying the nature, peace and quiet, and talking to people who lived there. *Permaculture Farm Perak* is a project similar to the one in India - people grow organic food and produce energy through reasonable use of the natural sources at their disposal, and they rely on their own skills. Moreover, there's an educational touch to the farm: they occasionally teach children from the nearby villages about organic farming and self-sustainability. At the time, the local authorities were trying to force them to leave their property because of an investor who had decided to process the piece of land, deforesting it for a personal profit. But those guys didn't want to give up so easily - a couple of months after our visit, they were still there, persevering and fighting for their cause.

We returned from the farm, and Chloe got back from Australia. The very same day, Sara, her ex-roommate from Berlin, joined us and would thereafter keep us company over the following three weeks. We spent a few days in Kuala Lumpur, went to Chilling waterfall with Patrick and had a great time, crossing the river and swimming under the waterfall like true adventurers.

"And then I headed for Thailand, where I spent the following two months," I said as I turned to the next slide.

Day 231

A Buddhist temple in the north of Thailand. It's 9.00 pm. Everyone was supposed to be in bed.
I took out the little black notebook in which I write my impressions from the trip - I hadn't opened it since we entered Thailand. I tried to catch up, writing in the dim light from a table lamp.

Our first stop in Thailand was Koh Lipe, a nice little island under the jurisdiction of the Urak Lawoi tribe (also known as Sea Gypsies), people of Malaysian origins who have since swapped their nomadic maritime existence for life on the islands in the south of Thailand. Today they mostly make their living from tourism and fishing, and their lifestyle isn't dissimilar from that experienced in small coastal towns around the world, with the compulsory afternoon siesta and days spent on the terraces and in front of their homes/huts.
Everything was peaceful and clean, cars were nowhere to be seen. The view was fantastic: heavenly blue sea, soft sand, colorful boats, blue sky and a few distant islands.
I'll remember this experience for as long as I live - I boat-hitchhiked for the first time.
Since the island wasn't very big, we thought we would manage to walk around it in a few hours. We didn't think that halfway through we would have to trek along a non-existant path and end up in a jungle in the island's interior. We bumped into a playful dog, who we hired to be our guide. Our destiny was in his paws. After about half an hour we were lost.
Realizing that we couldn't go neither left, nor right because of the cliffs that surrounded us, we managed after another half an hour to get down to a small beach. We had two options - we could either go back into the jungle to search for another way out, or swim around the cliffs to get along to another beach, if there was one. It was getting dark and the tide was rushing in, and then we noticed one of the local boats sailing just a hundred yards from us.
"How about trying to hitchhike a boat?" Messing around, I stepped into the sea, and stuck my right thumb out...
We chose Koh Tarutao as our next destination. It was much more isolated and quieter than Koh Lipe. The whole island is a national

park and there are only three restaurants in front of which you can camp. It was time to use my tent for the second time on this trip.

Koh Tarutao was declared a national park in the 1970s, but its history goes back a little further. The island was used as a prison for Thai political prisoners in the 1930s. During World War II, when all the connections with the mainland were cut, the prisoners and guards joined forces and started terrorizing the ships that dared to sail into their waters. By the end of the war they had managed to sink 130 ships, killing all the crew, without any exceptions. The British finally managed to chase them off and so the island was then populated by the fishermen and farmers.

Besides the restaurant which was open for a few hours a day, a public toilet and a shower, there was nothing on the island. We decided to make the most of it, enjoying the silence, swimming in the sea at a beautiful, empty beach, sunbathing in the bright sunlight. Our night swimming ended up with us admiring the natural phenomenon of glowing planktons, just like in the movie The Beach. Swimming under the stars, in a sea full of planktons that glowed just like stars, was such a unique experience.

I would usually wake up before the girls. Every morning plenty of trash had washed up onto our beautiful beach, so I decided to roll up my sleeves (which I didn't actually have) and asked at one of the restaurants for some garbage bags so that I could spent the following hours litter-picking along the shore: plastic bottles, pens, candy wraps, flip-flops... all kinds of stuff. The Universe (through the restaurant's staff) treated me to a free breakfast. I did the same thing every day until the beach was clean and the bags full - and also my stomach.

We also went to a waterfall and returned home after nightfall, with the moon and stars illuminating our way.

In Trang we couchsurfed and hitchhiked for the first time in Thailand.

Everyone drove pick-ups and hardly anyone spoke English, but as in many countries in this part of the world, they were perfectly familiar with the concept of hitchhiking. The procedure was always the same - we stood by the road, smiled as a pick-up pulled over and rolled down its window, said hello in Thai, gave the name of the town we were going to, and we could then tell by the driver's face whether or not he was going in our direction. If it was good news then we smiled and hopped into the back part of the pick-up without saying a word. The sun was scorching, the wind was blowing, and we had to watch the road, being careful to bang on the roof at the right moment to let the driver know that we wanted to hop out.

Unlike the two islands that we had previously visited, Trang was relatively unknown on the Thai tourist map. We decided to enjoy the local food, even though we had some difficulties in the restaurants when we tried to explain that we didn't want to eat meat. We were all vegetarians - Sara and Chloe for several years, and I since we arrived in Thailand. In fact, I just carried on with my habits from India, where I only ate fruit, vegetables and fish for more than three months. I didn't find it difficult to adapt to the girls' tastes, so buying food and cooking together was a lot easier.

I also discovered my favorite food ever - mango & sticky rice. The recipe was simple: mix rice, coconut milk, sugar and fresh mango.

Ton Sai, a beach near Krabi, was our fourth destination in Thailand. It was a perfect place for rock climbing, some more time to enjoy the beaches and the end of Sara's three-week adventure as a third wheel.

"Are you awake?" She whispered, carefully entering my cottage.

"You crazy woman, you know you can't be here!" I answered cautiously, keeping my voice down. "What if we get caught?"

"I don't care, I can't sleep," she murmured, laying on the thin mattress, turning off the light, moving onto her side and hinting to me for what to do. "You'll be the big spoon, I'll be the small."

I laughed, lay down beside her and fulfilled her wish.

It was our third day in a Buddhist monastery that we had come across quite by chance.

We split from the main road and followed a dusty pathway which led us to Vipassana monastery in the middle of the forest. Its name was such an obvious choice - the *Forest Monastery*. We took a short walk, our surroundings growing greener and greener, next to us a murmuring brook was running, a toothless old man wearing a Buddhist saffron-yellow robe smiled at us, the birds were chirping, and stuff like that. We arrived at the entrance and stopped.

We didn't know what the rules were once we were inside, in fact what we did know about *vipassana* meditation was a bit intimidating. Basically, you're totally isolated from the rest of the world, deprived of all possessions; complete silence and no eye contact were essential, men and women were strictly separated, meditation sessions were strictly organized, we had to get up at 5.00 am and things like that.

"I have an idea," I clapped my hands. "We'll find a place in the yard to draw lines on the ground."

"What kind of lines?" Chloe asked.

"Just ordinary lines," I replied. "We'll draw them on the ground using our fingers, a stick or a spoon, it doesn't matter. One line will mean that we want to stay, and five lines will be a signal to get the hell out of there."

"What happens then?"

"If the total number of lines at the end of any given day is seven or more, then off we go," I concluded.

We miraculously agreed, but as soon as we entered the monastery we realized that there was no need to follow my amazing plan. Men and women were hanging out and talking. We joined them and they gave us some basic information: the meditation wasn't strictly controlled, there was a lot of free time, men and women weren't separated, we could stay for as long as we wanted, we each had our own cottage and everyone could freely use their own stuff. Apparently, this was the most liberal *vipassana* center in the world.

Above all, just like all monasteries of this kind, it survived on donations.

We found the head monk as he was taking a walk and we greeted him with the typical gesture - bringing our palms together. We addressed him as *Master* and he called us *Oztrayleeya and Croaysher* to address us. He was a really nice guy, bald, and with smile permanently upon his face. The only problem was that we barely managed to understand every third word he said, but since we'd come here to grow spiritually, we managed to establish communication on a higher level - body language, plenty of nodding and smiling. It always worked.

He showed us the cottages that would be our home for the coming days.

"Everyone sleeps in their own cottage," he winked at us.

We were given the clothes we would be wearing while in the monastery: light pants and a white T-shirt. The cottages had a toilet, a shower, a ventilator and a thin sleeping mat.

There were some things that weren't allowed: killing any living being, stealing, sexual contact, vulgarity, drugs or smoking.

Although there were very few rules, we obviously couldn't just abide by them. By her entering my cottage, we risked getting caught and expelled. Chloe obviously didn't care about that. Neither did I. I had her by my side, and for weeks now this had been the most important thing in my life.

I loved her endlessly and enjoyed spending every minute with her - so much that I felt like I didn't need anything else. Except for maybe oxygen and water. I had given leave to my logic and common sense from the moment we kissed at the airport in Kuala Lumpur, and let my feelings take over. I began to lose control. I was vulnerable. I was lost. I was irrational. I was stupid. I was in love. I was everything I thought I'd never be. For all those years I was sure that this state of mind belonged to the past, and that those feelings were long gone.

But it turned out that she had just taken them with her that time we parted ways in Berlin. And now she had brought them all back.

"Tomislav, be cool!" I told myself that time when she headed back to Australia after only two days in Kuala Lumpur and said she would be back soon. The very same evening, I was sending her drunken emails, declaring my love for her, picking stars from the sky for her. I told her everything that I'd wanted to share with her over the years but had never got the chance to say.

Once I'd sobered up, I knew I shouldn't have done this. I shouldn't have exaggerated, I should have taken things slowly and there was no need to say everything that was on my mind. I knew this, but as soon as I saw her face, felt her presence, fell in her arms, thought of the feelings I had for her - everything I planned fell apart. I felt as if I was driven by an invisible force and I couldn't do anything to stop it.

Day 232

"Good morning, honey," I whispered in her ear after waking up to the sound of the huge gong that gave the sign to everyone to gather in the dining room.

"I dreamed a cool dream," she said turning to me. She was already awake. "I was in a crowded hall and some guys showed up on a stage. Each of them had the appearance of a god - Christian, Muslim, Jewish, and so on. Together, they sent a message to the audience: Mother Nature asked us to be your spiritual leaders on this wonderful planet, but you completely misunderstood us and screwed up. Now we're worried that we're going to lose our jobs because Gaea[6] is coming to do an audit and won't be best pleased with what she sees."

"Some people in the audience were marked with black dots," she continued. "The Gods told them that they'd screwed up big time and that there wasn't any hope for them. Some had white dots and the gods were proud of them because they'd done plenty of good deeds during their lifetimes. Others weren't marked with any color."

"Well, let's get you out of my cottage so that they don't give you a black dot," I told her, leaving the cottage and giving her the green light to quietly follow me.

I understood her dream very well. Basically, all religions are the same, but individuals and institutions had misused them for ages, instead of insisting on cooperation that could lead people to a higher cause - respect for each other and saving the planet that had been entrusted to us as a gift for safe keeping. We had turned the world into such a twisted place and it was only a matter of time before Mother Nature showed up to tell us off.

We went to the main hall, where each day began with the rice offering ceremony with the monks. Some 20 participants would sit on the floor in this big hall, and in front of each of us lay a white brass plate with a spoon and some rice. The monks soon arrived, four of them, and approached each and every one of us with a bowl into which we put a spoonful of rice as a sign of respect. After each of us had put four spoons of rice into the four monks' bowls, we could finally go upstairs and have our breakfast.

The food was strictly vegan: no dairy products or eggs, let alone

---
[6] *goddess of the Earth in Greek mythology*

any meat. It fit perfectly into my Thai vegetarian adventure. We only had two meals a day; the first being the said breakfast at 7.00 am and the second a lunch at 11.00 am. And that was all the food for the day. Nevertheless, this food was really tasty, fresh and diverse, and we weren't even hungry. There was more than enough rice, vegetables prepared in all sorts of ways, tofu, and freshly picked fruit. All food was either bought with the money from donations, or, in most of the cases, received as a gift from the local people who every now and then would come for a blessing and, in return, brought something from their gardens.

After breakfast we had some spare time until the gong told us it was time for communal morning mediation. The meditation was practiced in three different forms in the monastery: walking, sitting, and, my favorite, lying. We were constantly combining the three modes, we would start with the walking meditation (to the unfamiliar passerby we would probably seem like a bunch of hypnotized lunatics dragging ourselves along the forest path), continue with the sitting one (which was quite unpleasant if your back wasn't accustomed to it), and finally we would end with the lying meditation (during which some of us would fall asleep, including the monks). Each phase lasted between half an hour and forty-five minutes.

We were free to use the time after the morning mediation to have some tea or coffee and socialize. Shortly after, a big gong would announce that it was time to congregate in the main hall. A lunch ritual was about to start. The procedure was quite similar to the one before breakfast, except that now the monks didn't approach us, but, instead, we would go to them and give them food. The girls were in charge of giving the blessing and presenting the gifts, while men would collect the bowls once the monks were done with their meal.

After lunch, our final meal of the day which is always full and delicious - rice, potatoes, pumpkins, tofu prepared in various ways, green veggies, watermelon, pineapples, mangos, apples and lychee - we had some free time to hang out with other monastery-dwellers. We met some who had only been there for a few days, others who were coming back repeatedly, and there was even a guy who had been living there for a whole year. The time spent in this peaceful place in the middle of forest made us realize why some people wanted to live there and kept coming back.

The sound of the bell meant that it was time for our communal afternoon meditation, which again consisted of walking, sitting and lying. And meditation, of course.

For the rest of the afternoon we were free to take a rest (although I wasn't sure what from), read a book from the well-stocked library or take a walk across the estate, but also to lend a hand with the chores, since there was always something to do: cleaning, raking up the leaves in the yard... If you wanted to, you could always find something to do. The time for this work/rest was over at 7.00 pm. when, for the last time in the day, the gong sounded announcing that it was time for communal *chanting* and meditation. Around this time, the power would usually go off.

The whole thing finished around half past eight, when you could withdraw to your cottage and take out your little black notebook to write down the things that had happened in recent weeks before you forgot them.

After Ton Sai beach and saying farewell to Sara, we arrived in Hua Hin, known as the summer residence of the royal family. Our only reason for visiting was because it was on our way to Bangkok, but there was also a nice, middle-aged Norwegian, Jon, our CS host.

He kindly received us in his four-bedroom villa, which also had a swimming pool, took us to the market and explained to us something that seemed to be a regular occurrence around the city streets. Namely, we spotted lots of Thai girls standing in front of the bars and clubs, watching us pass by with their big eyes wide open.

"It's a pure win-win situation," he started. "Middle-aged well-off Europeans come to Thailand looking for love, and the poor Thai girls welcome them, all caring and affectionate, wearing huge pretty smiles on their faces."

"What about prostitution?" Chloe asked suspiciously.

"It is definitely there," said Jon. "But this isn't what I mean, it's got nothing to do with sex. It's about relationships between older white men and young Thai women. Look at those two."

He pointed to a couple who was romantically holding hands and walking down the street. He was an older white guy and she was a young local girl.

"You'll see those sorts of couples all over Thailand," he continued. "There are several ways in which these two species get together,

and we're just witnessing one of them at the moment. The girls chill out in front of the bars, the guys come in, buy them a drink, pull a move on them, they get to know each other, and then both sides decide whether or not they're compatible to spend a night, week, month or lifetime together. And it really works: one side gets what he can't get in Europe - a beautiful, young, caring companion, and the other side gets what she can't get in Thailand - an easier life, with promises for a bright future. My brother met his wife in the same way. They've been happily married for years, and they have a cute young daughter."

I knew exactly what he meant. It was an example of a sugar baby arrangement as we call them.

However, it was the first time that I'd looked at this concept from a different perspective - without judging the other side. I looked at this from a practical angle. Like most people seeing a young, pretty girl in the company of an older man, I tended to think it was ugly and immoral. That she was only with him for his money.

But why did I think that? In fact, was it any of my business? Did their relationship cause me any harm? Why couldn't I just notice it, avoid any negative thoughts and just carry on with my life? If two people are old enough to use their own heads, if nobody is forcing them to be with someone else, why should we care about their choices? What is this voyeuristic drive in us that stops us from resisting?

"It's not just about money," added Jon, interrupting my thoughts. "Many Thai women prefer white men because they find them exotic."

"It always makes me laugh," I said. "White men and women want to tan their skin, while naturally tanned people want their skin to be lighter. Young people want to grow up, and the elderly are trying to be young again. The grass is always greener on the other side."

"That's right," agreed Jon. "Add onto that the fact that many men over here aren't the best spouses. Many of them have mistresses and don't treat their significant others with respect they deserve, which fuels an additional argument for these local girls. It doesn't mean that white guys won't cheat on them or abuse them, but the chances for something like this still seem slighter. And that's not to mention the other positive aspects, like their families' well-being. If they marry a white man with a good passport, their children will have much better conditions and more opportunities in life than those who stay in Thailand. And since families here really stick together through thick and thin, the rest of the family can expect some form of assistance if their daughter or granddaughter marries a rich man."

No matter how hard I tried, I couldn't find anything to fault this. Of course, if both parties agree to it, without coercion. Just like with other prejudices, I decided to be non-judgmental. Just because I stick to some principles, it doesn't necessarily mean that other people have to agree with me.

It was very hot in Bangkok so we didn't spend much time there. We stayed with some fun Americans, met a few interesting people with whom I celebrated my birthday, Chloe gave me a ukulele as a present and I pulled out a cracked tooth that I didn't feel like fixing.

We visited Wat Pho, the Lying Buddha, experienced the chaos on the Bangkok streets, and headed to the north, which once again confirmed that I wasn't a fan of big cities, unless I stay there for a very long time, in which case I'm sure that I could find a way to like them.

We went to Nakhon Sawan for two reasons - it was on our way from Bangkok to Chiang Mai, and we found a CS host there. The town is known for... hmm, I'm not really sure actually. However, we instantly grew to love it. The moment we arrived there Claire, our host, took us to have some mango & sticky rice, and it was the biggest portion I'd ever seen. We watched the sunset in what must be the biggest and most entertaining park in the whole world: people were jogging around the lake, playing badminton, soccer, basketball, a bunch of lady boys were kicking ass at volleyball and some elderly ladies were doing aerobics and tai chi. Then suddenly, it all got a bit Twilight Zone-like. A loud melody started to echo through the entire town: everybody stopped what they were doing, and stood motionless. At first, we thought it was some kind of mass hypnosis, but Claire explained to us that it was just the national anthem. It was played every day at the same time and everybody would stop whatever they were doing to pay respect to the king and to their country. I'm telling you - it was scary.

Claire was really fun. She had been living there for a year and a half, she had a Thai boyfriend (it was the first case in which the guy was the local, and the girl was the foreigner), she was teaching English and earning good money, and soon she would return to the USA to continue her studies. We killed time during the evenings in the same way I did while I hosted CSers in Zagreb: playing board games. On the second day of our stay, we borrowed Claire's motorbike so we could visit a nearby Buddhist temple up on the hill above the town. We went at sunset, when we had finally plucked up enough courage after spending the whole day in front of a fan.

Phitsanulok. We arrived there in the back of a truck. We visited it for all the same reasons as the previous town. This time our host was a local girl, who lived with her parents, two aunts and 10 (ten!) dogs a few miles outside of town.

We had our happiest day since we'd arrived in Thailand during our stay in Phitsanulok. Songkran was being celebrated, the New Year in this part of the world. Normally, the celebration lasts for three or four days - during the hottest period of the year. The celebration consists of splashing water on other people. Now, this might sound quite innocent and simple, but try and imagine the whole town out on the streets, armed with buckets and 20-gallon barrels on their trucks, water guns, and hoses. Only then will you have some idea of the chaos, laughter and fun that definitely couldn't be described as innocent.

Together with our host, her friend and her cousins, we rampaged straight towards the main street. Needless to say, we didn't make it there and were already soaking wet. And smiling. We gradually made our way along, splashing water from the trucks at passersby, and the funniest moments were when two trucks stopped at the traffic lights - a war broke out between the passengers of the trucks that lasted until the light turned green. We soon discovered that some participants were upping the ante - they had huge ice cubes in their barrels so that the water they splashed on others was ice-cold.

That was where things got serious. Your first reaction was to look for a stand where you could buy ice, so that you could match your opponent's arsenal. Revenge is a dish best served cold, they say. Well, ice-cold is even better.

You're treated to loud music, dance, and quite a lot of alcohol by your comrades, and colorful powders get rubbed on your face - we witnessed all these things on the battlefield in the middle of the main street. Everyone was having a whale of a time, without any complications - splashing water on baking hot day. Chloe and I agreed that all wars should be resolved like that: the opponents should be given buckets of water: whoever is wetter by the end of it is the loser.

After a whole day of partying we were invited to a traditional Thai lunch. Shortly after lunch, our host put three chairs in the backyard and three grannies came out and sat on them. The other people, carrying buckets of water, got in line and tipped the water over the grannies' heads. They told us that this was indeed the main point of Songkran, besides marking the beginning of the annual rains - a blessing and paying respect to the elderly.

Chiang Mai. It took us one ride to get there, after just four minutes of trying to hitch a lift. Moreover, that ride was in a truck with an English guy called Alan, his Thai girlfriend and their young daughter. We were finally able to communicate with the people who were giving us a ride - usually, we were either in the back part of the pick-up truck or our driver's English was as proficient as our Thai.

Chiang Mai is, among other things, known for the chaos typical during the Songkran but, fortunately, we managed to avoid it. One day of Water War was plenty. Besides, the tourists in Chiang Mai took the whole thing too seriously, arming themselves with water guns and taking head-shots. That was way too aggressive for my taste, especially since they used the water from the nearby dirty brook - good luck opening your eyes or mouth there!

We met with a couple of acquaintances from Bangkok, went for a stroll through the center, and tried some street-food specialties. I didn't try any insects, though. I was a vegetarian.

For the final two nights we stayed with a guy called Kevin, a New Zealander and a photographer whose face was dominated by a moustache which he hadn't trimmed for more than 30 years.

"Ante died, we're going to the funeral tomorrow," I got an email from my mother. My uncle, whose moustache I loved most in the whole world. Cancer. I felt so sad and powerless. Far away from them all. Even though my presence wouldn't have changed anything, it was hard being away at moments like this. Having said that, it would probably be even more difficult being close.

During our last day in Chiang Mai we took some photos of the temples as proof that we had been there. Also, for the first time, we treated ourselves to Thai massages - we were massaged by blind masseurs.

Pai. The road that took us from Chiang Mai to Pai was really winding. We crossed 65 miles by passing through 762 corners. That's almost twelve corners per mile. It makes you feel dizzy and even begins to chafe if you're at the rear of the truck.

Pai was our home for just one evening, although the place was ace, and our CS host was really cool. He made a living as a chef on a boat, while he spent most of his time in his wooden house in Thailand, the rent of which was ridiculously low. Unfortunately, he didn't cook anything for us, but he did take us to a vegetarian restaurant where we only spend 30 bahts (about 1 dollar) for a meal consisting of rice and two servings of mixed vegetables.

We spent the afternoon walking down the streets, that weren't so numerous, and then the following day we rented a scooter and drove around the place. We saw a couple of sad, shackled elephants and visited a waterfall. On our way back we stopped to try a juice we'd never come across before that was being sold in one of the yards.

We had barely parked our scooter, when, suddenly, a guy from the yard came recommending me to park my scooter somewhere in the shade, after which, with a smile on his face, he offered us a table and brought us a glass of the ice-cold, red nameless juice, served boiled potatoes, peanuts, green mango, bananas, fresh coconut and a bottle of wine made of the thingummy fruit. With question marks hanging above our heads, we wished each other bon appétit and dug in. After a few minutes a couple approached us and sat at the table right next to ours, but we invited them to join us. They told us that they had only come across this place the day before and were coming back for more. It was an all-you-can-eat buffet with bottomless drinks, and you give as much money as you could. Plus, all meals were vegetarian.

We made small talk and then took some photos of a land crack - indeed, there were three of them. The story goes like this: the owner woke up one morning in 2008, only to discover a huge hole in the middle of his property. Then he made a smart move - since the estate was on a dusty road that lead to a waterfall, they decided to turn their misfortune into a tourist attraction. And it seemed that they knew what they were doing - donations were paying off. The guests felt that they had to give something, and they were so friendly and kind (they would fill your glass of juice at least four times - that I can vouch for!) so you end up giving them more money than you would pay for a meal in a restaurant with fixed prices.

Through Couchsurfing we found a farm where time seemed to have stood still. There was no electricity, no hot water and no sign of civilization whatsoever. However, there was plenty of silence and interesting people, who spend most of the year on the farm. The time had come for bathing in a small creek some one hundred yards from the farm, cooking and helping with everyday chores. That was exactly what we needed after nearly 1,200 miles on the road, mostly in the rear parts of pick-ups, in +40°C.

    A break from all this travelling. That was what we were doing on the farm, and after we left. As we went to get some water from a supply in the nearby village, we saw a sign by the road: Tam Wua Forest Monastery.

Day 1000

"In Thailand, there was another first for me: actually driving the car that I hitchhiked, because the driver was completely wasted," I went on with the story by changing the slide.

The photograph showed me sitting at the steering wheel of a Thai pick-up truck, with my then shaved head. I had a young monk shave it for me. There was nothing spiritual to it though, I just did it for practical reason. Treating an infected cut on my head (a consequence of the close encounter with the surf board in India) was a lot easier without hair.

We left the monastery and headed to the south, to visit another CSer, when a truck pulled over. There would have been nothing strange in that had the co-driver not been totally wasted. He kept turning around, telling us about his job, smiling confusedly and drinking one beer after another. We found him hilarious, especially when he was constantly stuttering and couldn't remember the right word, but the highlight was when he couldn't open his next can of beer. It was only a minute or two later that he realized that he was holding it upside down.

And then, after one of the many toilet breaks, the very same drunk co-driver took over the wheel. At that point there were five of us in the car: the drunk driver, the sober co-driver, driver's sister (who we had picked up in the meantime but who kept quiet), and two passengers who were scared to death: Chloe and I.

It was dark, a light rain was falling, the road was bendy and bumpy and took us through a thick forest next to the border with Myanmar, and our driver (whom in this state I wouldn't have trusted even with a pointless task guarding the Queen's corgis) was confidently driving into each of the bends. Chloe and I exchanged worried looks realizing that we had to do something to put a stop to this nonsense. It took us some time to figure out what to do next, but it came to us when the driver was trying to change the CD while another car was heading straight for us in the opposite direction.

"Sorry, could you please stop the car?" I asked politely, trying to hide the fear and panic in my voice. Chloe held her head in my arms, too terrified to watch the road and the inevitable disaster that was about to unfold.

"Don't worry," stammered the driver. "I'm a taxi driver during my free time, I know this road like the back of my hand. I could drive it with my eyes closed."

Having heard that, Chloe pushed up against me even harder, while I looked at the other passengers in disbelief, thinking how they were idiots to let a wasted person take the wheel.

"Haha, I'm sure," I said, trying to sound cool and calm. "But I've never driven a car in Thailand, so I'd like to try it out. And you must be quite tired..."

"You want to drive?" he exclaimed in amazement. "No problem!"

He stopped abruptly and we swapped places.

Even though my driving license had expired, even though there were police *check-points* ahead of us, even though I hadn't driven a car for nearly a year, even though I had never driven a pick-up, even though I had never driven on the right side of the road, I got straight to work. There's a first time for everything. There's only a last time for dying.

It took me a couple of minutes to get used to shifting gears with my left hand and driving a vehicle that big, but I made it. The former driver was already snoring in the back seat putting his right leg up onto the right side of my seat, wriggling around every now and then like a dying frog and hitting my right arm. I couldn't believe it and all I could do was laugh, while his sister was thumping him every so often to stop any further wriggling.

"The last place we visited in Thailand," I said, "was Mae Sot, where we spent a few days at an orphanage. There were about one hundred kids, most of them were from Myanmar and had either been abandoned or their parents were so poor that they had to give them away. Most of them technically don't exist since they have no documents, and some of them don't even know when they were born. They don't want them in Myanmar, and in Thailand they end up as sex slaves or, in slightly better scenarios - in an orphanage like the one that we visited."

The orphanage was run by a man who was a political refugee from Myanmar. He started with a dozen children some years ago. He'd even been offered asylum by the US government but he turned it down since he wasn't allowed to bring his kids with him. He found himself a place in Thailand where he could do what he really wanted to: spend his life helping all those kids who wouldn't stand any chance of a normal life if it weren't for him.

We had lunch with the kids, spent a few hours with them, having a really fantastic time with the music of ukulele and a dance or two. Chloe ended up with *tanaka* on her face, a cream made from tree bark, which is used for medical, cosmetic and traditional purposes. We laughed a lot and, given the entire situation, only cried a little.

"That was it from Asia," I changed the slide. "After more than seven months of traveling across Asia, the time had come for a new continent - Australia."

Day 274

"My late mother and I bought this land together," said my new friend Pauly, beginning to describe the history of his place to his new guests.

I'd been in Australia for a few weeks, but it was only now that I started feeling like I should feel when traveling - I was happy, fulfilled and excited. Up to this point I was staying in Cabarita, a beautiful town on the east coast, at Chloe's parents' place, and I hadn't really done anything worth mentioning. I was hanging out with Chloe and her family, trying to find a job. Since I only had a tourist visa, nobody wanted to take a risk and hire an illegal immigrant.

Chloe got a job in Jindabyne, at a ski resort in the south of the country, so she went there to seek her fortune.

"A part of me is looking forward to the time that we'll spend apart," Chloe said excitedly as she was sitting in the car that would take her to her temporary employment in a Mexican restaurant six hundred miles away. "We've already been together every day, 24/7, for three months, I think that it will do us good to have some time alone."

After saying goodbye to her, I headed for Nimbin, which was only about an hour away. This is the most famous hippie village in Australia and was where I was listening to Pauly's stories around a campfire.

"The main goal was to create a tribe that would live in harmony with the beautiful nature surrounding us," he continued. "We started off with only one tipi, and after just a couple of years there were already twenty of them, with more than thirty people living there full-time. Men, women, children, the elderly, we all lived there as one big and happy family. We founded a tribe called the *Star Earth* tribe."

"Anyone who has accepted our way of life was welcome. Whenever someone arrived here, we would show them the way to the river, just to spend some time there and feel the energy of the place. We had a guidebook with a detailed description of our lifestyle and we'd share it with anyone who wanted to stay with us. Someone would show the newcomer around the estate, explain how the kitchen and toilet worked, what the daily activities and chores were, and if they liked it and if they decided to respect the rules, the whole tribe would welcome them in."

I knew exactly what Pauly was talking about, since I had passed the initiation a few days before when I first arrived. The tribe split up a few years ago though, after Pauly's mother Judy died. Judy is a special story - she was one of the founders of MardiGrass, a movement that fought to legalize cannabis, and was the first person to hand over tax payments to the Australian government for the sale of cannabis. Besides that, she was a political activist: every year she would hand business plans to politicians and try to show them the ways in which we could all benefit from legalising an innocent herb like cannabis, instead of treating it like the spawn of Satan. Pauly moved here permanently with the desire to renew this philosophy.

I discovered it through CS but when I finally arrived, all I could see was two empty tipis, two sheep and a tin house in which Pauly lived with his wife Fabi and nine-month son Atlan - the only members of the *Star Earth* tribe.

They welcomed me with a hug and suggested that I head down to the river where I could spend some time and then come back when I was ready. I did exactly as I'd been told. I sat on a rock by the river and soon felt the magic of this place. I took a few deep breaths, smiled at the foliage that surrounded me and got back to the house, just in time to roll up my sleeves and lend a hand to my hosts with changing the roof tiles.

We spent our days at work around the house and the estate - we changed the roof tiles and erected a fence around what was meant to be a garden. I dug a channel around the house to drain the rain away, chopped some wood and did other things like that. No chemical products were to be used on the estate, including soaps, shampoos, detergents, tooth pastes or deodorants. Thanks to solar panels, we had electricity and hot water.

"During the first three days of your stay on the estate nobody had to participate in the tribe's activities, so they had a period to adjust, rest and simply observe the environment," continued Pauly. "After three days, you joined the rest of the tribe and helped with the work on the estate, or better put, with the games on the estate. This is the word we actually use for work. The game. What game shall we play today? Let's pick up fruit in the woods! Let's play cooking, wood chopping and other things like that. This means that work doesn't exist and nobody *has* to work. We encourage people to keep watching, listening and learning. Instead of asking, observe the way the things work and then join in. But if you're not sure about something, don't hesitate to ask."

There were still a few guidelines by which they lived. Those guidelines were simple, and their beauty lies in this simplicity. Respect and appreciate. Share, communicate and create. Be patient and responsible.

The key was in the old Buddhist saying: "Before enlightenment, chop wood, carry water. After enlightenment, chop wood, carry water."

"We respected each other's privacy, despite not having any walls or strict boundaries between who owns what," he continued. "Everyone who arrived at the farm chose the sound of their bird call, which was used when approaching another person's space or when approaching a group of people who were in the middle of a conversation. If you wanted to join them, you let them know using your bird call. If you got an answer from someone in the group, you were welcome to join them. If you didn't get an answer, you could have another go and try the call once more. But if there's no answer after the second attempt, you don't go there, whatever the reason may be."

"Also, if there are two crossed sticks in front of the entrance to someone's tipi you aren't supposed to make a sound. Two crossed sticks are a universal sign for not being disturbed. The person inside could be meditating, or working on something important and needs to concentrate; or a couple could be making love. Love always comes first, always. It's number one. There's also a 'no wake up' rule, everyone is free to sleep as long as they want or need. You only wake other people up if there's an emergency."

"Every member of the community shared their own talents with the rest of the group - one would do the morning yoga, somebody else would offer meditation sessions. Someone else would cook, others would do the dishes, or collect nuts on the estate, and someone would chop wood, or do the laundry, while others would teach the kids or go to buy groceries in Nimbin from time to time, or go to the spring to fetch water. As for finances, each member contributes to the budget for living expenses by giving a fixed sum every week. Most of them have either a part-time job or sold their hand-made products, sometimes even the fruits grown on the estate. There have been more than 2,500 macadamia trees on the estate. The goal was to be self-sustainable, so as not to depend on anyone or anything."

"Before and after each meal, people would play the drums and sing. Everyone would eat together, gathered in a circle, and would start eating together once every person had been served. The leftovers, if there were any, would be distributed equally. We took a *siesta* in the afternoon, which is the hottest time of the day. We're spiritual, but not religious. We don't worship any god, but rather ourselves, each other and Mother Nature. We're grateful to sun for coming out every morning and to the moon for lighting our way at night, to the water from the spring and to the food."

"All decisions were made in the circle. Everyone had the right to have their say and non-violent communication was encouraged. All problems, which were rare, were resolved within the family. Everyone was given a second chance if they damaged the community, but not a third one."

It was wonderful to hear these stories. They sounded perfect.

This mini community in Nimbin was my second first-hand experience with the hippie philosophy and their way of life. I gained my first similar experience two years earlier when I visited Beneficio, a hippie community in the south of Spain. I liked what I heard, what I experienced and everything they advocated. Love, altruism, respect, peace, the environment, and freedom. Traveling was encouraged, and hitchhiking is a way of traveling popularized by hippies. They experiment with soft drugs.

I parted from everybody and went over to my tipi to do some serious thinking.

Was I a hippie? I shared the same philosophy and lifestyle as them, and if I had to choose an affiliation to any group of people then I would probably choose them. Was I supposed to stay on this farm and become part of their tribe? Live off the land, reject technology, let love flow freely? Talk and listen to stories around the campfire, stop using soap, sleep in a tipi by the river?

I looked at my plush sheep. I recalled its (or rather 'our') story. Both of us left our flock, where there were shepherds and guard dogs, and we started to travel the world and do what we wanted. We were looking for answers, our purpose, our place under the sun

- our flock.

"The time's still not right, what do you say?" I said, stroking its head, turning onto my side and closing my eyes.

We still hadn't found our flock. We weren't ready to join someone else's. It seemed most likely that we would have to establish our own flock. Whatever this might mean.

I opened my eyes and grabbed my phone.

Tomorrow I'm meeting a Croatian friend, we're going to the south. Just say the word and I'll come to you - I sent a message to Chloe. It was one of the many that I had sent her these days.

I missed her. She was the main woman in my potential tribe. I wanted to share all my happy moments and thoughts with her, I wanted to wake up next to her and go to bed with her by my side. I wanted to be responsible for her happiness, or at least be wherever she was happy. I wanted her to feel the same.

"*Word*," she texted back.

Day 276

"This is going to be great!" Janica said, her face all aglow as we slowly climbed to a height of thirteen thousand feet in a bumpy little plane. I was looking out of the window, enjoying a lovely sunny day over Byron Bay, trying to ignore my sweaty palms and racing heartbeat. The instructor told me what to do, attaching himself to me as he jokingly left one of the buckles undone, waiting for my response. I was terrified. I'm sure this joke works every time.

"If anything happens to me, you'll have to meet my mom and tell her what happened," I told her. It was only yesterday, after entering the tipi and sliding into the sleeping bag, that she revealed her plan to go skydiving, asking me if I wanted to join her.

"No way!" I replied without any hesitation.

The reason was very simple. I was afraid of heights. My legs were wobbly, my head was spinning, and I was terrified. But I didn't tell her that. I recalled in the silence my first trips and those stories about fear, and how the only way to beat my fears was to face them. To try out what I was afraid of and see if there was actually anything to be afraid of. A parachute jump could certainly mark the end of my fear of heights.

Or the end of my life in general.

"Actually, I will!" I replied soon after.

I closed my eyes and took a deep breath, just like they taught me in the Buddhist monastery. I was trying to rationalize the whole situation, understand that the statistics were on my side, that there was nothing to be afraid of. Since this didn't seem to help, I tried another tactic - the tactic of imagining the worst-case scenario. What if I die? It would be a terrifying ten seconds, as I would realize that the parachute wasn't going to open before I hit the ground. That wasn't so bad. I would be sorry for my parents and my other grieving relatives, but I would be dead anyway so it wouldn't be too big of a problem for me. I'm going to die anyway someday, so why shouldn't it be now? If ever in my life I was prepared to die, it was definitely at this point. If it had happened a few years back, when I still had too many dreams, unfulfilled desires, question marks in both my mind and my heart - things wouldn't have looked good. But as my dreams became reality, wishes came true, and the question marks turned into full stops, my curiosity was stronger than my fear of death. I had already experienced so much life, so it would be interesting to find out what was on the other side.

"It's time," said the instructor, patting me on the shoulder.

Using our combined strength, we crawled to the plane's open door and got into the position for jumping. Gazing into the abyss, I decided to forget about everything and try to experience something new, unknown and frightening with eyes wide open and without thinking. I put on a smile and winked at the instructor, signaling that I was ready.

"Isn't hitchhiking dangerous?" Janica asked when we were sat in the SUV, on our way to Sydney.

"How long have you been skiing?" I answered with a counter-question.

"Probably since I was nine," she said. "Why?"[7]

"How fast do you go when you're downhill skiing?" I went on, avoiding a direct answer to her question.

"I can get up to about 80 miles per hour," she replied. "Why?"

"Because you fly down the mountain at 80 miles per hour with just a helmet to protect you. Because you've jumped out of a plane, gone under the knife so many times, and after all this you're asking me whether hitchhiking is dangerous."

She just smiled, put her headphones on and focused on the road.

"I hope you don't mind," she said soon after, pulling the headphone away from her left ear. "I like to listen to music while driving, and there's no cassette player in this car."

"Go ahead," I said, closed my eyes, and fell into a deep sleep, exhausted after an intense day.

"Here we are!" she woke me up as we entered Sydney. "I've booked a hostel in the city center, do you also want to sleep there?"

"I have a friend in the city center, I can sleep on his couch," I lied. I didn't have enough money to afford a night in a hostel in the city center. Telling stories about not having enough money that would provoke guilt and possibly lead her to offer to pay for me wasn't an option. I would manage somehow, although it was almost midnight. "Just drop me off near your hostel and I'll walk."

---

[7] *It's probably worth mentioning that my travel companion was none other than Janica Kostelić, four-time Olympic gold medalist and six-time world champion.*

She stopped the car, turning the hazards on, and helped me to get my stuff out of the trunk.

"I'm so glad that I joined you over the past two days," she said. "Although we haven't spent that much time together, and what we did was mostly in silence. But that's exactly what I find most important about people I care about. How I feel with them when we say nothing at all."

"I'm so glad you did, Janica," I replied, giving her a big hug. "Thank you for everything, I'm sure I'll see you around!"

I put my backpack on and started looking for a place to stay. Other travelers had told me that the price of the cheapest accommodation in Australia was at least 30 dollars, which meant three days of food, drinks and other travel expenses. I needed an alternative.

I stopped next to a bench where an elderly man was sitting with guitar in hands, awkwardly plucking the strings. At least two of them were out of tune. His huge backpack lay next to him, with piled up clothes and shoes jutting out. I tossed a dollar coin into his guitar case.

"Excuse me?" I asked when he was done with the song. "Do you know anywhere I could sleep for free around here?

I didn't want to give up and look for a hostel, but I knew that a developed country like Australia probably had rules, laws and heavy fines for camping and sleeping in the city center. This busker looked like he had quite some experience of sleeping on the streets.

"Sure thing," he replied. "A few of us sleep in that little park, you can't miss us."

"Thanks very much," I replied happily and set off in the direction that he had indicated.

I found the park and noticed a couple of homeless people in one part. Taking out my mattress, I inflated it, unfurled my sleeping bag, crawled into it, wrapped a clean T-shirt around the sheep and made it into a pillow, hugging my backpack just as I was going to hug Chloe the following day. I soon fell asleep.

Day 278

"See you soon!" She looked at me with those innocent-naughty blue eyes as I was leaving her room, less than forty-eight hours after I had got there.

I stopped, slowly turned around and looked into those eyes once again.

"You know, this is exactly what you told me in Berlin too," I said.

She was silent, because she herself knew that. She also knew that I knew. She knew almost two and a half years had elapsed from when we said our goodbyes in Berlin to the meeting in Kuala Lumpur.

Looking at those eyes, I had a feeling that this time it would take considerably longer.

I turned away, bowed my head and left the room.

"I'm not sure if I want you to stay here," she said the night before, in a bed that was far too small.

"What do you mean?" I was confused. I was still suppressing the sentence that she had said when she was leaving Cabarita to go southwards. In my mind, spending those few weeks apart was more than enough. It was enough for me to realize that I missed her, that I wanted to be with her, because it made my life so much better. I had been without her for years and for me it was stupid to spend time apart while we were so close. I'd already been asking around for jobs and I really planned to stay.

"I enjoy spending time with you," she said quietly.

"But?" I knew that there would eventually be a *but*.

"But... I also enjoy spending time without you," she said, somewhat more quietly.

Bam, a dense silence followed.

I knew what it was all about. I knew because I was usually the one who said these words in almost all of my past relationships. Or at least I thought about saying them, because I was too cowardly to say them out loud.

I was so immensely sad, but also angry. At the same time though, I couldn't blame her - for two reasons. Firstly, I had done the same thing on so many occasions, so how could I blame someone for doing the same to me? Secondly, I knew that it wasn't because of her or us, it was all because of me - I was crazy in love, lost, unreliable, addicted and possessive. I knew that my happiness, my joy and my sadness came from one single source. From her. From our time spent together, our relationship, the touches, words and love we shared. I knew I needed her like a drug, she had become an essential part of my happiness. No matter how hard I tried to ignore it, she didn't feel the same about me.

I couldn't have acted any differently. My feelings were too intense, for some unknown reason they were out of my control. I'd got lost. I'd lost myself in us. How could you then blame someone for not wanting to spend their time with a person who no longer exists? How could I blame her for wanting some time for herself?

So, without talking much, I picked up my stuff and left.
Outside a new day was dawning and light snow was falling. I put on the hat and gloves that I'd bought in a second-hand shop and stuck my left thumb out.

Day 311

Away from everyone, I lay down under a tree at the foot of Uluru and shed a tear.

From the moment I got closer to the huge red rock, I was filled with the place's invisible energy. It was incredibly strong and extremely sad. I felt that the rock was silently telling its tragic story, and I listened carefully with compassion.

It talked about the evil and injustice of people.

Even if I only noticed the other end of the human spectrum and the kindness of strangers, I knew what it was talking about. I knew about the atrocities that human beings were capable of committing at the expense of their brothers and sisters, other living creatures, and nature.

Please Don't Climb, said a large sign at the foot of Uluru where, at the moment of our arrival, dozens of people were climbing their way to the top.

The magnificent rock has been a sacred site to the Aborigines for thousands of years. Today, you can climb it, even though it was against their customs. The reason was money. The Australian Government is concerned that prohibiting climbs up Uluru would result in a significant drop in the number of tourists. However, they don't seem to care about the consequences it may have on a culture which has been almost entirely ruined.

"I just have to climb it and admire the view from the top," Simon said. "Besides, I read that the Aborigines no longer consider this rock sacred anyway, some of them have even climbed it. Look," he pointed to the dark-skinned kids who were climbing the rock barefoot and messing around near its foot.

"Do what you want," I said. "Although I don't know much about the Aboriginal culture, customs and beliefs, I believe that it's a sacrilege for most of them."

I didn't want to impose my viewpoint upon him since I knew he wouldn't change his mind anyway. I know many people drive thousands of miles to see the red rock, and once they hear about the fantastic view from the top, they feel like they have to climb it, coming up with all kinds of excuses.

Jean Baptiste wasn't sure whether to climb the rock or not, but he finally decided against it and set off on a two-hour walk around it instead. In the opposite direction from me.

We had been inseparable for three days and three nights. After a late-night drive with some cowboys, I spent the first night by a gas station, where I was sniffed by a dog, couldn't hide from the rain, had bats in the tree top above me and where a barefoot man nearly stepped on my head. I spend the second night in Mount Isa, at a CS's place, while the last three nights were with the two of them, camping and sleeping in Simon's car. We spent days driving monotonously across the Australian outback, while we endured cold nights at the free roadside rest areas. We didn't drive at night, fearing that a kangaroo might jump out onto the road and smash into the car (there are twenty million kangaroos scattered across Australia). We cooked, ate, drank and slept together for about one thousand miles. We planned to do the same for the next one thousand three hundred miles, and then we should be in Darwin.

We met Grant, a guy in his fifties, who had been cycling across Australia for the past three months. He had started in Perth, cycled through Melbourne, Sydney, Brisbane, Townsville, and his final destination was again Perth, he was supposed to get there in two months.

"My wife started to get on my nerves so I wanted some time to myself," he said.

However, he was not alone, he traveled with a friend, whose ashes he was carrying in a small urn. This was also an honorary tour for his friend. We saw a sharp kitchen knife attached to the wheel by an adhesive tape.

"To protect myself against the black guys, just in case," he explained. My cowboys had also told me to watch out for the black guys as we were saying our goodbyes.

I had attributed this to mild racism, until, the day before we visited Uluru, we had arrived in Alice Springs, and the scene left us stunned. The Aborigines were roaming around the city center and the suburbs just like zombies, intoxicated by cheap alcohol or from sniffing petrol, which was even worse.

"Puppies for ten dollars!" A visibly drunk local guy shouted, callously throwing a puppy around. The puppy was whining in pain, until a lady pulled a banknote out of her wallet and handed it to a guy, saving the puppy from further pain. The Aborigine stumbled away to a nearby liquor store.

The scene made me immensely sad and got me thinking about the causes of all this. The consequences were there for everyone to see, but the first step in solving the problem was to define its cause. In this case, the cause was very obvious - several centuries of racism, the oppression of indigenous peoples, belittling their customs and beliefs, and finally taking their children away for *australization*, which my female driver had told me about a few days earlier. No wonder that the lost Aborigines, just like their American cousins, found opiates to be the easiest escape from this harsh reality.

"How can I change the world?" I quietly asked the rock, wiping a tear from my cheek. I listened and felt the sorrow she radiated. I grew more and more optimistic. I didn't let anything stand in my way. I was convinced that there was still hope for this world. I was convinced that most people were good. I was convinced that, being united and educated, we stood a fair chance of defeating evil.

"If you want to change the world, start with yourself," the rock replied.

"Done!" I answered confidently. "I forgot everything I had previously learned and started to learn things again. I changed myself, my attitudes, and my beliefs. I've been traveling, absorbing new experiences, observing things from different perspectives. I can say I've changed for the better."

"Bravo!" The rock replied, without the anticipated irony in its voice. "Then now get down to the business of changing the ones closest to you."

"I think I've done that too, it was a natural progression," I continued. "My parents, friends, acquaintances, everyone had the opportunity to open their eyes and hearts by listening to my stories, getting to know people from all over the world with those with whom I hung out in Zagreb."

"Then find a wider audience," the rock persisted.

"I've already done that," I persisted too. "I have thousands of followers on Facebook, they're reading my blogs, watching my photos and streaming my videos. I think I've managed to pass my cheerful and positive experiences of the world and its people on to them, and so change them and their view of the world."

"Then you have no other choice," the rock said, "but to get involved in politics."

I laughed out loud, got up and continued to walk around Uluru. I couldn't stop smiling. Not because the idea was stupid and childish, but because, quite some time ago, I had discussed this idea with a friend and even came up with a theory as to how one could easily succeed in politics.

"I don't get these idiot politicians," I told Nina, visibly upset at one of the many newspaper articles that pointed out their idiocies. "And it's all so simple."

"So let's see, what would you do if you were a politician in power?" She replied, starting one of our endless conversations that were used solely for the purpose of wasting time instead of studying for exams in college.

"Like I said, it's very simple," I replied confidently. "I'll give you an example from my own life. In my fourth year of high school, I became student council president. The student council was composed of all the class presidents in our school, and I was the first among equals. As the president, I wanted to do something that would have a positive impact on all students. I called a meeting of the class presidents and invited them at their next class assemblies to ask their classmates to write their proposals for what they would like to change at school, what could improve their education and high school life. Once all the students had written down their proposals, the class president would collect the papers, reject the stupid proposals that would inevitably crop up, and make a list of the top five to ten proposals, which they would pass on to me. All of the twenty-or-so classes did it. I took the proposals and linked them into one list that I then presented to the principal."

"And then?"

"Almost all of the proposals were smoothly adopted," I said proudly. "We managed to extend our snack break from fifteen to twenty minutes, shorten the last two lessons in each period by five minutes, were given a corridor for graffiti, started to play music during the breaks between lessons. Although it was nothing sensational, it meant an awful lot to the pupils. It showed us that things could work out really well if we got organized, if we knew exactly what we wanted and if we duly presented our requests to the decision-makers."

"That makes sense," she agreed. "Maybe you should be traveling across Croatia, collect people's ideas and present them to the decision-makers."

"Yeah, I could," I said. "I could go hitchhiking, couchsurfing across the country... I think that five to ten years would be enough to meet most of the people and to visit every village in the country. However, the plan falls apart when you see what our politicians are like and when you realize that they place their own interests ahead of the will of the people, when you realize that they would wipe off their asses with those proposals. They should be defeated in their own battle, on their own battlefield - in the elections. If I were to take a tour across Croatia, meet people and listen to their problems, I could even run for a position in a city council, or in the Parliament. People would know who I am, they would know they can trust me."

"I get it," she said thoughtfully. "But what would you say to all these people, how can you solve their problems? You're an ordinary man, you don't know much about all spheres of society, trade, economics, health care..."

"I'd visit successful companies, colleges, international experts, and would ask them a question: what would you do in your respective field if you had the power in your hands? I would gather a hundred economists and prepare a summary list of their ideas. I would do the same for health care, economy... Actually, I don't have to know anything, just like when I was the president of the student council. I just need to be a liaison, a link between the people, experts and legislators."

"Then you have no other choice," she said, "but to get involved in politics."

Realistically speaking, it was a naive, utopian and almost unrealizable idea. I would have to face so many obstacles along the way, so much criticism, belittlement, constraint. Which was exactly what happened when I started considering traveling the world.

I laughed out loud once again, realizing where I was. At the foot of Uluru, the sacred rock of the Aborigines, on the other side of the world. Perhaps no idea is actually that stupid, naive or impossible. Perhaps the only way to check it is simply to try. Just like all other things in life, after all.

So my next potential life goal is: getting involved in politics! I wrote it down into my little black notebook, smiled again and moved on.

I met up with my French friends shortly after that. Simon showed us his panoramic photos he had taken from the top of Uluru, but some strange defiance in me didn't let me take a look at them. We jumped into the car, drove to the place where all the tourists would go to see the color of the rock transform into various shades in the sunset. We took some photos, and then went to a free camping area, where we spent the fourth night in a row sleeping by the road. We bumped into some Gray Nomads (retired people who pour their retirement savings into a motor home or caravan, and enjoy their hard-earned money by travelling around Australia) and shared our camp fire with them, while they treated us to some toast at breakfast time.

Since the ticket for the national park where Uluru is situated was valid for three days, we decided to visit Kata Tjuta, too: an enormous rock formation 15 miles west of Uluru. Many people considered it much more attractive than Uluru. Unfortunately, we didn't manage to see whether that was the case or not since, just as we passed the road to Uluru, our car broke down.

Simon, the car's owner, was desperate and tried everything to get it started, but in spite of help of the good people who pulled over to try to help us out, Simon had to go to a mechanic.

"Maybe I shouldn't have climbed Uluru," he told us later that evening over a beer, dumbstruck by the bill for towing and repairing the vehicle, which came to a little more than a grand.

"Maybe you shouldn't have," I confirmed. By then I had already heard a few stories about the *curse of Uluru* and the things that had happened to people who didn't treat the Rock with enough respect, those who carved their initials into it or picked up stones from the formation as souvenirs. I had refused to believe in such superstitions, until we drew a link between Simon's climbing the rock and the malfunction of the car.

"The most important thing is that you learned a lesson," said Jean Baptiste, optimistically raising a bottle of beer.

We spent that night in the official camping area at Uluru, and it was the first time that I paid for accommodation in Australia. We paid seventeen dollars for the chance to pitch a tent, with the three of us all squeezed in together.

The camp also had a restaurant, but this was too expensive for our standards. Since the kitchen closed at 9.00 pm, I asked the guy who worked there what they would do with all the leftovers.

"We'll throw them away," he said.

"Could you give them to us instead of throwing them away?" I asked him pleadingly. "We're hungry."

"If I do it, I could lose my job," he replied sadly, looking around.

A few minutes later, as my stomach started to growl, I watched in silence as the guy threw away the food in trash bags.

Forbid food waste or somehow distribute it to those in need. I wrote it down in my little black notebook and we all went to bed.

Day 324

"Welcome back again, bro!" Two familiar smiling faces greeted me and gave me a hug in Fremantle, the final destination of my three-week hitchhike across Australia.

These two smiling faces belonged to Keveen and Gina, my friends from India. They had arrived in Australia some months ago, found jobs, and come across an elderly couple who were seeking somebody to housesit while they were in Europe. They had free accommodation and hourly wages of twenty dollars, so they were in a position to make the money needed for the project that they were planning to run in Mexico the following year.

All they had to pay for was their food, and they even managed to minimize this expense.

"Let's go and get some groceries," they said.

"Isn't it a little late to go to the supermarket?" I asked. It was already 10.00 pm. and I was sure that all the shops would be closed.

"We actually do our grocery shopping after hours," they winked at me.

We showed up at a big supermarket that was closed and started searching for food in the large green bins. Just like at Uluru, a lot of food was thrown away on a daily basis. Supermarkets are responsible for so much food waste because, at the end of the working day, they throw away what they won't be able to sell the following day. After five minutes of rooting around in the dumpster, I realized that there was a small fortune: a bunch of fresh fruit and vegetables that were still neatly wrapped. All of them had the same flaws - the packaging was damaged or there was a little scratch or they were starting to go over here or there, which meant that they couldn't stay on the supermarket shelves that were constantly full. In another dumpster, we happened upon baked goods: bread and pastries in all different shapes and sizes. Most of them were in their bags and still had their price tag on. These products often cost as much as ten dollars.

"We're not going to take it all, of course," said Keveen, after he jumped out of the dumpster. "We've got enough to cover this week, and there are other people who also get their food this way, so it wouldn't be right if we took it all, especially if we cannot eat it."

How many people would have something to eat, how much less food would be thrown away, and how much money would be saved if we dealt with this problem this way? Is this the best thing that our supposedly intelligent civilization has been able to come up with when it comes to dealing with the food surplus? Shouldn't there be a more dignified way of getting this food to its final recipients - the hungry people - given that the supermarket chains are throwing it away anyway?

"Where did you go, what did you do, who did you meet?" My new hosts started firing questions at me once we settled down in the beautiful house that they were looking after. "Do tell!"

"Oh, I don't know where to start..." I sighed. "So much has happened since we last met in Varanasi..."

Little by little, I told them about everything that had happened to me over the past few months. Nepal, Malaysia, Thailand, Australia. Breaking up with Tanja, meeting Chloe. They were listening carefully, observing me with curiosity in their eyes. They laughed when I told them something funny and looked downcast when I told them something sad.

"Since I didn't want to wait until the car was repaired, I decided to keep going on my own," I went on with my story, telling them about my experiences from Uluru. I didn't forget to mention the food that had been thrown away in the restaurant. "The next day I hitchhiked to Alice Springs, couchsurfed with a host there and then headed for the north."

"A really cool guy, Alex, pulled over for me. He was carrying a surfboard in the car, heading for Darwin, which was almost a thousand-mile drive. On our way there, we exchanged our travel stories. This guy had been traveling around the world for two years, he had already sailed across the Atlantic Ocean, and was left penniless in Nicaragua after he was mugged and had a knife drawn on him, and so gave up the last 150 dollars he had. But that didn't stop him, he used an old banana cake recipe that he had, and started selling them on the street to get through the next few months. We also alternated behind the wheel, even though I still wasn't sure whether or not my driving license was valid in Australia. We spent one night in the middle of a forest - I slept in the driver's seat and he was in the passenger's seat. If someone had come across us in the morning, they'd have thought that Leonardo and Kate spent the night there, just without the palm print on the steamed up window."

"We stopped by in Katherine, refreshed ourselves at a natural spring and finally arrived in Darwin. I ended up roaming the streets of Darwin at 10.00pm, looking for a park where I could spend the night. It made me feel uneasy since I'd heard that Darwin had the highest crime rates in Australia, putting even Alice Springs in second place. Looking for a place to stay, trying to get a discount in hostels and walking the streets again, I passed by a girl."

"Hi, how are you?" she asked, approaching me on the main city street.

"I've been better," I said looking around, trying to make sure that she was actually speaking to me. "Do you ask everybody you come across how they're doing?"

"Not really," she beamed. "But I'm in a good mood."

"She asked me if I wanted a cigarette, and I accepted, even though I don't smoke cigarettes. Her company made me feel better, and you never know what can come out of a random meeting of this kind. She had recently returned from a trip across Europe, and when I told her that I didn't have a place to stay in Darwin, she took a look at my CS profile on her mobile, called her roommate and asked him for his blessing. So I had a place to stay for the next two nights."

"Haha, that sounds great!" Keveen and Gina hung on my every word.

I told them how I ended up in Batchelor, in a home belonging to a couple that had picked me up as I was hitchhiking and how we spent the evening watching trashy horror movies. Then, I also told them about hitchhiking a tourist bus going to Litchfield National Park and spending the day with people my age from all over the world, how I got myself rides with the Grey Nomads and a Swiss guy with whom I spent one night in a camping area somewhere in the north of the country, about bumping into Grant, the cyclist whom I had met before, and about everything that happened along the way.

I told them about a ride with Glen, a lawyer who specialized in defending the Aborigines.

By the time I got into Glen's car I had only met a few people of Aborigine descent. Some of them had fit perfectly in the Western lifestyle and weren't much different from anybody else, apart from the color of their skin. Some of them were half-naked, with vivid colors on their bodies, they played *didgeridoo*, entertained the tourists, took photos with them and earned a living that way. The others were addicted to alcohol and sniffed gasoline, and could be seen in most of the cities wandering aimlessly down the streets.

Glen was the expert for this unassimilated element.

"I'm originally from Melbourne, for the past couple of years I've been working in the north and west of Australia," my driver began his story. "I married an Aboriginal girl and we have two beautiful children. I was a partner in a large law firm with over thirty lawyers, but I decided to leave, go back into the field and try to make a change. I probably don't have to tell you that both of these moves - marring a humble Aborigine girl and swapping the comfort of a legal practice for the gloomy everyday of traipsing from one court house to another - were met with accusatory looks of my friends and acquaintances."

"I've been there, done that," I added.

"My holy mission is to keep Aborigines out of jail," he continued. "In Western Australia, the Aborigines make up about four percent of the population, but the situation is quite different in prisons: almost half of the prisoners are Aborigines. And if you want to talk about young offenders, almost 100 percent of them are Aboriginals. The system wants more police officers, stricter laws and more people behind bars. My goal is to convince them that it's all about prevention. The government is fair enough: every now and then they invest some money in the prevention, social workers are on the streets talking to the kids, but none of these efforts are enough. They'd much rather spend a couple of million building a new prison than invest that money in the prevention. You always hear that same old maxim - if you can't do the time, don't do the crime!"

"Over the past twenty years that I've spent defending murderers, rapists and thieves, I've come to realize that very few people are truly evil. There were very few people who really enjoyed hurting other people. Most of them were marked by a childhood trauma, abusive parents, and a lack of understanding from their environment, so crime was their easiest option. Sometimes the only one they had."

We also talked about the white Australians who, in my opinion, enjoy the highest standard of living in the whole world. The economy was excellent. The minimum hourly wage was 16 dollars. Most of them had a beautiful house, a nice car, surfing equipment and ate in the finest restaurants. And these things make them happy. However, that's only on the surface. "The divorce rate is soaring," said Glen. The suicide rate was one of the highest in the developed world. They consume large amounts of alcohol and drugs.

"Sometimes I think that ordinary Australians are jealous of Aborigines," he continued. "They watch them walk around carelessly, without a job, without having to worry about the mortgage or if they've got as much as their neighbors. After all, this is their country: why should they pay for a permit to live here? The Australians see it as a threat - they have to work hard so they can afford all the things they own, they have to pay off the mortgage and owe money to the bank; why wouldn't the Aborigines be just like that too? It's not fair that they can be so carefree, without the typical Caucasian worries."

"In Australia, the racism isn't institutionalized like, let's say, in South Africa, it's much more subtle, but it's still there. Don't get me wrong, even if Australians are ill-tempered by nature, they also have a softer side. If they see a young Aborigine who has made an effort to accept their lifestyle then they'll accept him and be supportive. The greatest responsibility lies with the media that isn't especially fond of the Aborigines, so a lot of people gain a negative opinion of them from the very outset. This results in strict laws, one of which prescribes a minimum prison sentence of one year if you commit a felony three times, which also applies to under-age perpetrators. Although, at first, this might seem fair - if you rob someone's house three times, you deserve to go to jail for a year - the usual perpetrators are drunk kids who break into the houses of rich Australians. Also, in most cases they hardly steal anything important - sometimes just food. So they end up in jail, which they leave, as it has been proven, in a worse state, so they then repeat the crime."

"After all, it all boils down to the fact that the Australians don't understand the Aborigines, they don't understand their own history. We were too busy whitewashing the whole thing, instead of studying it thoroughly and trying to establish a peaceful and sustainable co-existence."

After that educative ride, Glen left me by the road and carried on his way, taking care of his wife and children, or defending the sins of a national minority - either way I wish him the best of luck.

I was telling Keveen and Gina about being picked up by two French girls whom I joined on a camping trip to Wolfe Creek, a giant crater with a diameter of 950 yards, which makes it the second largest crater in the world, if you're counting those craters where bits of meteorite have been found.

Unfortunately, Wolfe Creek is far better known for its eponymous horror movie, partly based on Ivan Milat, the hitchhiker murderer. In the movie, three backpackers (two girls and one guy!) ended up as victims of a maniac who confined them to his house, tortured them, and eventually killed two of them. When I heard that the guy was the only survivor, I was a little bit relieved.

I told them about my visit to Broome, where I enjoyed a spectacular view: a wonderful sunset with camels carrying tourists upon their backs, walking down the endless beach. Camels had been mostly imported from India and Pakistan during the second half of the 19th century, helped to build mines and telegraph lines by carrying supplies to remote towns. But when engines came along in the early 20th century, they were released into the wild and now roam freely throughout Australia. It's estimated that there are about 300,000 camels, and fifty of them work in Broome, on Cable Beach.

"A young trucker picked me up," I recounted, finishing my story. "So here I am."

"Oh!" Keveen sighed. "So much has happened since we last met."

"So what's next?" Gina wanted to know.

"In a few days I'm flying to Kuala Lumpur to extend my visa, and then I'm coming back to Australia to try to earn some more money before I leave permanently," I replied. "My original plan was to go to New Zealand and try to hitchhike a boat to the Americas from there, but that plan has fallen through because I'd have to wait for a New Zealand tourist visa for four months, and sailing across the Pacific is almost impossible. A route to the east isn't the best idea, and flights are darn expensive."

"How about Africa?" They suggested.

"Hmm, Africa," they had got me thinking.

I looked at the map of Africa and the visa requirements for some of the countries. The situation wasn't bad at all, you could get most of visas for the countries in the east and southern Africa on the borders.

Poseidon was merciful too: in a month's time, a bunch of boats would be crossing the Indian Ocean from Southeast Asia or Australia to South Africa. So I said to myself that, even if I failed to find a ship looking for an inexperienced crew member, I would still be able to stay a little longer in Australia, try to make some money and then fly to Africa. Those flights were twice as cheap as the ones to the Americas.

Now I had to plan my trip to Africa.

Day 1000

"After staying in Fremantle and visiting Kuala Lumpur, I returned to Australia and ended up in Melbourne," I explained, continuing my presentation. "I decided to stay there for some time. It had been a year since I started traveling around the world and I'd grown a little bit tired of constantly changing places. I couldn't find any ships that sailed to Africa, and I felt good in Melbourne. I'd even found a job."

I turned to a new slide showing me wiping the floor in a restaurant kitchen.

"So, one morning I took a seat in McDonalds, where I went to steal Wi-Fi every day," I continued. "And I noticed a brief ad: *Kitchen Hand Wanted. Full-time hours. Apply ASAP*. Since the restaurant was pretty close to where I was, I picked up my stuff and got going. Running out of breath, twenty minutes later I introduced myself to the head chef."

"I've come to discuss the kitchen hand ad," I told him.

"Have you ever worked in a kitchen?"

"Yes," I replied without hesitation. "In Croatia, Turkey and India."

"When can you start?" He asked quickly.

"I can start right away," I answered even faster.

"Great, go ahead," he handed me a rubber apron and showed me the dishwashing station.

"So I got another job in Australia, cash in hand work" I continued. "I lived in a house with nine other people and slept in a tiny room where they previously kept a projector for showing movies. It didn't have any windows and you couldn't enter when the mattress was on the floor. I didn't have to pay the rent in cash but in the left-overs that I would bring from the restaurant at the end of my shift."

"I visited every corner of the city, riding the trams without buying a ticket, just as I would do if I was back at home. I inquired about the possibilities of extending my visa, whiled away hours in bars, drinking cups of coffee and pints of beer, and hung out with old and new friends in the parks. I visited the nearby tourist attractions. One day, just as I was about to buy a second-hand bike, I received an e-mail."

Tom,

As luck would have it, crew plans changed and I can now offer you the berth on This Side Up to Africa. Are you still looking to go to Africa or have you found a boat yet? If you are still interested, we'll pick you up in exactly three weeks on Christmas Island.

Captain Mike

"It made me wonder. Should I stay in Melbourne, perhaps earn enough money to pay off all my debts or should I go and start the greatest adventure of my life, sailing across the Indian Ocean? I had to think long and hard about this one. So after four, five...," I took a breath and deliberately paused for a moment, "... minutes, I knew exactly what to do."

My long and hard thinking made the audience chuckle, and a moment later, I showed them a photo of a thirteen-meter sail boat, safely docked.

"I worked for another three weeks, earning enough for the plane ticket to Christmas Island and then waited for the captain and the two members of the crew."

Day 420

"There are two especially beautiful days in the life of a ship owner," the captain told me as we turned off the engine and raised the sails, leaving Mauritius behind. "The day you buy it and the day you sell it. Not necessarily in that order."

I laughed, recollecting how my experience of sailing on this boat was quite the same. I was ecstatic when they invited me to sail with them, but I was sure I would be so much happier once we landed in Africa.

I took out my little black notebook to write down the captain's words of wisdom. But then I just continued to write about what had happened during my month on the high seas.

On Christmas Island, where the cheapest accommodation cost over one hundred dollars, I was supposed to spend a couple of days waiting for the boat and its three-member crew - my new family. I hitchhiked a ride with a car that brought me from the airport to the island's main port, and the driver informed me that there were some abandoned military barracks up on the hills behind the harbor, and that it would only take ten minutes to get there on foot. I occupied one immediately by putting my inflatable mattress down inside. I had got myself a new place to stay.

Near my barracks, there were showers, a free public toilet, a supermarket and... well, that was actually it. It was a small settlement. However, I'd heard so much about it lately. In Australia, a lot of politicians talk about illegal immigrants who come to Australian territories on ships from Indonesia and seek asylum. Most of them end their long journeys precisely on Christmas Island, and in December 2010 one of those ships ended up crashing into the rocks that surround the island, killing 50 people. A memorial had been erected some ten meters away from my barrack.

The following morning I had an opportunity to see what it all looked like in the flesh: a nearly disintegrated fishing boat with 50 people wearing fluorescent vests accompanied by military ship was docking in the harbor. The refugees were mostly from Sri Lanka, but often from Iraq, Iran, Pakistan and Afghanistan. They had to cover thousands of miles from their homelands just to reach Indonesia, where they boarded these vessels and got smuggled to Australia. In most cases this way of the cross was expensive, so the passengers were sponsored by their families who would sacrifice everything just to enable this one member of their kin to embark on that long journey in search of a better life.

The story was awfully sad, especially when you witnessed the nationalist attitudes of some Australians, cursing the illegal immigrants and telling them to go back to their boats and return to wherever they came from, just as the Aborigines were asking them to do the very same thing. It would be funny, if it wasn't such a tragedy.

I didn't see much of Christmas Island, which doesn't have more than 2000 habitants (the refugees don't count!), 70% of whom were of Chinese origin. The island was discovered on Christmas Day in 1643 and has been under Australian jurisdiction for the past 50 years. Since it was basically uninhabited up to the end of the 19th century, Christmas Island is renowned for its great variety of flora and fauna (two thirds of the island were declared a national park) and it is best known for the annual migration of red crabs, which was due to occur just a few weeks after I left the island. It's estimated that they number up to 100 million.

Other than migrating crabs, there were some other places on the island worth visiting, but since the island was too big to be explored on foot (especially when the temperature was over 40°C), there were no cars so hitchhiking was out of question, and renting a scooter cost 50 dollars per day, I gave up this idea. I spent my days observing the ocean, waiting for my ship, just like a woman who was waiting for her husband to come back from sea. I spent my nights drinking rum, just like a sailor impatient to see his wife again.

On the fourth morning, at the crack of dawn, a sailing ship entered the harbor. It was the first one since I'd got to the island. I had a strange sensation in my stomach - that could be it. I quickly gathered all my stuff, left my little barrack, and went down to the harbor. As I was getting closer, the name of the ship became clearer. This Side Up. That was it.

While I was anxiously waiting for the crew to lower the dinghy into the sea and come ashore, I was growing ever more excited, but also nervous. Those were the three people I would be spending the next month and a half in a really confined space, which, among other things, would be swaying from left and right, back and forth.

Relentlessly, on and on. So I met captain Mike (USA), Sebastien (Belgium) and Li Ti (China). They didn't seem like the sort of people who would throw me off the ship in the middle of the ocean, leaving me at mercy of sharks.

After going through the customs formalities, I left my luggage on the ship and they gave me some basic information: how the toilet worked, where the groceries were stored, how we should cook and stuff like that. Since the thirteen-meter sail boat offered rather limited space (there were only two cabins with beds - the captain slept on the stern, and Seb and Li Ti slept on the bow); I would have to sleep on a bench in the hallway. This was the moment when I said goodbye to any kind of privacy and comfort for the days ahead. If I had paid any money for this then I would have asked them for a refund. But given the circumstances, I really didn't have a choice.

The captain wanted to know about my sailing experience, and I had to tell him a white lie saying that I had sailed quite a lot in Croatia, but that I had never gone so far so as not to be able to see the land. Hearing that, the captain just smiled. Since I didn't know him that well I wasn't sure if the smile meant kid, you've got no idea what you're getting yourself into, or the red mist was descending over him from having a totally inexperienced crew member when he was about to sail across the second largest ocean in the world.

Seb and Li Ti asked me if I ever suffered from sea sickness - as if they knew what I had been thinking for the past two weeks.

Sea sickness, which I'd only heard about in the worst terms, seemed like a problem that was impossible to solve and which I was very likely to suffer from during the journey (the storms and accidents involving other ships didn't even cross my mind). The two of them suffered from sea sickness the first couple of days, but after that they were all right. I also felt a bit dizzy after a couple of minutes in the cabin, but I hoped that I would only be seasick for the first day or so. I didn't want to be one of those people from the stories I'd heard: one man even threw himself into the sea because he couldn't stand feeling sick anymore.

I took the crew inland, where they took a shower for the first time in five days; later we went to the supermarket to stock up on supplies (this was my only expense during the journey across the ocean: paying for the one quarter of the groceries we bought), and to the Internet cafe where I informed my mother that I wouldn't be in touch over the following 5 or 6 days, until we reach the next island. I thought about making a video with my last will, but I didn't want to tempt fate. Besides, I didn't have much to leave behind anyway.

We spent the night in the harbor and after a morning walk in the nearby forest, another shower and lunch on the ship, we raised up the anchor and set sail towards the setting sun. We had to travel 600 miles to get to our next stop: the Cocos Islands.

There are three main rules when sailing: stay on the boat, don't hit anything, and the mast must be facing the sky at all times.

The last rule was the reason why our sailboat had been named "This Side Up". Also, there were two arrows pointing upwards to avoid any confusion. If the mast was facing downwards then it only meant one thing: evacuation. If you had enough time, of course.

We didn't have any difficulties while casting off from Christmas Island: the island protected us from the wind, we managed to witness a gorgeous sunset, and as soon as we were on the open sea I got ready for the first task in my sailing career - pulling up the sails. I felt a bit awkward to ask what was I supposed to do and by doing so admit that I had no experience whatsoever in sailing, so I simply did the same as the rest of the crew. Luckily enough, the main and head sail were successfully up, the wind was pushing us forward so we started sailing at a speed of six or seven knots. By the way, if you were travelling at a speed of 1 knot you would cover one nautical mile in an hour, which is slightly more than one standard mile.

The sails were up, engines turned off and coordinates entered into an autopilot, so we could finally have some rest, after those exhausting four minutes of work. I was waiting for the captain to give us some more assignments, but he just sent us to bed and told us that he would take the first shift on night-watch.

Easy for him to say. Whenever I closed my eyes on my bench-bed, the rocking of the boat that I had never experienced before would wake me up. After one strong wave, I panicked, got up and went to see the captain, asking him whether we should start with the evacuation. He just told me that we had good speed and the sea was relatively calm. Calm? 9 foot waves, the boat rocking on all sides, with groceries sliding all over the cupboards, and he called this calm? What had I got myself into?

After the captain's shift ended, it was my turn. The night-watch consisted of a series of three-hour shifts between 7.00 pm and 7.00 am, during which you had to keep an eye on the boats in your surrounding area, and you could either see them with your bare eyes or on the radar. After that, I finally managed to get some sleep. I did wake up a few more times, expecting that the rest of the crew would do the same, but it didn't happen.

Morning brought lighter wind and smaller waves, which made me happy, even if the rest of the crew wanted stronger winds to help us sail to the next destination as soon as possible. Nobody gave a damn about my paranoia. Enough whining, I said to myself, I'm on a sailing boat that is taking me to Africa for free, under the leadership of a captain who can teach me something about sailing. Make the most of it!

Captain Mike was cool: he had plenty of patience with us rookies: he readily explained everything we wanted to know; as a matter of fact, he answered our stupid questions more than once, taught us how to tie sailor knots and loads of other things. When he was young, he had been a rock star in America, performed with a couple of bands. He'd been the only person who had crossed America from the southernmost to the northernmost point of the United States on a Harley. He'd been a millionaire. He'd had it all, and then all of a sudden, arthritis spelled the end of his career. He bought a boat and set off to a trip around the world with his wife, but she came back home because on the way to the Galapagos, she got terribly seasick and there was no sign that she would recover soon. Since at that time they lost almost all of their life savings during the financial crisis, they decided to sell the ship. But the crisis didn't abate and there were no buyers in sight. This was why the captain had been sailing alone over the last couple of years, taking along wanderers like me to help him around the ship.

Sebastien was a Belgian cop. He quit his job when he realized that it didn't make him happy and moved to China, where he spent most of his time with his sweetheart, Li Ti. They got bored in China, so, just like me, they decided to make an unusual move - cross the Indian Ocean. They didn't have any experience in sailing the high seas either.

The thing that I noticed straight away was that our diet was relatively monotonous: our fridge wasn't working, we only had canned fruit and vegetables, our bread supplies were scarce and would only last another couple of days, and we just had some Indonesian biscuits bought in Bali for desert. We had a lot of pasta, rice and tomato sauce. On the other hand, it wasn't as if my standard diet was especially varied.

I had just one problem during the first few days: sea sickness. Just like with working on the sails, I was too proud to admit that I felt constantly sick. Seb and Li Ti had already got used to the sailing life, but I was new to it all. I tested my body and observed how it reacted. When I was lying in the cabin, with my eyes shut, I felt fine. Whenever I was standing or sitting with my eyes wide open I had a strange sensation in my stomach, and I'm not talking about romantic butterflies. When I was up on the deck observing the horizon I was fine. But as soon as I tried to read a book or spend some time in front of a laptop, it caused me nothing but problems. So, after these tests I either slept or watched the sky and the sea from the deck.

Still, a close encounter with sea sickness was inevitable and it was finally my turn to show off my culinary skills. I was just about to make some spaghetti in a tomato sauce in our damp little kitchen, that was always akilter, when, thinking about the nausea that was overcoming me and the quality of lunch I would serve I was surprised by a sudden wave. I came crashing down, along with a bowl full of water, and hit a few kitchen cabinets on the way. The result: a couple of bruises that would conceal themselves for a day or so and water everywhere. Fortunately, it hadn't been boiling.

I managed to prepare the lunch, but it was so awful that I had few regrets when I threw it back up just a few minutes later. My fellow crew members were very supportive: they didn't criticize the quality of the lunch in the slightest (in fact, they ate all of it), and they didn't make fun of how I fed the fish chewed up pasta and a tomato sauce that was a bit more sour than when I had originally prepared it.

While I was at sea, I had plenty of time to think. In fact, that was pretty much my main activity. The sails went up and came back down and we only had to change their position a couple of times a day at most. Night shifts only lasted three hours. We had rest of the day free. We slept a lot, read a lot and, well, thought a lot.

I also figured out how to describe sailing to someone who had never sailed across an ocean. Saying that, I think that it might be better not to know, because it might change their mind. Here goes.

You know flight simulators they have at funfairs? Get inside, wait for it to come on. Have the turbulence lowered to about 60%. And there you have it: that's sailing. But, you have to stay in that simulator 24 hours per day - cook in it, eat in it, drink in it, go to toilet in it and sleep in it. From one day to the next. Day after day after day... well, I guess you get the picture.

During the third day of sailing I finally started showing signs of recovery from my sea sickness and was in a much better mood. I was even able to have a conversation with other crew members that were longer than three sentences. One day we saw a cargo ship in the distance and contacted them by radio - that was the only contact we had with the outer world in five days, the time it took us to get to our first stop: the Cocos Islands.

The last 12 hours of sailing were the worst: we had to put down the sails so that we could slow down and avoid arriving at our destination in the middle of the night. Since we had to put down the sails, our boat was at the mercy of a strong current and ten-foot waves which made it sway back and forth as if it was made of paper. The groceries started falling from the shelves, Li Ti spilled sauce on the floor, Seb tried to help her, but all he did was spill his dinner all over the kitchen too. It felt as if we were caught in the midst of an earthquake.

Since the wind was very strong and there was an awful downpour, we discovered that the ship had sprung leaks in several places, two of which were right above my bench-bed. Still, on a brighter note, at least the ship wasn't leaking beneath the water line: that would've been a much greater problem.

As we were approaching the island, the sky was clearing, it completely stopped raining, the wind died down completely and nature suddenly shone in all its splendor.

The crew were lost for words, exchanging looks and smiling at each other, reading each other's thoughts. We had arrived in paradise.

We dropped anchor and spotted a few small rock sharks looking for leftovers. We sat on the deck simply enjoying the colors of the sea, the palm trees not far away from us and the white sand while we waited for the customs control. We also noticed a small vessel covered in sponsors' stickers. The customs officers who had arrived in the meantime explained to us that that vessel belonged to a Dutchman who had arrived the very same morning from the east, having rowed all the way.

We burst into laughter but also paid our respect to his adventure, especially since this was the third ocean he was crossing in this way. The officers' gestures implied that they thought the guy was a bit looney. They told us one of his anecdotes about several sharks which, a few days previously, had kept him company in the middle of the ocean, swimming around and bumping the bottom of his vessel with their snouts, curious to discover what kind of animal was crossing their territory.

And we had thought we were on a great adventure!

We spent the rest of the day wandering around the soft beaches of uninhabited Direction Island, one of the 24 islands that formed an atoll, with endless coconut palms and other exotic vegetation. Only two of the islands are inhabited and they have 600 inhabitants.

The following day we visited Home and West Island where we actually got to see the inhabitants. They weren't much different from people living on the Australian mainland. There were no topless dancers, colorful flower necklaces, fruit cocktails... it was actually quite disappointing. We replenished our stocks, careful to avoid the fresh fruit and vegetables since most of it cost up to five dollars per piece! I found the only Internet café on the island so I managed to let my folks know that I was safe and that I would be off the information superhighway for the following three weeks or so until we made landfall again.

I couldn't even begin to imagine what they must had gone through during my sailing, especially since I'd spoilt them by getting in touch every day, almost without an exception.

I have to admit that I was sad on the third morning, when we pulled up the anchor and set sail towards the west. It wasn't because we were leaving one of the most beautiful places I'd ever seen, but the very opposite - because it didn't impress me much. True, the Cocos Islands were probably the most beautiful place I had ever visited, but you get used to all this beautiful scenery. After a while it becomes something common, even mundane.

I was sad because there were three weeks of non-stop sailing ahead of us.

As the old saying goes: There are plenty more fish in the sea, usually used when someone dumps you.

Well, we disproved that theory. During our whole trip, we managed to catch two plastic bags and just a single fish that we had to eat the very same night since we didn't have a refrigerator. Where have all the fish gone? There was no sign of dolphins, whales or sharks. Every now and then a flying fish would end up on the deck, sometimes missing us just for a few inches.

When the nights were calm, I slept under the stars, in the cockpit. It felt good to be in the fresh air, I just had to be careful and watch out for the waves which could easily splash me. Beside the stars which were amazing (although still not shiny enough for my liking, I'm very picky), the reason for sleeping in the cockpit (and being there during the whole day) was the foul smell coming from the inside of the boat. The sewage ejection pump was broken, which resulted in a blocked sewage pipe and a very bad smell. My bench-bed was next to the very source of this beautiful aroma.

Ten days, plus the five days that we had needed to get to the Cocos Islands. That was the time it took me to start seeing the sea as my friend. We synchronized our watches, we started to talk: we became one. I didn't see it as a necessary evil, as an obstacle, but as a big brother who had decided to show me the way and keep me company to my destination.

It was obviously typical Stockholm syndrome. I had befriended my kidnapper - the ocean. As a matter of fact, sailing resembled serving a prison sentence in a number of respects. Not that I had ever been in one, but I'd seen them on the TV. I even developed a theory that prison was way better than sailing across an ocean. You couldn't get off the ship, just like you couldn't get out of a prison. You share the space with a bunch of people you cannot choose, which is again just like in prison. You are counting down the days till you're free/reach land. But on a ship you have to cook for yourself, while in prison you don't have to do that. That's a plus for prison! You get to eat fish more often in prison. That's already two pluses. A prison doesn't sway back and forth all the time. Three pluses. In prison, there are no storms that keep you wondering if you will get out of all this alive. Well, that's already four pluses. There are no lightening strikes that could hit the ship and cause the sort of damage that, as our captain used to say, could leave us in the middle of the ocean. You couldn't receive any visitors on a ship. There is no communication with the outside world. You get to shower, on average, once every five days, and it is usually in salt water so washing with soap is problematic. Now we're already at eight pluses in favor of the prison. On a brighter note, there's no one lurking just behind you while you are soaping yourself on a boat. One plus for life at sea!

Life on a ship isn't that difficult, it's just monotonous. I had thought that sailing across an ocean sounded like the adventure that happened once in a lifetime, one of the biggest things in I could do, something romantic... but it wasn't. If I had to use one word to describe my experience, the word monotony would first spring to mind. I managed to read the entire Lord of the Rings trilogy, and a couple of the captain's books and started editing my video clips.

It took us 18 long days before we saw the land: Mauritius! We arrived to the harbor, did what we had to do for the customs, and I was given a stamp which meant that I could stay there for the next 15 days. Looking at all the stamps from different countries, I realized that I would soon run out of blank pages in my passport.

Once I got the stamp, my only thought was to buy a local SIM card for my mobile phone and call my parents. Never had 18 days elapsed during which I didn't communicate with them. In fact, my previous record was five days, which was the time it took us to get from Christmas to the Cocos Island during the first leg of our trip.

My mom's cell kept ringing. Dad answered it. He'd never answered my mum's phone. In a split second dark thoughts ran through my head. What could have happened during all that time? Soon, after we'd exchanged few words, I guessed that mum had seen the unknown number on her screen and didn't want to answer it by herself so she handed it over to dad. Their lost sailor son was safe and sound! They just started to worry because some nasty storm had hit the United States: it didn't matter that I was sailing across a completely different ocean...

After the conversation was done I fulfilled my second biggest wish: to eat and drink like a glutton. Eighteen straight days of eating pasta in tomato sauce were too much by now. I indulged in some junk food, fresh fruit and vegetables, cold water, ice-cream. I felt like a kid in a toy shop.

I got back to the ship and the three of us cleaned it, while the captain had to see some repairers because there was some work to be done on the ship before we set off. The verdict was reached: we would spend an entire week in Mauritius.

The moment the ship was spick-and-span, maybe even a few seconds before, I dashed away with a small rucksack on my back, saying goodbye to my boat family. I went to visit my new, couchsurfing family. Maja and her husband Xavier, a Serbian-Mauritian couple would be my hosts. A smile, hug and a beer at a local supermarket: it was enough to feel at home again. I ate bread and cheese. I went to Xavier's sister birthday party. In the evening I was in a big, warm (non-rocking) bed. This is what I call happiness.

The following day we moved to the beach, into the house of Xavier's grandparents. This was the place where I'd be resting for the following week, going on a few short kayak trips to an island that had been declared a natural park, to dinners with their friends, to a party accompanied by drums and a campfire and other stuff like that. I didn't explore Mauritius and I wasn't too interested in its history and culture. There was really nothing new.

However, a walk down the streets got me back into the good old chaos. I was starting to feel that I was reaching Africa: there was no more of Australia's order and cleanliness: the streets were colorful, full of aromas and sounds; people gave you curious looks; everyone was hopping on and off of moving buses; everyone was selling something. I'd seen it somewhere before: I knew, in fact, that Africa, with few exceptions, would be like a copy of Asia. I would once again become a rich white tourist, as opposed to the image of a wanderer and a homeless guy that I had in Europe and Australia. That was the image I learned to appreciate.

I wasn't sure if I wanted to turn back into a rich white tourist. While on Mauritius I got an offer from another captain to join his catamaran on its way from South Africa to the Caribbean Islands, only a few weeks after we were scheduled to arrive in Africa. If I was there then I wouldn't necessarily be a rich white tourist. I'd perfect my Spanish in a few months, and once you know the language everything is easier.

Still, it would mean that I would have to skip Africa. Also, it would mean a minimum of another month and a half of sailing across an ocean. Most importantly, it would mean giving up on the agreed meeting in Kenya.

After a few days mulling it over, I finally made up my mind. I decided to spend a few months in Africa, give it a chance. I would have *to put aside the fact that I didn't feel like travelling and that I may be wasting my only chance to visit the continent that had always been the most appealing to me. Never mind, things would fall into their place, like they always do.*

Meanwhile the sails had been repaired, our supplies of groceries renewed, I got myself a new stamp in the passport, and we were back on the sea. It will take us two weeks before we arrive to Durban, on the eastern coast of South Africa. The captain feared this very part of our journey the most; he said we'd feel as if we were in a washing machine once we were south of Madagascar.

I closed my little black notebook, thinking about how I had managed to squeeze the whole past month into just a few pages that someone would read in a little more than ten minutes.

All this is such an illusion: photos from the trip, travel films, blogs and status updates on Facebook - all of it. You edit the photos, enhance the videos, shorten the stories and only tell the most interesting details. But you'll never be able to catch the moment when you first saw something, or catch your feelings at that moment. You'll never be able to shoot an authentic video as the very fact that you're shooting it puts the whole situation into a different context, taking away its freedom and natural beauty. There is no story that I'd be able to retell exactly as it happened, to accurately recreate its flow, intensity and my feelings.

The real truth, the real beauty is everything that happens between the shooting of these photos and movies, between telling these stories. It's all those things that you cannot catch on camera or write down. It's everything that cannot be told.

I put my notebook in my bag and returned to watching the open sea.

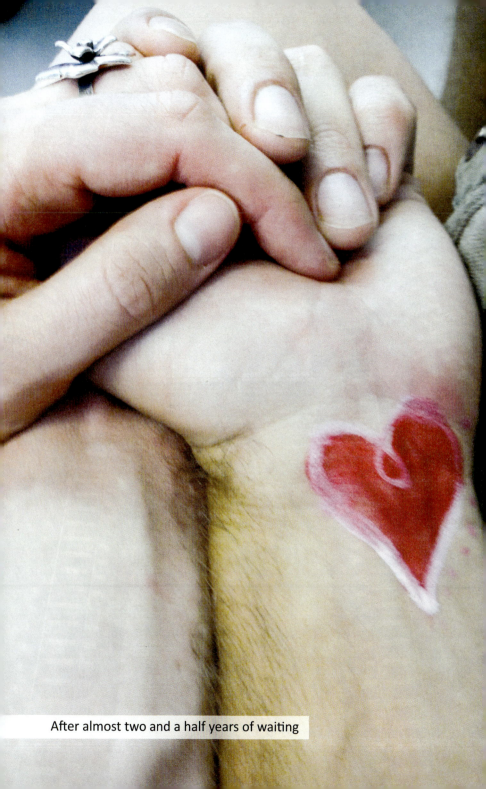
After almost two and a half years of waiting

The Petronas Towers

Koh Lipe, Thailand

A girl and a puffer fish

Hitching a ride in a boat for the first time

Stone yoga

Koh Tarutao

The hardworking beach cleaner

A Thailand sunset

Hitch-hiking in Thailand

Ton Sai and rock climbers

Posing in an Indian dhoti

Songkran

A monk in a Buddhist monastery

Getting my head shaved

Forest Monastery's wonderful surroundings

Walking meditation

Meditating lying down

At the wheel of a pick-up we flagged down

With the kids at an orphanage

Cabarita beach

Pauly and his family in Nimbin

Tallow Beach

Byron Bay's lighthouse

Janica and the sea

Dolphins

A photogenic lizard

Skydiving

Janica and I graduated

My yard in Brisbane

A professional traffic diverter

Karlu Karlu (the Devil's Marbles)

My overnight stop

Uluru

An apology to the holy rock

My favourite bench

The view from my favourite place

Kata Tjuta

The consequences of bad karma

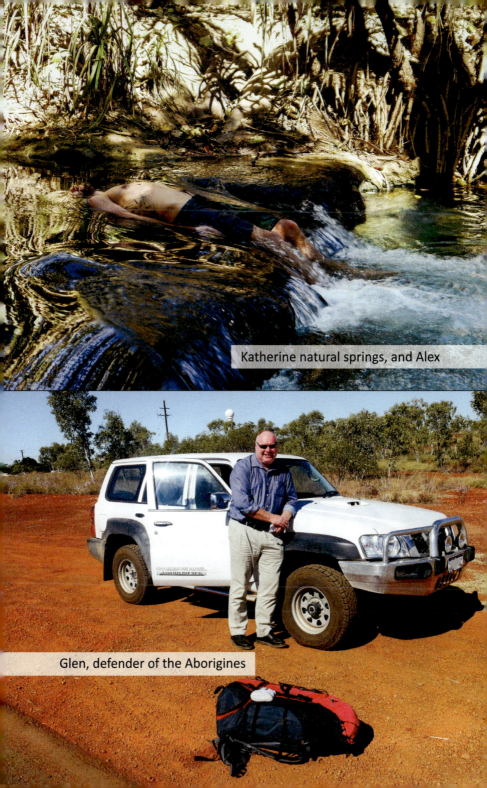

Camels on Cable Beach

The most beautiful twilight

A dog-dingo cross

Keveen and the fruits of his dumpster diving

Freemantle

A sweet girl on the beach

Melbourne

> Stonnington Area > South Yarra > Hospitality > Other Hospitality > Ad ID

chen hand

A job advertisment

Date Listed: 04/09/2012
Last Edited: 04/09/2012
Address: South Yarra VIC
Advertised By: Private
Job Type: Part-time

kitchen hand work. full time hours . good wages. apply asap

Visits: 9

The kitchen-hand

I'm rich!

My home on Christmas Island

The first real sailing of my life

Towards the setting sun

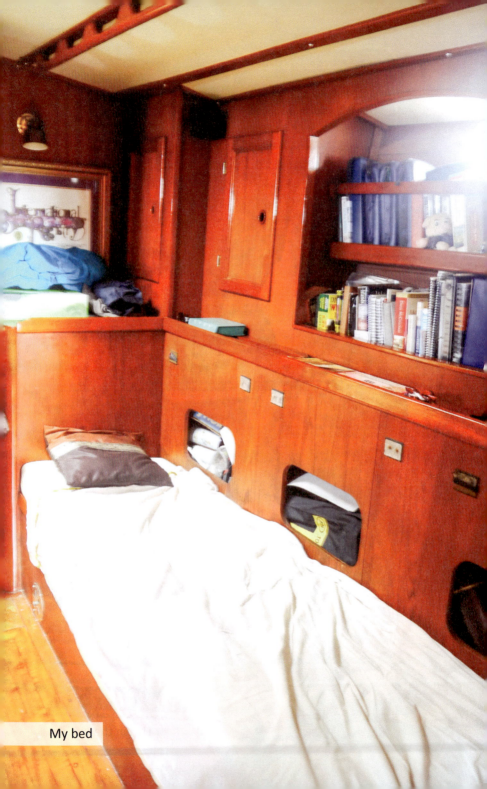

My bed

A madman who was rowing across the ocean

A heavenly beach

Another heavenly beach

Yes! Yes! Yes! I want to travel!

Mauritius

The one and only fish we caught

Day 1000

I didn't talk too much about crossing the Indian Ocean, instead showing the audience a four-minute video, which conveyed it so much more effectively. After all, I needed a break from talking.

I looked at my phone, and noticed that I'd got an email. From Chloe.

Without opening it, I put my cell phone back in my pocket, took another sip of water and got ready to resume the lecture.

"I arrived in South Africa forty-five days after leaving Christmas Island," I changed the slide, showing a photo of me kissing the ground. "I didn't stay long in South Africa, just a few days, which was enough to enjoy the luxury of staying in a gay hotel that I came across on CS. They normally only accept gay guests, but I guess they liked me, so they made an exception."

I'll never forget the moment when I entered my big hotel room, threw myself on the clean, soft bed, and showered in the marble bathroom after a month and a half of splashing myself with salty water on the ship's deck. I still remember this experience as one of the highlights of my entire trip. So now you see what a lack of basic conveniences such as a bed and a shower can do to you. It can make you happy once you get them back and teaches you to appreciate the small things in life.

"After South Africa, I visited Swaziland, a small kingdom best known for its recent new law that bans high-flying witches from hovering at an altitude above five hundred feet so as not to hinder air traffic."

My host, the only pale skinned volunteer in Ngomane, a small village in the north-east of the country, shared many other interesting facts about her everyday life experiences in Swaziland with me. For example, Swaziland has one of the most horrific statistics that I've ever had the misfortune of encountering. More than a quarter of the population is infected with HIV.

Also, being the only white woman in the village she was always the center of attention. She received at least ten marriage proposals each week, and each of her suitors promised her one more cow than the last. When arranging a marriage, a groom's father has to give a certain number of cows to buy his son a wife.

She hadn't accepted a single offer so far, and told me one of the reasons. The night before the wedding the groom invites his wife to his home, and when she falls asleep he would sneak out of the house, and his place would be taken by women from his family. They would take the poor girl's clothes off, dress her in traditional clothes, give her a spear, and paint her face. After that, they would take her to a place where their cattle is fed and then would harass her until she bursts into tears. Once she's married, there would be no more tears. *I'm coming out of debt, I'm going into debt*. This is the sentence the future wife has to repeat over and over again, which is supposed to symbolize her leaving her family and entering a new one. In this beautiful way women would wait for the sun to rise, and the wedding could finally take place.

Another interesting fact related to marriage in Swaziland is an annual parade where topless virgin-dancers dance every year in front of the king who, at the end of it, would choose one of the girls as his new wife. The king, known as the last absolute monarch in Africa, currently has 14 wives and often treats them to nice gifts, expensive trips abroad and things like that. I found it a bit too extravagant for a country in which two-thirds of the population live in poverty and misery. However, this doesn't stop children, girls and women from gathering every year in an impressive number (in 2012 there were 80,000 of them) and chanting slogans such as *I'm a virgin, come and test my virginity!* or *We don't want political parties in Swaziland!*

Brainwashing at its best (or worst).

"After Swaziland, I visited Mozambique, where I didn't stay too long either," I changed the slide, showing a photo of a truck under which I spent one night."

It was after a day during which I covered nearly six hundred miles, mostly with an exhausted driver who had been on the road for the past 14 hours. I kept asking him questions, telling him stories and putting his favorite song on repeat to keep him awake. He dropped me off in some village at midnight and advised me to look after myself.

The streets were dusty; there were no lights: the only sound was coming from a little bar playing local folk music. I successfully avoided the curious glances of passersby who were walking along holding beers and found a police station. I got acquainted with the guard, then noticed a broken-down truck, the side-car of which was meant for me and my self-inflating mattress. I immediately fell asleep. A gentle drizzle woke me up in the middle of the night so I moved under the side-car and, with the exception of a curious dog, there were no other disturbances during the night.

"There's one particular reason why I love this photo," I continued, recounting my only story from Mozambique. "People often ask me which were the most original or dangerous places where I've slept during the trip. My usual answer is under this truck in Mozambique. Sounds dangerous, right? Most people say: *I could never do that*. The thing is that everyone could do it if they had to. If somebody showed me this picture five years ago, I would have reacted the same way, saying that I could never do it. Almost nothing you do on a trip requires particular courage, including sleeping under a truck. You just have to end up in a village in the middle of the night and pragmatic thinking takes over, looking for the easiest and safest solution."

"I then arrived in Malawi, where I finally stayed a little longer."

Day 463

"Mister Kanyenya!" My buddies greeted me cheerfully as I walked up to them on the street.

"Hi, guys!" I said, stopping at a kiosk that had a large tin bowl with pieces of fried goat's meat. I pointed to the pieces that I wanted and the chef took them, put them on the side, and cut them into small pieces, seasoning it all with salt and passing me a fork.

Every day, without fail, people would gather and start their day by eating and talking things over on the dusty road a few meters from the entrance to the camp. In the morning, they served the cuts of meat that went off the quickest, like offal, and other parts of the freshly slaughtered animals would be prepared across the day.

They called this meat and the way it was prepared *kanyenya*. Since I came back to the scene of the crime day after day, they started calling me Mister Kanyenya. It was my first African name. In fact, second. Before that, they called me *Muzungu* like any other white man. This unique name made me feel good, for the first time in Africa. It made me feel as if I belonged here, at least in part.

Until I arrived in Cape Maclear my biggest wish was to be black. Wherever I went, the eyes of the local population were fixed upon me. I had experienced this in Asia, but there are many more white tourists there so a pale complexion isn't as sensational as it is in most of Africa.

I always try to fit in when traveling, to be like a local and get by in my new environment, to be inconspicuous. Here, though, it was all but impossible. You were always special, always noticeable, you were always a rich white tourist. The division was more than obvious, and the only times when you could feel part of a group was when you were with other people of your own race, or at least with people who spoke your language. Otherwise, wherever you went, you provoked a reaction. Even if it was the most positive reaction possible, it was still a reaction, which made you realize that you didn't belong.

The exception was if you stayed in one place for a long time. You learn the language, dress like a local, eat local food rather than Western stuff, and get in the routine of the locals.

That was exactly what I tried to do here, on the shores of Lake Malawi. I mastered the basics of the local Chichewa language, wore the same clothes every day, and ate kanyenya. I even stopped taking my antimalaria pills, since they didn't really guarantee that you wouldn't get malaria, and they were known for causing, to put it mildly, terrible side effects. I acted like a local - they don't take the pills until they get malaria.

One element of my efforts to turn into a local was to play bao.

"Let's play one round," said Moses, one of my *kanyenya* friends, after we had eaten.

I followed him to the camp and sat down at the table. There was a wooden board with 32 holes and 64 stones in front of us. I had seen locals from all over the village playing bao all of the time, so I was destined to master the game: anything to make myself feel more local, or kill some time, which was passing at a typically African pace - slowly.

Moses, who in both his appearance and mannerisms was a spitting image of Kareem Said from the television show Oz, was teaching me to play the game. He was mysterious and quiet, always keeping a low profile. He drank imported beer, which was a sign that he wasn't an ordinary local. Locals always drank local beer from a carton, which needed to be shaken before opening. He showed me the game's different tactics and approaches and we spent hours together. We talked about life in Croatia, life in Malawi and life in Cape Maclear.

"Sometimes I regret that tourism arrived to our small village in the first place," he said, beating me yet again and rearranging the stones into their starting positions.

"But why?" I was curious and surprised because it looked as though tourism had brought a lot of good to the village, boosted the local economy and raised living standards for ordinary people.

"I'll give you an example," he started his story, making his first move of the new game. "Do you know those kids who play music on improvised instruments and entertain the tourists with their cute renditions of Western songs?"

"Of course, they come here every day," I replied. "They're great, they sing well and play good music and try to be creative. I gave them a few coins and bought them something to eat."

"Those kids don't want to go to school because of you and people like you," he said.

"What do you mean?"

"Why would they spend ten years of their lives going to school if they can make more money than the adults around them by performing for wealthy tourists?" He pointed out. "In the short term, there's nothing wrong in earning some money this way and supporting their families, but in the long run, it's a road to disaster. In a few years' time, they will no longer be cute kids entertaining tourists; they will be uneducated adults, probably alcoholics, who will be dwelling on the good times from the past over a carton of beer. Just like these *beach boys*."

At that moment, two of the many locals that made a living by walking up and down the beach and annoying the tourists walked past us. They scoured the camp, looking for foreigners who were still sound asleep. They noticed Moses and me, exchanged a few words and carried on. I knew they were very well organized, divided into ten groups of ten people. In Cape Maclear there are ten accommodation units, so they rotated every week and did their business in front of each accommodation unit. They were really well trained. And very annoying. Although I had already been there for a few days, they were constantly trying to sell me the same things.

"These kids are just one example, perhaps the most banal, the most innocent one," continued Moses. "But the money from tourism only ends up with a few people, who spend it either on alcohol or on prostitutes. The majority of the population isn't that fond of tourism. It does them more harm than good."

"So how can we change this?" I asked after another quick defeat.

His theory gave me a lot to think about. Did we actually hinder their community, even if our intentions were good? If we give money to a beggar on the street, do we actually discourage him from finding a job, are we actually helping finance the mafia that is often behind all of this? When we raise money for a humanitarian cause, are we actually telling the state, which should intervene in such situations, that it doesn't have to do this because we, ordinary people, will try to solve the problem ourselves? When we donate money to charity or a church, do we know where the money really ends up? Can we be sure that our donations go to a good cause?

"Only by changing the mindset," his answered simply. "Although it's not always easy, people need to think about their actions and try to assume what kind of reaction they will provoke."

"What would that look like in the case of Cape Maclear?" I asked, looking for a concrete proposal.

"It would be very simple," he replied. "We should directly help those people who normally just get peanuts out of the total profits from tourism and encourage others to do the same."

"But why don't those people simply start their own business in tourism?" I continued, unrelenting with my questions.

"Competition isn't good for the job," he laughed and let me know what he had in mind as he took a look at another *beach boy* who was coming our way.

Over the next few days, I discussed this topic with other guests at the camp, encouraging them to spend their money sensibly, suggesting sites for them to visit, telling them how much they should be paying for different things.

Prompted by my good relationship with the guests, but also because her business was going through tough times, the owner of the camp offered me the assistant manager's position in exchange for free room and board. I accepted the offer without hesitation. I wanted to change things, and I was finally given the opportunity. I immediately gathered the staff of the camp together, just like in my high school days, trying to get their suggestions for improving the business - I was looking to find out if we could offer the tourists services and products at our own premises, without involving the *beach boys*, and how we could improve cooperation between them and the owner. The main problem was that money, crates of beer, food, pieces of fruit and other things would go missing from time to time. The employees were hesitant and reluctant to give suggestions to improve the business, and the problem with the owner boiled down to her lack of trust in them.

So things were going round in circles.

The days passed by. The harder I tried to improve and change the situation, my relationship with the camp's staff grew colder. They grew more disinterested. Even more frustratingly I assumed they were obviously okay with the situation since they could steal and fabricate stories to the owner, who was completely helpless in a foreign environment. I didn't let anything stand in my way. I decided to stay as long as I could and change some things. Things like catching somebody red-handed in lying or stealing, firing them, starting all over again with new staff and new rules.

Until one morning, when I experienced a painful disillusionment.

"Mister Kanyenya!" One of the *beach boys* called to me as I was having breakfast. "Let's have a little chat."

A group of ten beach boys lined up on the beach and waited for me to come. I could easily guess what they wanted to talk about.

I got up from the table, took my plate with me, and headed toward them with food in my mouth. I was walking leisurely, relaxed and carefree. As much as I could.

"Rumor has it that you have decided to stay here, manage the camp, and change some things," the leader of the badass group said.

"Yes, the owner offered me a job to improve the camp's business," I replied, smiling with food in my mouth. "Besides, I like Cape Maclear and the people living here." I looked at them, making it clear that I was alluding to them. I was hoping I had hidden the sarcasm in my voice. I didn't want to add fuel to the fire.

"Listen, man," the Boss continued. "We've been doing business here for years. We make our living and put food on the table for our families from what we sell to the tourists, the souvenirs and boat trips, and by organizing barbecue-parties on the beach and stuff like that. And all of a sudden you, a *Muzungu*, rock up and make yourself a local. If you continue working on your small noble project, you'll ruin our business. We've gathered here to have a word with you and kindly ask you not to do it anymore."

He didn't hide his sarcasm.

"Are you asking me not to do my job properly?" I said. "To sabotage my employer, to lie to the tourists when they ask me for fair prices of certain products and services?"

The idea of joining them crossed my mind for a moment. The idea of crossing over to *the dark side*. What if I joined them to earn my commissions? It would make it easier for them to approach the clients, because the tourists were more likely to believe *one of them*, we would make a dream team. Together we could spend our easy money on alcohol and prostitutes.

"We're not asking anything from you," the Boss said. "We just wanted you to know about the situation in Cape Maclear. We're the ones pulling the strings. We control everything: accommodation facilities, local shops, and the police. It would be a shame if someone made us make some unwanted moves in order to protect our business interests."

He winked at me, and walked away, signaling to the others to follow him. The transition from sarcasm to threat was swift and painful.

I sat in the abandoned boat on the beach and rolled a spliff. Malawi Gold, just one of the products that could be bought from the *beach boys* in small bags at high prices, even if this could be easily avoided with a little bit of effort.

It didn't take long until I figured it out. There was nothing I could do. There was nothing I could change. I was just passing through. No matter how good, noble or revolutionary my ideas were, soon I would be gone. There is a lot more you have to do if you want to change things. It takes a lot of effort, time, and education in the real problems and potential solutions. Here, in the middle of the Dark Continent, the only thing you can get is a beating. At best. At worst, they could call the police and have me locked up behind bars.

This was something I couldn't allow to happen since my date in Kenya was rapidly approaching.

Day 1000

"Besides Cape Maclear, I visited several other places in Malawi," I went on with the story. "I was walking around through remote villages, staying with locals, and playing with cute kids in the streets."

I spent my last days in Malawi camping in my tent, surrounded by countless fireflies, waiting for a boat that would take me across the lake to get to Tanzania. In a nearby hostel, I met an Israeli who had been staying there for several months, doing what I was supposed to do in Cape Maclear - he was in charge of a hostel in exchange for bed and board.

"How did you deal with the challenges?" I asked him one night over a game of bao, after recounting my brief managerial episode.

"Not so well," he said with a sour smile. "As soon as I arrived I asked one of the waiters to walk a bit more frequently among the guests and ask them more often what they would like to drink. The waiter was lazy, so I fired him after a couple of warnings. A couple of days later, the police came knocking on my door. They rummaged through my room, found three marijuana seeds and arrested me."

"For three seeds?" I asked, inhaling the smoke.

"For three seeds," he replied, exhaling the smoke. "They didn't care that I was suffering from malaria, they only let me go after I agreed to pay twenty thousand kwacha, which is quite a tidy sum over here."

"I'm so glad I left in time," I said with relief as I exhaled.

I spent a few days playing bao with the new waiter in the hostel, met a couple who were walking from Cape Town to Cairo (it took them ten months to get to Malawi) and a girl who was licking her lollipop very seductively. When I asked her for directions to the place I was going, she answered *two thousand*. I guess she wasn't fluent in English, but it was perfectly clear what I could get for those two grand.

"I crossed the border between Malawi and Tanzania by boat," I said, changing the slide, "illegally, with sugar smugglers."

It was my first contact with Swahili and an expression that perhaps best describes Africa: *pole pole*. It best translates as: slowly, take it easy, you've got time, be patient.

When I showed up on Saturday with a backpack, ready to cross the lake, there was no customs officer on duty, which meant that I couldn't get my passport stamped nor leave Malawi. *Pole pole*. Sunday was a non-working day for both customs officers and smugglers. *Pole pole*. A new boat was expected to set off on Monday, and the officer was expected to be at work. But then a storm arrived with heavy rain. *Pole pole*.

On Tuesday, I finally arrived at the Tanzanian side of the lake, crowded with people who, under torch lights, unloaded the sugar from the boat into trucks. There was no sign of civilization, let alone a customs officer who was supposed to issue me with a visa.

Pole pole.

"Fortunately, the smugglers knew the customs officer on the Tanzanian side, who let us into his home and stuck a visa onto one of the remaining pages by candlelight."

Day 496

I think it's time to go home.

I was lying in bed in the middle of Tanzania, shocked by this sentence, even though I had written it down myself.
I just continued to write.

I don't feel like travelling anymore. I don't feel like discovering new places. I don't want to just get to know new people superficially. I don't feel like staying in Africa where I'm a complete stranger, obviously. I don't have any energy left. I don't have any motivation. I don't have any inspiration. Nothing makes sense anymore.
I have traveled across four continents. I've sailed across the Indian Ocean. I've found a couple of places that I could call home. I beat my fears. I met incredible people. I've learned more than in eight years at college. I've tasted foods and drinks that I didn't even know existed. I put my mind and heart in order.
I experienced a moment of self-sufficiency on a truck.
Is there some reason that keeps me on the road? If we put aside the fact that I named my journey "1000 days of summer", there wasn't any other reason. Apart from my ego. The ego that would consider my premature return back home a failure. I'm trapped in my own freedom. The whole philosophy of my journey came down to one thing: being free. Having the possibility to make a choice at any time. Not to follow others. Not to listen to what other people say.
If I was to play by my own rules, the person who had been planning to travel for 1000 days wasn't there any longer. I was somebody else. So I didn't have to listen to that old me.
I would like to do something. Something concrete. I would like to create, to build something, and change the world for the better. And I don't feel like I'm doing this. Not anymore. Not here, in Africa. I tried to do something in Malawi, it didn't end well. I came to volunteer and work with beautiful kids in an orphanage in Tanzania and soon realized that I was useless. After all, what do I have to offer? I can play with them, but they can also play with each other. I can talk to them and teach them English, but they have teachers who are professionals in that field and who can teach them much better than I can. I can love them and they can love me, but I'll soon be gone -

and then what?

What do I have left? Travel the rest of Africa? Sail across another ocean? Hitchhike a plane? Travel across the Americas? Discover a few more magical places? Meet even more wonderful people?

All this somehow seems pointless. It's not a challenge. I feel like I could be using my time more productively.

It is time to go home.

Day 514

"How about staying in Tanzania?" Benjamin asked me while we were preparing one of our many dinners together, after I had told him about my travel problems and the idea of returning home. "Maybe you could help me with my business?"

He was born in Iran, raised in Sweden and moved to Tanzania three years ago. Although he lived a comfortable life in northern Europe, he swapped it for a three-bedroom house which had no furniture, except for the beds. They say that the things you own end up owning you, and he really lived by this maxim. He bought all his groceries in the neighboring local stores, he hosted couchsurfers, he was fluent in five languages and had his own travel agency in Arusha, at the foot of Kilimanjaro.

His travel agency was different to any other.

"Just like you, I graduated from the Faculty of Economics, had a successful business, and even won a hundred thousand Kronas on a Swedish television game show, but that didn't do it for me," he began the other night, recounting his story. "I also traveled a lot and, during a trip to Tanzania, I noticed a wide disparity between the prices tourist pay for packages and the standard of living experienced by locals employed in the tourism sector. It didn't take long for me to figure out the catch: ordinary people rarely profit from tourism."

His story reminded me of the one I had experienced in Cape Maclear, and I filled him in about it.

"The situation is the same everywhere in Africa," he confirmed. "The staff working on most of the tours in Tanzania, like climbing Kilimanjaro, are on minimum pay, sometimes even less. They depend on the kindness of visitors and their tips. I didn't like it at all so I decided to come back here, use my knowledge of business economics and change the rules of the game. I threw myself into research. I was determined to learn as much as possible about Tanzania and its beautiful sites. About its history, people, and traditions. I decided to move here and start an agency that would be different from all the others."

"What do you mean by different?" I was curious.

"It's very simple," he smiled, "The plan is that all of the profits get fed back into to the local community and projects that benefit the community."

"So you decided to start a non-profit travel agency?" I asked with surprise. I was trying hard to remember whether I had ever heard anything about non-profit travel agencies in college, but nothing came to mind.

"That's right," he beamed.

"But what do you gain from this?" This was my first question. "You'll have your company, you'll do the work, but you won't reap the rewards?"

"I'll take a monthly salary," he said. "But, of course, it shouldn't be much higher than similar salaries in the industry. My monthly salary as a manager is two hundred dollars and, frankly, I don't need much more."

I couldn't believe my ears. There had to be a catch. Someone was working in the tourism industry, had his own company, advertised it to bring people from all over the world - and didn't make any profits at the end of the year? I couldn't understand it.

"I see that you're thinking about money and profits", he remarked, reading my thoughts. "Try to look at the bigger picture for a moment. The agency staff are paid above the average salary in Tanzania, so they don't depend on tips. My employees are happy. We don't break the strict rules of the national parks to motivate tourists to leave us more tips, 99 percent of the funds are spent and stay in Tanzania, and we have a zero carbon footprint."

"Sounds good," I confirmed.

"So where is this leading to?" He asked.

"Happy customers?" I blurted out.

"That's right," he smiled. "A happy customer will recommend us to their friends. And we have competitive prices, because our main goal isn't accruing extra profits, so in a few years' time, when our customers recommend us to others, these tourists will be able to choose whether they want to get the service done by the well-paid staff who don't depend on tipping, knowing that all the company's profits get ploughed back into the local population and their projects, or, for the same price, pay for another rich foreigner's house or a filthy rich local. Over time, in order to become and stay competitive, other companies will have to change the way they do business and adapt to us."

"Sounds like a great plan!" I said. "Not only do you do what you love..."

"But I'm also doing something worthwhile for this world," he finished my thought. "Imagine if the whole world worked according to this principle. Imagine if everyone, besides doing what we love, also did something good for their community and the world in general. What if we moved away from a strictly capitalist way of thinking and doing what is economically justified? Wouldn't the world be a wonderful place? Like, what if we decided as a society to stop producing deadly chemical weapons, and make our scientists who enjoy tinkering with test tubes in their laboratories focus their work on nobler goals. After all, it only takes common sense and decision making."

"Common sense and decision making," I repeated.

"That's why I made a common-sense decision to start my own community-based travel agency," he said. "I decided to start a business that wouldn't necessarily allow me to buy a beautiful house with a swimming pool and a new car, but that would be sufficient to meet all my needs. At the same time, the local community would benefit from my business, which means that we would all be more connected. There won't be a big difference between my lifestyle as the owner of the business and other people like my employees. This means we'll be more connected, happier and more satisfied."

It made sense, at all levels. After all, we're all in pursuit of happiness anyway. Whether we were trying to find it in love, work, travel, or whatever else. But can you still be happy once you've achieved your goals? What happens when we find ourselves at the top of the mountain, with a beautiful view, and realize that we've got what we wanted? What happens when we finally win the heart of the love of our life? What happens when we find a job that we love and earn all the money in the world?

I think everybody should get rich and famous and do everything they ever dreamed of so they can see that it's not the answer - said Jim Carrey, a famous comedian. I think that this was exactly what Benji and I were talking about. This is the meaning of his travel agency, and maybe life in general. Sharing his wealth with others. A character in the book *Into the Wild* wrote almost the same thing before he died: Happiness is only real when shared.

If you're number one, the champion, the winner, the rich man, but one in a million - how can you enjoy it if the people around you are always lagging behind, losers and poor? How can you enjoy life if everyone around you is suffering? How are you going to share your happiness with them, how will anyone ever understand it?

I took my little black notebook and wrote the following lines.

Three steps to create a happy and fulfilled life:

1. *Find out what you love to do.*
2. *Do what you don't like to get to what you do.*
3. *Find out how the world could benefit from your work.*

P.S. Make a concerted effort not to lose too much time on step 2.

I finally answered Benjamin's question. "Maybe after visiting Kenya, I could come back to Arusha and help you out around the company. I could learn something, see what it looks like in practise, gain some experience that will help me in the future. I really could stay here for a while."
He smiled and carried on cooking.

But then I received an email from my mom: *Are you on Skype? It's an emergency!*
I frantically tried to connect, but only managed to establish a connection after six failed attempts. The image was blurry, I could only see the outline of somebody's palm of their left hand. And a ring.
A ring!
My brother's smiling face and the face of his girlfriend, now fiancée, said it all. Happy parents were standing in the background. They had only one question: "Are you coming to your brother's wedding?"
"I don't think I'll be coming back here after visiting Kenya," I briefly replied to Benjamin. As usual, he just smiled.

Day 1000

"After Tanzania, I arrived in Kenya, where I had one of the most important experiences of my entire trip," I announced, continuing my talk with the next photo. "My father Mirko came to visit."

"My father had never traveled before. Not counting visits to former Yugoslavia countries, he'd only crossed the border once, and he'd only flown once, from Zagreb to Croatia's second biggest city, Split, back in 1991. However, from an early age, he had a wish, a dream. His dream was to go on safari in Africa. Every time we watched documentaries about Africa, mostly about animals, he'd say: 'If I ever go on safari, I'll be able to die in peace!'"

At every lecture I have ever held, every time I say those words, I get a lump in my throat, so I can barely say it. There is no particular reason for that, it's not like my father died and that I fulfilled his last wish or I don't know what...

"When I realized that I was going to visit Africa, I called him and invited him to join me so that I could take him on safari. I still had some savings left from Australia and I also had the money from my sponsors, so I could afford it, and I knew it was something that he would never get around to doing himself. He just replied: 'You've got it!' And a few months later, he arrived in Nairobi."

Day 523

I was walking down the road and my only company was the zebras, antelopes and wildebeest which observed me with curiosity. It was a beautiful day - sunny, but not too hot. There was no sign of civilization anywhere. How pleasant it was to hear the sound of silence.

After Benjamin and Arusha, I arrived in Nairobi to wait for my father, who was about to land in a few days' time. At the same time, I got an offer over Facebook that I simply couldn't refuse. An unknown girl offered me a Maji Moto gift card. This is the eco camp run by the Maasai warriors. She'd been there a few months earlier and had won a free two-day stay for two people and decided to share her prize with me.

The kindness of strangers.

My idyll was interrupted by a wildebeest which was standing still in the middle of the road, some 100 yards in front of me. I stood there, thinking about whether I had ever heard of a case in which a person had been attacked by one of them. Even if I couldn't recall any specific warning or any horror story, I didn't continue my carefree walk. Like a chicken, I waited for it to move and thought about my options of escape or self-defense in case it launched an attack. The only thing I had to hand, though, was a half-empty bottle of water.

After a few minutes the wildebeest simply took off. I thanked it for that and promised that I wouldn't be telling any stories about me being brave and making it run away by shouting at it or charging towards it. And I won't tell anyone that the wildebeest was a chicken. That wouldn't be fair.

Two hours later, I arrived at the thermal spring that the Maji Moto were named after (Maji = water, Moto = fire), exchanging smiles and short instructions with the stark naked locals who pointed me in the direction of my accommodation.

"How did you manage to find us?" The chief Sankale asked, visibly surprised.

"It was easy, I walked six miles and asked people in the village for directions," I replied, with a smile.

"None of the white men have ever arrived alone, on foot, like you," he said, showing his large, pearly-white teeth again.

"Take some rest, you've arrived home."

That was exactly what I did.

Shortly afterwards, a Dutch family showed up. They planned to spend the following two days there. We instantly hit it off in the improvised restaurant with a beautiful view of the savannah. They bought me a beer and this was the beginning of a beautiful friendship. I can be easily bought. Even with a warm beer.

When the sun slowly began to set, it was time to take a walk. The guide showed us how to make a toothbrush with a branch, which plant can be used to fight back against nightmares, which leaves can be used instead of a deodorant or toilet paper, the potential uses of aloe vera and other stuff like that. I really enjoyed the tour. I was thrilled to see the cooperation between man and nature, this coexistence. Mutual respect. It was something that has been lost in the developed countries, something that people are only just starting to think about.

"The Maasai are not religious," began our amiable guide, giving a short presentation. "We believe in Mother Nature. She provides us with everything we need. She is the only one we can rely on. She has never let us down. The sun brings us happiness every morning. Without exception."

We listened carefully to the guide, hanging on his every word. When you think about it, those attitudes seemed logical and all *primitive* people on all continents shared them. All of them believed in one god - Nature. Even the silliest members of these tribes realize that Nature is everything. Without nature we can't exist, but we could still manage without everything else.

So, the question we need to ask, in that case, is who is actually primitive and who is developed? Are the people who live modestly, in harmony with nature and who are able to survive even in the most extreme conditions primitive or is it actually those people who are relentlessly destroying that very same nature and who wouldn't be able to last two days without electricity and a nearby supermarket? Can we really consider those people who feel the need to give their god a name and promote it as if it's the one and only as developed, or those who worship the one that is always present and visible to everyone?

"The Maasai are polygamous," Chief Sankale said over the campfire after he had finished singing some traditional songs. "This is so for one simple reason, the animals in our environment are also polygamous."

We all laughed, knowing that it must be true, but also because it was the most convenient solution. High mortality rates in infants and warriors in the past remained the main reasons for polygamy. The women who lived in the same household were supposed to take care of the house and the chores together - the more of them there were, the more hands there would be to help out around the house. If one was sick or having a baby, others would be there for her and help her.

"We don't differentiate between the wives, just like we don't differentiate between the days of the week," said Sankale, sharing his wisdom. "The only difference is the number of cows you have to pay for them."

Just like in Swaziland, cows took the place of money. When arranging a marriage, a man has to use this four-legged currency to pay the father for his bride. The average price for a wife is seven cows. They could live without money, but they couldn't live without cows. The Maasai people lack a concept of love in the sense of butterflies in the stomach, the irrational and infatuated sense. There is no jealousy either. Or at least so they say.

We sat around the campfire for hours, telling stories about two extremes.

Sankale told us that they only ate beef, mutton and goat meat and drank only milk, water and cow's blood (they claimed that it gave them strength). He said that they picked fruit from the trees when there was something there to pick, but that they didn't eat any vegetables since they didn't cultivate the land for farming. In turn, I told them about the growing number of vegetarians in our society, who only ate fruit and vegetables.

This was something he couldn't understand.

He said that they only slept four hours each night and walked sixty miles per day to find good pastures for the cattle. They couldn't afford to take a nap after lunch because a lion might attack one of their cows. I explained to him that people in our world didn't walk that many miles, and those who did, would probably run it on a treadmill in the gym. I told him that people didn't spend enough time in the sun, but that they happily went to tanning studios that imitate the sun. I also mentioned that people in our world either ate so much that they developed obesity or starved themselves to lose weight.

These were all things he couldn't understand.

He said that they always had something to do and that the responsibilities were evenly shared out. Men take the flock to graze and go hunting, while women take care of the house, children and livestock. I told him that we were working hard to achieve gender equality at work, and that men and women were almost equal.

This was also something that he couldn't understand.

But he definitely didn't understand it one little bit when I told him how many people couldn't find a job.

"There just aren't enough jobs," I said.

"Nonsense," he replied. "How can you say that? There's always something to do if you want to work."

Was Sankale right? Is there always something to do, but some people just don't want to work? Have we become too picky and lazy in the Western World? I knew about the high rates of unemployment in Croatia, I knew that some of my college mates were now on the dole, and I knew that a lot of people lacked the necessary skills for the in-demand jobs that were out there. But was all this a good enough excuse for not having a job?

"Anyone who doesn't have a job can come here, I'll give him work," said Sankake, laughing out loud.

He told us that he had killed three lions and that he had been chosen ahead of his 36 brothers to be the chief. While killing lions is rare these days because the lions themselves have become an endangered species, the Maasai warriors still stick to this tradition. Whoever kills a lion receives great honor within the tribe. He also told us that if men want to become warriors they have to train for seven years in the African wilderness. The training for the women only lasts four years. One part of their initiation is circumcision. During the ceremony they can't even blink if they don't want to lose face.

"If they can overcome this fear of the knife they won't be scared of anything," he concluded.

"What about circumcising girls?" I asked.

"Well, yes, circumcision is still practised here. It marks the transition from childhood to adulthood," said Sankale in a serious tone. "But rules are starting to change, and now the girls have a choice. My eldest daughter was the first girl in our tribe to refuse circumcision. She started a trend, although most girls still insist on it to preserve the tradition. But we've come to a point where it is okay to say no."

"Also, the number of young people who go to school is constantly rising," he continued. "As a chief, I get to decide who will go to school and who will become a warrior. If a family has four kids, two of them will go to school, while the other two will become warriors. If it were up to the kids, all of them would become warriors. It's a matter of prestige."

"Do you miss out on anything in life?" I asked. "Is there anything that you would want to take from us Westerners?"

"No," he replied without hesitation. "It's true, we use some of your things to make our lives easier, but we're perfectly satisfied with what we have."

"What would you do if you came to Europe on a road trip?" I continued with my questions.

"I would go to the zoo," he said, "and ask them to give us back our lions. Lions don't belong to the zoos, they belong to the wilderness. Our, African wilderness. After bringing the lions back, we would try to do the same thing with the cows."

Other than lions, the Europeans were also taking cows from the peaceful Maasai tribes. In that sense, they believed that all cows in the world were actually theirs. I paused for a moment, not really being in the mood for laughter anymore. I tried to explain to them that it wouldn't be a good idea.

"But why?" They asked me.

I started describing the conditions in which the cows were forced to live, as well as the majority of other domestic animals. I told them about the farms where cows spend their short lives in a space so narrow that they could barely turn around. I could sense a sad silence and a lack of understanding so I quickly shut up.

Really, what the hell's wrong with us people? Why are we being such assholes to the environment, animals, and other people? Why did we build a world in which on one side people die every day from malnutrition, while on the other they die from obesity? Why in one part of the world do people die from preventable diseases and lack of medicines, while in the other they die from excessive doses of those medicines?

So many things are wrong in this world we're living in. It became crystal clear to me in an interview with primitive people who drink cow's blood, believing that it gives them strength.

"Are you up for an African jacuzzi?" Sankale asked me when the Dutch had gone back to their tent.

"When?" I asked.

"Now," he said, throwing me a towel.

We went to the thermal spring. There was nobody there at this late hour. We took our clothes off and immersed ourselves in the natural hot bath. The view was spectacular: the countless stars glistened in the sky, which finally shone in all its glory...

Day 541

"So?" They all exclaimed at the same time as we sat down for coffee. "How was it? Tell us all about it!"

I ordered a beer even though it was 1pm. I hadn't had a beer for far too long to be able to resist.

I was in Zagreb. It wasn't really one thousand days, but it felt like it was. Maybe even more. My mother, aunt, grandmother, brother and his fiancée - they were all sitting around my dad and me. We had arrived back from Africa just an hour earlier and they were waiting for us with a big welcome sign at the airport. It was strange to see them all together, even though we often saw each other on Skype.

It was sunny, but chilly. After returning from sub-Saharan Africa, it was a welcome change.

"I'll let dad do the talking," I replied and took my first sip. I didn't feel like talking because I knew I would have to tell the same story a thousand times over during the coming weeks. Besides, I knew that dad, who was full of much more impressions than me, would be happy to take the floor. It was so nice and relaxing just to lean back and watch them in silence.

"Where should I start," said my old man. "All I wanted was to get to Kenya in one piece. This was what I was most afraid of. Luckily, in Istanbul I bumped into a Croatian guy, who saw I was completely lost so he helped me get to my connecting flight. There's not much to say about the flight. The food was average, miniature. And you couldn't even smoke in there."

"Did the plane shake around a lot?" Mum asked.

"Nah," he replied, exhaling cigarette smoke. "Just enough to lull you to sleep."

"I would have died," she said.

"And that's why I didn't invite you to Africa in the first place," I reasoned.

"The biggest problem was when we arrived in Nairobi," continued dad. "The people on the plane just handed me a piece of paper and told me that I had to fill it in. So I asked myself how the hell I was going to fill it when I don't know a word of English. I walked around the airport like a fool, with this bit of paper in my hands. Fortunately, there was a black guy, black like coal. He approached me, said something, then took the paper out of my hands and started filling it in. I just handed him my passport, he filled the form and then holds out his right palm. The guy wanted money!"

We burst into laughter.

"But, what could I do - I gave him a dollar. He assumed I had more, but I didn't give it to him! I made my way to the customs, they asked me something, I just smiled like a fool," dad continued. "I probably looked so miserable and lost that they let me go. I still have no idea how I managed to find my luggage and the exit, where this little jackass was waiting for me."

"And what was that like?" my aunt asked.

"Well, fine," my dad said. "We hadn't seen each other for year and a half, so what was it supposed to be like?"

I remembered the moment we finally met really well. Especially after the last time we had been together, when we'd parted in tears, with a heavy heart full of guilt, the night before I set off. Dad's arrival in Nairobi was perhaps one of the biggest victories in my life, for several reasons.

This man had lived for almost thirty years just to fulfil the dreams of my brother and I, and I had now finally managed to make one of his dreams come true. I had finally managed to drag this man, who had been fighting tooth and nail to convince me to give up my trip around the world, out to his own dose of wandering in Africa. I had proved that my lifestyle, no matter how different it seemed from anything he had ever imagined, was not destined to failure.

I knew I had made it when I saw his face at the airport in Nairobi, and felt his firm embrace. The firmest ever.

"So we got into a taxi and went to the hotel," he continued. "Everything was upside down, they drive on the other side of the road, but the hotel was nice. I took a short nap, then we went for a walk around the city. He was walking like the boss, in front of me. So he took me across the road, we went to the stands where they were selling their knick-knacks, but Tomislav didn't let me buy anything - he said that it was all too expensive. We'd buy stuff from the Maasai when we were on safari. The next day we joined our group. We got into something that was like a mix between a truck and a bus, and went on safari."

"And how was it?" My other aunt wanted to know.

"I don't know how to explain this to you," he looked up at the sky, searching for words. "It was just so unreal. It was as if I'd become a child again. The other fourteen people in the group spoke English, but I just kept on smiling. The only way I could talk to anybody was when Tomislav was standing next to me to be the interpreter."

"I still can't believe you were in Africa," my brother said. "I hope you're aware that you can't get on his case about traveling any more?"

"That's why I asked him to come," I said.

"What about the animals?" Gabi asked.

Gabi had given me a bar of *Animal Kingdom*, a traditional Croatian chocolate that has a sticker of an animal under each wrapper, as soon as I'd arrived at the airport. They knew how much I loved chocolate. I took it out of my bag, unwrapped it and looked underneath to check the sticker. Number 220. A llama. I could see the Andes in the background. Machu Picchu.

"That's a sign, Gabi," I whispered. "Perhaps that will be my next destination."

"It was so surreal," my old man continued. "For years I've watched African animals on TV, and now they were there, just a few meters in front of me. We saw a bunch of zebras, antelopes, wildebeests, giraffes, monkeys, those pink birds at the lake, leopards, we even saw two lions. And we walked past a group of six rhinos - the guide told us she had never seen them so close. We drove past the animals and sometimes even walked next to them, at least those that wouldn't eat us. When we weren't watching the animals or driving around in the bus, we all had our tasks. They divided us into four groups and we took turns with cooking, dish washing and cleaning the bus. We had to wash our clothes by hand."

"When was the last time you did your own laundry?" I asked my dad as we were washing our shirts and pants in water and detergent at a makeshift camp.

"Before I got married," he replied. "It must've been more than thirty years ago."

"Tell me one thing," I asked him. "How did mom manage to take care of the three of us, while working full-time, cooking, cleaning and doing all the other chores around the house? Filip and I didn't lend much of a hand."

"Honestly, I have no idea," he admitted.

"You guys were too good to us as parents," I continued. "You always tried to make it easier for us, to give us everything we need. But at the same time, that's why we grew up into people who don't do household chores, don't know how to cook and are lazy when things need to be done. Now you understand why I had to go. I needed to grow up and become independent. I needed to make my own path in this world without my parents' help, without anyone I know."

He didn't say anything, and thought about my words. He had to tacitly agree with me because there simply wasn't any room to disagree. I was right.

"See Dad, this is one of the reasons why I'm travelling," I said, squeezing the excess water out of my last t-shirt, chuckling and returning to the camp.

"We slept in tents all the time," he continued.

"You may have been sleeping peacefully, but I'm not so sure about everybody else," I said. "You were snoring so loudly that I didn't know what I was more worried about: if nobody could get a wink of sleep, or if a lion would hear you from the other side of the savannah and come get us."

"Now you know how I feel every night," my mom added.

"Anyway, we also visited the Maasai warriors in a village," dad continued, ignoring our interruptions. "They showed us around, told us about their customs, their way of life, showed us how they use some of the plants for medicinal purposes, and taught us how to throw spear to kill a lion, if one happens to be coming your way. But the best, I mean the worst, was when they put us in a livestock pen, and then their women, dressed up in colorful clothes and wearing jewelry, stood in a circle and started to sing. Also, I've never seen so many flies in all my life!"

He stopped telling the story and tried to pull a face to show his disgust at the swarms of flies that just wouldn't leave us alone, but he couldn't make the right one.

"To be honest, the life of these Maasai people isn't so different from life in the Croatian countryside a few decades ago," concluded my old man. "In their culture, the woman's place is in and around the house, while the man is the one who goes out to earn a living in order to feed the family. They're attached to their savannah, just as we're attached to our karst. For centuries, we relied on nature for everything we needed: food, clothes, shoes, medicines, everything. They compete by jumping up into the air to win a woman's heart, just like how we threw stones over our shoulders. They sing their traditional songs, just like how we have Ganga songs.[8] Although we look different, talk different languages, believe in different gods, eat different foods, and have different traditions, we aren't so different after all."

I liked Dad's story and his conclusions. He had just confirmed what I always knew. I could be telling him about my travels and all the lessons I had learned along the way, the kindness of strangers, the exaggerated fear of unknown countries, the similarities between all the people of this world, but the real thing is when you're actually there, on the ground, experiencing all this. When you experience it for yourself.

"And so, after eight days on safari, we headed to Subukia to pay a visit to father Miro," he went on with the story. "We got there by hitchhiking."

"You what?" My grandmother spoke for the first time since we had sat down.

"Hitchhiking, Grandma," I replied. "See how dad raised me the wrong way - he also hitchhiked!"

"Yeah, this little one screwed me over," he sighed. "He said that we would have to wait for the bus by the side of the road, and asked me to pretend to hitchhike so that he could take a photo of me. We didn't stayed there for a few minutes, and my hand started to hurt, but he was still messing about with the camera. I realized that it wasn't a joke. And then a car pulled over."

"And then?" they all asked at the same time.

"Well, nothing," he said. "Tomislav had a word with the driver, who was going in our direction; he told me the bus was coming god knows when, so we got into the car and set off toward father Miro."

I remembered father Miro, who welcomed us with a smile. We crossed the last 15 miles in his Land Rover, driving along a non-existing road. Father Miro explained that the road tended to change when it rained. With the sounds of Croatian musicians playing on the tape recorder, I must admit that I felt somewhat nostalgic.

I was thinking about this bumpy ride as dad was retelling how we settled into a house that was actually a Franciscan monastery run by

---

[8] *Ganga is a traditional style of singing in rural parts of western Herzegovina. A lone singer performs a line and at the end is joined by others who climax in a wail.*

father Miro Babić, who has been a missionary in Africa for the past decade. In this magnificent building, atypical by African standards, we met some volunteers who were focused on the same goal - helping the Little Home Orphanage, home to a few dozen children, with its health issues.

Besides building the orphanage and holding mass in the surrounding villages, he also focuses on maybe the most important project - the education of the local children. He restores schools, raises funds for textbooks, and also helps a nearby clinic that manages to operate despite not having full-time medical staff.

"There are sixteen churches in Miro's parish," dad continued. "In each church, mass is only held once a month. There's also another priest, so each of them holds two masses on Sundays. And get this, the mass doesn't have a set start time, just when the priest arrives, because it can take hours for him to get there during the rainy season."

Pole pole.

"We had such a good time. We went to the orphanage where we played with the kids, and I could finally talk to people in Croatian. Every night we sang and played music. And we played five-a-side soccer, and celebrated Miro's birthday," said dad approaching the end of his story about his African adventure. "And then, two days before I was due to fly back, this little one told me that he was coming back home with me."

"How did you decide that?" My brother wanted to know.

"Well, I didn't want dad to travel alone, since he was going to have an overnight layover in Istanbul. Who knows how that would turn out," I replied.

There was also another, least important reason for my return. Apart from getting tired of traveling and my brother's wedding, there was also the email that I got from my friend Darija.

So... I'm having a surgery on Monday, keep your fingers crossed that I wake up! :*

Having read this e-mail, I went for a walk down a dusty street, sat under a tree and made a decision - I was going back to Zagreb. I decided not to hitchhike through Ethiopia, Sudan and Egypt, as I had originally planned, so as to get there just in time for my brother's wedding, but instead opted for the simplest and fastest way - taking a flight.

"What are you going to do now?" My brother asked me while we were waiting for a green light on one of Zagreb's streets. We had visited Darija and headed home. It was about to be my first night in Zagreb in almost a year and a half.
"I've no idea," I answered honestly. "I haven't thought about..."
BANG!
We suddenly exchanged looks - it sounded like a gunshot.
We got out of the car and saw a large stone that was still rolling down the road. Someone had thrown a rock at our car that had left a visible dent on the roof. We exchanged puzzled looks, got in the car and made a U-turn at the next traffic light. We slowly went back and pulled in just in front of the entrance to a garage, where we saw two guys who started to run as soon as they saw us.
Filip got out of the car and I followed straight after him. We gave chase to the fugitives.
We didn't know who they were, we didn't know why they had thrown a stone at our car, we didn't even know whether they had been aiming at us, but we still ran after them through the dark underground garages. Everything seemed so unreal. A few days earlier I had been in Africa. In Nairobi, a city that doesn't enjoy the best reputation, and everything had been fine. I had finally come home, to my home town, my beloved Zagreb, and I still hadn't slept a single night, yet here I was, forced to run after two scumbags who were throwing stones at cars for no apparent reason.
Would we be able to catch them? And if we got them, what would happen next? Could we be so sure that those guys wouldn't be waiting for us around a corner with a knife? Could we be so sure that they weren't actually two Jiu Jitsu masters who would break our legs? Maybe this was just a scam, a tactic they used to nick cars in Zagreb? Where were the keys? And if none of that was true, then what? Once they got cornered against the garage wall, would I try to beat the hell out of them? Me, a pacifist, a hippie, a traveler with so many interests, who loves all the world's people?
The situation was utterly unreal.
Fortunately or not, they managed to escape. They jumped over some wall and ran off into the dark.

"Isn't it funny?" I asked my brother as we were driving back home in the car with its damaged roof. "Isn't it fucking funny?"

"Welcome home!" he curtly replied.

Welcome to Swaziland

Cape Maclear

Otter point

Inquisitive kids

Hippos

Kanyenya

Bao

Cactus-tree

A hammock with a wonderful view

Kids in Livingstonia

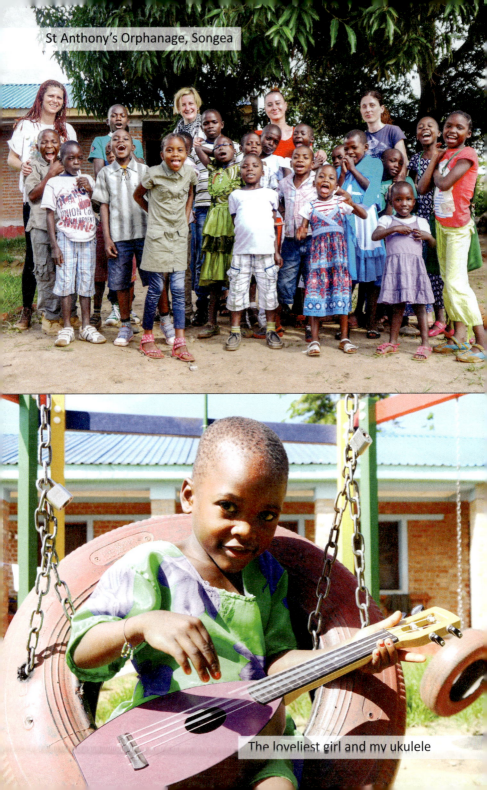

St Anthony's Orphanage, Songea

The loveliest girl and my ukulele

Kilimanjaro

On the way to Maji Moto

Masai feet

Our photogenic guide

Batman, a Maasai warrior and Zagor

A warrior dance

On safari

Rhinos up close

A giraffe

A crocodile

Father Miro and me, a pair of musicians

A warm welcome at Zagreb Airport

Day 1000

"I went back to Zagreb, attended my brother's wedding, but soon went back on the road," I said, resuming my talk.

The truth was that at that moment I really didn't feel like traveling. Tired of it all, I was considering my alternatives. I wanted to start something, create something, and I had plenty of ideas, but also a huge obstacle. My debt from my days as a stockbroker was still hanging over me, even though I had managed to cut it by half since the beginning of travels. I was still fifteen thousand dollars in debt.

Before embarking on new projects I had to get rid of this burden. There were two ways to do this. One option was to get a job in Croatia or abroad and save up some money so that one day I could repay the debt. The other option was an easier way out of this situation - I could continue to travel. If I continued to travel, I would also continue to receive sponsorship money that I could use to repay my debt, just like I did before.

Traveling for money didn't sound right. My story would certainly lose its point, and I would lose my credibility, everything I stood for - doing what I love, no matter what. Being free.

I remembered my little black notebook and looked at what I had written under number two.

Do what you don't like to get to what you do.

Maybe I should travel or do something I didn't like in order to get the money that will allow me to do what I love in the future?

"A few months after returning to Croatia, I bought a ticket to Peru," I said.

I opted for a compromise solution. I would continue to travel, but at the same time I would change my style and tactics. I had the most beautiful memories and experiences from the first "540 days of summer", from the places where I stayed for a longer period of time, at least a couple of weeks. This meant that I had to slow down a bit. To stick around a little longer. To scratch deeper.

I decided that South America would be my next destination. The flight to Peru was the cheapest. I had been considering crossing the Atlantic Ocean, and now I had the valuable experience that would help me to find myself a boat, but after I had seen a video that I recorded while sailing across the Indian Ocean any desire for this had died. The idea of going to North America crossed my mind, but since my passport was covered in stamps and visas from Pakistan, Iran and Iraq, I had a feeling that the American border guards wouldn't be welcoming me with open arms.

There was also the language. I had very fond memories from Asia and Africa, but I almost always felt like a stranger there, like somebody who never really belonged there. Besides the obvious differences between the locals and me, language proved to be a major barrier. My Spanish was okay, so I guessed I wouldn't face such a problem in South America, where many countries shared the language. It certainly wasn't like in India or Africa, where people in each province used their own distinct dialect, which further complicated communication.

The Amazon. The jungle. This was one of the few places that had always attracted me, one of those places that I really wanted to visit. Maybe I could stay there for a while, live with a tribe, be completely in the hands of Mother Nature, and work on spiritual experiences.

These were all excellent reasons for leaving. Since I didn't feel like traveling, I would instead try to exist in a foreign country, but without traveling around too much. It was time to settle down for a while.

All those reasons became even more convincing when I realized that I would have someone to share all this with.

"I didn't travel to South America alone..." I said, changing the slide.

Day 662

Lima's airport, the arrivals terminal.

I'd been in the capital of Peru for a week now, but I wasn't really taken by it. It was cold, foggy and gloomy. The city was big, overcrowded and noisy. There was no doubt that I would have been long gone if she wasn't supposed to be landing any minute now.

When you think of it, it was really funny that I came to the other side of the world to wait for a girl I had met a month earlier next to the Manduševac fountain in middle of Zagreb. With my headphones on, I was playing a game called 'which-song-will-be-playing-when-I-see-her', keeping an eye on the sliding doors that were opening and closing.

I listened to a few songs. And then a few more.

Another one started with a familiar intro. One of my favorite songs. It took me back to Christmas Island and observing the open sea. The waiting process, just like now. Except that back then I was waiting for a boat to sail me across the Indian Ocean. Now, I was waiting for a girl with whom I was about to travel across South America.

Any minute now, my ship is coming in...

And of course, at that very moment the doors opened and I caught sight of a familiar face. We made eye contact. She was wearing glasses. For the first time since I met her. They were too big for her small face, but they suited her. She smiled at me, I smiled back. It was a smile that broadened when I thought of the song title. A hug. We got into a taxi that would take us to our first home in South America.

"How are you?" I decided to start the conversation with the most original question in the world.

"Lost. Confused," she answered, obviously quite tired after two days spent in airplanes and in airports.

"How come?" I responded, with a serious face. "I mean, we met a month ago and you've had ten whole days to leave your life in Croatia, buy a one-way ticket, get on a plane, fly to the other side of the globe and meet a man you barely know, carrying only a backpack."

She smiled. That was always a good sign.

I knew that, despite this smile, her mind was wandering. It was exactly a month since we met. She added me as a friend on Facebook, I automatically accepted her request and flicked through her photos to see if I knew this Maria or whether she was one of those people who added me after reading my blog. She seemed very familiar, but I just couldn't put my finger on where I had met her. When I saw the photos of her standing barefoot, with dreadlocks in her hair, just like a little gypsy, somewhere in South America, I had to investigate who she was.

After a few clicks I found out, it was Iva from the Croatian soap opera Forbidden Love. I didn't watch the show (and even if I did, I would never admit it), but it was hard to avoid it over all those years of flicking between channels.

Then I sent her the first Facebook message.

Hey! :) I see you visited South America a few years ago... I'm off to Peru and I'm planning to stay there for at least a year. I wonder if there's anything that I shouldn't miss. A place, a person, something? Bye, T.

The reply came back the same day.

Over the past few weeks I've been thinking about contacting you so that we can meet because I feel as though I've met you before... I guess these sorts of thoughts bump into each other and sniff each other out somewhere up above, even before they happen :) Is it just Peru or are you crossing the whole of South America? I can write you a longer message when I get everything in order, we could even meet, but I'm actually thinking of heading back out to this beautiful place again...

We met by the Manduševac fountain, had a drink at a bar at the bus station, and talked about life.

"Can I see you again?" I asked as we were parting, giving her my raincoat so she could stay dry cycling home.

"And why do you want that?" she asked, almost snappily.

"Well, you have to go give me my raincoat back," I said. "And perhaps I could talk you into coming with me in Peru."

"I've been seeing someone for three and a half years," she said, looking down at the ground. "It's pretty serious, we live together."

"Well, my longest relationship lasted exactly three and a half years," I jokingly said.

She smiled, turned away and went home.

Eighteen days later, the night before my flight, we were laying on the grass in Zrinjevac park.

"So, are you coming with me or not?" I asked, finally expecting a definitive answer. Since we'd meet, we'd been strolling along Zagreb's streets almost every day, dodging this subject.

"Give me ten days and wait for me in Lima," she said, looking up at Zagreb's summer sky.

Day 664

"No!" Maria screamed as three guys sneaked up behind us, snatched our backpacks that had been resting on the bench and vanished.

I instinctively got up and ran after them, just like I had done that night in Zagreb a few months back. I was confused, I only knew that I was in an undesirable situation, that I had a strange feeling in my stomach and that I was chasing after three guys who wanted what belonged to us.

"Hey!" I shouted as loud as I could, judging that this exclamation would be comprehendible in every language. I hoped that a random passerby would help me, stop the thieves, intervene somehow.

But that didn't happen. We ran through the half-abandoned market, those three guys and I. I felt that I was gaining on them.

"Motherfuckers!!!" It came out of me so heartily, instinctively, fluently, completely naturally.

Best of all, it worked! The slowest of the three thieves, the one holding Maria's backpack, obviously scared by the foreign curse coming from his rear, threw his quarry to the ground and suddenly divided from his accomplices.

"What a rookie," I thought. "If he had split with the backpack in his hands, it would have been his. I would have carried on running after mine since I thought that there were only a few books and some vegetables that we bought earlier that morning in Maria's. By comparison, there was a small fortune in my backpack: a laptop and a camera."

I ran by her backpack, convinced that she was behind me and that she would pick it up in a few seconds. I had to do the other half of the job. The thief without anything in his hands turned right and left me staring at the back of the fastest among them. The leader of the group. The Man. The Big Dog. The one who showed no intention of dropping my backpack. He was some ten yards in front of me.

I kept on shouting as loud as I could, still hoping that someone would stop him while he was leaving the market and stepping out on the street. He made a sharp right turn and I looked to follow suit.

I couldn't remember the last time I had run like this or whether I had ever done so. At the very moment I was turning hard right, my poor body, unaccustomed to this kind of leg-work, lost its balance and I fell flat on my face in the middle of the street.

The fall was sensational. If there was somebody to tape it and upload it onto the Internet then there would be a bunch of people laughing their heads off. Some of them would probably have slowed it down and rewound it, just to admire the majesty of the movement. I got up off the ground and raised my head, only to see the kleptomaniac open the gate to someone's yard and go inside.

Lame, exhausted and still in severe shock, I ran after him, brusquely opening the brass gate. A young girl was standing inside. She was about ten years old. She had to have seen which way he went.

"Dónde está?" I asked her kindly and gently.

The girl burst into tears. Maybe I hadn't been that kind or gentle after all. I might actually have shouted a bit and had a rather crazy look on my face.

I left her there and got into the first house still with a crazy look on my face.

"Dónde está?" I kept shouting.

"Quién?" The people who lived there asked me quite shocked.

I left the house and entered the next one. By the looks on their faces it seemed to me that they didn't know anything about where he had gone, but also because my Spanish was so lousy that I didn't know the words for 'thief', 'backpack', or anything else that could help me.

The yard was closed off on all fours sides, surrounded by 3 or 4 houses and full of half-dilapidated rooms. He had a 15 seconds head start on me so he could have gone either way. I entered a few more of the rooms, interrupting people on their afternoon siestas, without finding that guy.

A fair crowd had gathered outside. I saw Maria standing there, without her backpack. Stammering, I told her to go back to the market and find it since it was somewhere on the floor. I went back into the yard. Everybody was there. A couple of families. The little girl in tears. I apologized to her, this time in a soft, gentle voice. A security guard had called the cops. Maria came back with her backpack. Somebody had picked it up at the market and returned it to her. My faith in humanity was restored, at least some of it. A little more when I learned that she had all the documents, her passport, and a couple of hundred dollars that she had brought with her.

As expected, there was no sign of the thief. Plenty of cops came and we snooped around a bit. Everyone knew those kids, but what could we do? The police station. Reports. All those stupid things.

I was sad. I was sad because I'd lost my two most valuable material possessions, and I was also sad because of how those guys had behaved. I was sorry because of everything.

"Well, that's a great start to our adventure, isn't it?" Maria stood in front of me and smiled as we were walking down the street. "Everything will be alright."

She hugged me, kissed me and put her hand in mine.

Day 671

"If someone had told me a month ago that I would soon be in Peru, I would have told them that they were crazy," Maria said while cleaning the windows. "But if someone had told me that I would soon be in Peru, cleaning dirty windows and sweeping dirty floors I would have said that, in that case, I'd be the crazy one."

I looked out through the now clean window and liked what I saw. Along with a very busy Maria, there was endless blue ocean and the desert, filled with vast heaps of brown sand. Between these two extremes, there was a row of palm trees.

"Crazy or not, it's great that we can go whenever we choose and that nobody is forcing us to do anything," I replied, scrubbing the floor.

The great thing was that both of us accepted openheartedly those *crazy little things*. To come to the ends of the Earth in the middle of a long-awaited Croatian summer, to be robbed in a park in Lima, hitchhike down the longest road in the world, get food poisoning and, in the end, clean houses in exchange for food and board. It hardly sound like an ideal choice. But it was *our* choice. We knew that we were free to do whatever we chose, so in that sense, scrubbing the floor didn't seem like hard work. Stay or go, whatever we felt like doing.

Mancora, Peru's second most visited destination, has two faces. It is the place where young *gringos* come for the sun, sand and surfing and a few additional things which are easily accessible: the only thing you need to do is to exchange a couple of pleasantries with the local boys who, with a smile on their face, ask you their well-rehearsed questions: "Do you speak Spanish?" "Where are you from?" "Do you surf?" "Do you smoke weed?"

Another face of Mancora was altogether more classy, and could be seen in the people living outside the center, in the part of the city leading to our hotel. On the beach area that stretched for about three miles, there was a great number of hotels, apartments, and huts with one thing in common - the higher prices. Families with pale skin, men with golden chains around their necks, women with large sunglasses, bottles of champagne next to deck chairs on the beach.

The two of us we found our place just between these two extremes, taking a bit from both, young *gringos* who were in the area for the rich ones.

For a number of days now, we had been working a few hours a day, five days a week, in exchange for food and accommodation. As we stayed in the house for volunteers and we were the first volunteers who had arrived, there was a lot of work to be done: apart from the standard chores, the rooms needed some repainting, the windows had to be cleaned, and the floors needed to be swept every day due to the sand drifts.

Our working days became routine. After waking up, we had breakfast, which was comprised of fresh fruit, followed by a few-hours work in the house for volunteers or in the hotel. We would make small houses-lamps, color the details on the walls in strange color combinations, build a wooden fence in an outdoor shower and help in the kitchen. The local craftsmen, who had been working around the hotel, soon became our buddies. Even though at first they were surprised to see a pair of gringos working alongside them, we were soon listening to Peruvian music together out of an old cassette player, cracking jokes in broken Spanish, calling each other *'Maestro!'* whenever we passed by each other, and that sort of thing. A real little family of workers!

Every day before sunset, we would walk down the beach to Mancora. Always accompanied by the wonderful sight of a massive yellow ball gently sinking into the ocean, we would see all kinds of things: from a dead sea-horse washed up on the beach to a sea-lion, which having got out of the sea, looked up constantly at the sky and decided to die.

The center was always lively, full of people selling fried chicken, cooked corn, quail's eggs, fried bananas and *empanada* - my favorite local food, which reminded me of a combination of my grandma's donuts and cheese-pie. We were regular customers in the local *Mercado*, where we would buy our groceries for dinner. We usually ate dinner at a different place each evening - on the beach, next to a church, in the middle of the main square... We became familiar with every bench in Mancora.

But more than getting to know Mancora, Maria and I got to know each other. Until we arrived in Peru, we hadn't spent a single night together, and now we were practically inseparable. It wasn't necessarily our choice, but things just turn out that way when you travel. The only time you are alone is when you're in the toilet, although even this isn't always the case. One small hotel room where we stayed before coming to Mancora didn't have a toilet door, so if one of us had to use the bathroom during the night, the other couldn't help but hear everything that was going on.

It definitely wasn't a typical way of getting to know your partner. There was no make-up, beauty products or choosing the moment when we would be together - just the hard truth.

"Maybe this is the right way," I thought one evening, as we were sitting on the roof of our volunteer house, watching the stars. The moon was as thin as it could be and it was quickly lost beneath the open sea. "All of my past relationships started in the same, ideal way. I liked a girl, a girl liked me. When we were together, we would always look great and shiny and happy, so because of the way it started, a decline was always inevitable. We would give each other everything we had, get used to the best, which usually had very little to do with reality. After a while, the sparkle would get lost along the way. This was when the painful process of sobering up normally started."

But this time, the situation was different. More relaxed. More realistic. Things weren't like in romantic movies, songs or novels - things were real. We were two individuals, attracted to each other, trying not to lose our selves in this coming together.

"Are we going to last?" I thought over one of my many glasses of Peruvian red wine and, still laughing, made a wager with the starry sky: "If there's a shooting star before she comes back with a new bottle of wine, I'll marry her!"

I loved to play in this way. I loved testing the universe, seeing if it was trying to send me a message, a piece of advice, or if it was predicting my future. I knew that the odds on us getting married weren't good. There were just a few stars, and she would only be gone for a minute or two at most.

I fixed my eyes on the sky. Footsteps were coming up the stairs.

"Look, a shooting star!" she exclaimed enthusiastically, entering my line of sight.

"Yeah, I saw it," I replied, looking into her eyes, knowing that I just lost the bet.

Or won it.

Day 714

"There you go, the video's done!" Maria said, closing the laptop lid.

"Ace!" I replied. "Now we're at the difficult bit - we need to find a good internet connection to upload it."

It had been a few days since we arrived in Iquitos, the largest metropolis in the Peruvian Amazon, after two days of sailing. We could have got there either by boat or by plane. We came without virtually any plans, but some plans found us.

Breaking through the hundreds of hammocks as we sailed into Iquitos, I got some signal on my cell phone and picked up nine almost identical Facebook messages from nine separate people.

I know that you're already traveling around the world, but this is definitely something for you!

It was a contest launched by a travel agency that was looking for a person for the *Best Job Around the World*, by which they meant somebody who would spend the next 12 months traveling the world, all expenses-paid, blogging about it, taking photos and making video clips. And there would be a good salary to boot - they were offering $100,000. To enter, you had to send a one-minute video, instead of a classic CV, stating why you were the best candidate for the job.

"Nah, it's just a marketing ploy," I quipped, sharing my opinion with Maria once I had told her what it was all about.

"So what?" She said. "It's not like you've got anything to lose. And it's not like we have anything better to do here in the middle of the jungle."

She was right. We had arrived there after a couple of weeks of road tripping through towns and villages, hitchhiking from Mancora, across the Andes, to the Amazon. We survived a ride during which our driver had overtaken a truck, driving uphill, crossing the double white lines. We experienced altitude sickness for the first time and tried a natural remedy against it - hojas de *coca or coca* leaves. We took the *death roads*, riding on top of a truck, together with several Peruvian families with whom we shared one thing in common - none of us dared to look down at the road and the canyons, hundreds and hundreds of feet deep, just waiting for a careless driver to make a mistake as we drove along the edge. We climbed up to Kuelap, the so-called Machu Picchu of the North, and were impressed by the view from the top, but rather disappointed by what seemed to be just a heap of rocks and what was left of some small houses.

Iquitos sounded like a secluded and exciting place, this was why we went there. But I also had one other plan for the Amazon, I wanted to try ayahuasca. I had heard and read all kinds of things about ayahuasca - it had been used for thousands of years by the indigenous cultures, mainly for medicinal purposes, and I had also read about hallucinations, expanding one's perception and consciousness under the influence of DMT and things like that. This, of course, attracted plenty of tourists. And the many tourists, needless to say, attracted numerous charlatans, locals who pretended to be shamans and ayahuasca experts, who wanted to milk the wealthy white visitors for as much money as possible.

"I want to try ayahuasca, but I want to do it properly," I said to Maria at one of the markets where they were selling it, or more precisely two of its main ingredients, and also the San Pedro cactus, another well-known hallucinogenic plant.

Whether by chance or not, one day, whilst we were drinking our first morning cup of coffee, five people from Samobor, a Croatian town not far from Zagreb, sat down at the table next to us.

"Tomorrow we're going to Tamshiyacu," the group's main man, Žac, informed us. "I bought 30 acres of land there, with a few houses, it's such a great place."

"What are you going to do there?" We asked.

"We're having ayahuasca ceremonies, what else?" he beamed. "Do you fancy joining us?"

We accepted their unexpected invitation and the next day, we were there. We finished filming the video for the *Best Job Around the World* competition in a single day and Maria edited it - we were now ready for ayahuasca, a healing plant.

Žac's estate was beautiful. There was a stream running through it, forming a small lake. It was surrounded by palm trees and there were the *cabañas*, little houses with thatched roofs. These didn't have any windows, their place taken by nets that served as the first line of defence against the jungle's worst predators, mosquitoes. A few trunks stood in for chairs and instead of a couch there was a wooden bench; there was a big foam mattress in the middle of the room that served as a bed and above the mattress was the second line of defence, another mosquito net. There was no electricity, no water, no network, no internet.

It really would have been heaven on earth if it hadn't been hot as hell in there. Also if the bloodthirsty mosquitoes buzzing about our heads had left us alone.

As the nightfall approached, we started to prepare for our first ayahuasca ceremony in the largest hut on the estate. We each had our own mat with *mapacho*, a Peruvian tobacco. There were also other things we might need: a bowl where we could vomit, a bottle of water, and a torch we could use to light the way to the toilet. One of the things ayahuasca normally does is cleanse the body of accumulated toxins, so we prepared ourselves accordingly.

Preparation for the ceremony shouldn't be taken lightly. Before the ceremony, you're meant to follow a strict diet that includes only fruit and vegetables (preferably raw), and you need to avoid coffee, cigarettes, and marijuana. It's also recommended that you abstain from sexual activities. All of this is intended to prepare your body for the cleansing.

Emanuel, a shaman from the Shipibo tribe, was also there, with us seven Croats. We sat on our mats. There was a soft candle light and the shaman started to sing and make a rustling sound in the pile of leaves. One by one, we came to him so that he could give us a small cup of the not-so-tasty potion. We lay down, the candle went out. With the sounds of the jungle, Emanuel was humming his relaxing, but scary song at the same time.

And then we waited for the potion to work its magic.

Minute after minute went by. Peaceful lying was interrupted by the occasional clapping sound caused by the irritating mosquitoes. The shaman was still humming his song and made a rustling sound. And then at one point he stopped and the journey began.

My thoughts began to run riot. To connect. To jump from one to another. Ideas started to multiply. There was chaos in my head. Every now and then a brilliant idea would flash into my mind, I received the answer to a vital question, and then jumped to another, equally interesting thought. At first I was thrilled by some thoughts, but then I became disappointed after losing them. It felt like a dream, but in such a way that all the dreams that I ever had were being fast-forwarded through my head. I was constantly waking up and trying to remember a dream, but I would then fall back asleep again, but still awake. It happened over and over again.

This might have lasted for two minutes, or two hours, I really don't know.

Maria brought me back to reality. She was lying next to me in silence, with her eyes closed. But besides her physical presence, I could also feel and hear her thoughts, which weren't nice. She was getting lost in her head and needed help. I put my thoughts aside and took her hand. She was sweaty, weak and lifeless.

I remembered all the stories I had heard about ayahuasca. Given that nobody had ever died from it, I tried to dispel my doubts. She gripped my hand, just briefly and weakly, and this reassured me. But we were still far from the end. I was lying next to her, choking in my own chaos, trying to help her mentally.

The cleansing began. I took my bowl and threw up in it. I got up and waddled to the toilet. The floor was moving, one moment I was filled with euphoria, and the next I was full of fear. My body started to shake and convulse, it really wasn't nice. Maybe I should have prepared better, followed the recommended diet and all that stuff.

However, the real horror followed after I came back into the room. Most of the people were up on their feet, gathered around one member of the group. Amongst all this chaos, all I could make out was his face but I could see that he was foaming at the mouth, and his girlfriend was holding his hand, completely pale. The shaman remained calm, sang a song in front of his face and tried to call him back to our world.

Maria was sitting, distraught by what was transpiring on the mat next to hers. I didn't know what scared her more, the chaos in her head or the scene around her. Slowly, I sat down and took her by the hand again.

"It will be all right," I said gently and smiled.

I could read in her eyes that she didn't believe me. She was looking into my eyes, but at the same time, she was looking *through* them. I couldn't begin to imagine what must have been going on inside her head.

The situation around us calmed down, our friend regained consciousness and cheerfully informed us that he had, quite literally, shat his pants.

"Why is this so terrible?" she asked helplessly.

"I don't know, but it will pass," I said. "Ayahuasca has never done any harm to anyone, it's all in your head, in your mind. It'll pass. We decided to try this and now we must be ready to accept the consequences of our decisions."

She closed her eyes.

I closed mine too and lay down. I allowed my mind to wander into the somewhat calmer chaos.

"I'd have exchanged five years of my life just to have it stop. In a heartbeat," she told me as we were heading out to our chalet at the break of dawn.

"Was it that bad?" I asked.

"It was even worse than that," she said. "How was it for you?"

"My body didn't like it," I said. "My mind was running wild, I couldn't focus, but as time went by, especially when the nausea went away, it all seemed to come together."

"What do you mean?"

"It's hard to explain. Among all of those thoughts that were racing through my mind, one seemed to constantly recur, telling me it was all okay. That I was on the right track. Telling me not to worry."

It was really difficult to explain my feelings, thoughts and insight of that evening. I just couldn't verbalize them into a meaningful whole. I couldn't simplify the lesson. It was a very personal experience, which wasn't supposed to be shared with others. On the other hand, I felt that my experience could be applied to any person, anywhere in the world, that we all shared the same fate, that we were all on the right track, that in this life there were no defeats or they simply weren't relevant for the whole story, for the bigger picture, for achieving a final goal, that in the end we couldn't lose and that in the end we were all together in this.

That we didn't have to worry, no matter what.

Day 754

Hey Tomislav!

We are delighted to inform you that you have qualified for the second round of our competition to win the best job around the world!
We hereby invite you to make another 2-3 minute video in which you present your home town or a town in which you are currently staying.
You have a week to send it to us. Best of luck!

I was lucky.
Not because I was one of the top 50 candidates in the contest, as this email informed me. That was to be expected, after we sent them a video created in the Amazon that made the Internet go wild. My one-minute video biography turned out to be a great success, partly because of the simplicity of the script, partly because of the scenes from all around the world that I had recorded over the past few years, and because Maria did a great job putting the video together. I also did a good job promoting it - I shared a link on my Facebook page, where people could vote for me, and I wrote to the Croatian media, so it was soon big news: *Croat in race for Best Job Around the World!*

I was invited to give a number of interviews for television, radio, newspapers and online portals. The likes and shares on my Facebook page skyrocketed. My face was all over the place, which resulted in one hundred thousand votes and meant I lead the race among a field of a few thousand candidates from all over the world.

It wasn't luck, but rather a well-designed and implemented plan. Luck was that we found ourselves in the most beautiful city in Peru, Cusco, right at the time when we were given a week to make the second video. And also that the following day we were planning to visit Machu Picchu.

We took the camera and spent a whole day exploring the capital of the Inca empire. In the morning, we hopped in a local van and traveled to Ollantaytambo.

Ollantaytambo is a cute little town built out of stones. Hordes of tourists go there every day because this is their last chance to get aboard the train that goes to Aguas Calientes (aka Machu Picchu village), from where you actually start climbing to Machu Picchu. Of course, you can also get on the train in Cusco, but it would cost you much more. From Ollantaytambo, you have to pay *only* 70 dollars for a one way ticket. This is why this route is dubbed one of the most expensive ones in the world, especially knowing that the distance you need to cross is less than 20 miles.

Besides being a regular stop for all those heading to Machu Picchu, you can find a lot of ancient ruins from the era of the Incas in the very town itself: terraces, mines, ancient walls and stuff like that. It's definitely worth visiting if time is on your side. It wasn't on ours. Our plan was to get to Aguas Calientes on foot. Even on the internet we couldn't find anyone who had tried to do the same thing and the lady who worked in the tourist office tried to scare us with stories about security guards who would chase us away and forbid us from walking on the tracks (which was the only possible route).

Since we didn't bring camping equipment (not even a flashlight for walking in the dark) and our destination was a good 30 kilometres away (at least seven to eight hours of walking), we planned to spend the night somewhere along the route. Several people in Ollantaytambo told us that we would see several private estates along the way, where we would be able to ask for bed. Being a full-time optimists, we had a cup of coffee, ate breakfast, took a couple of liters of water and set off around noon.

We hitchhiked a van to Piscacucho, the last village next to the railway accessible by road. It was located at the kilometre 82. According to the information we got, we had another 32 kilometres to Aguas Calientes, which was at kilometre 114.

Kilometre 82

There, next to the end of road, was the beginning of the famous *Inca Trail*, which hikers would take to get to Machu Picchu by foot over three-four days. However, you had to be prepared physically for such a mission and you needed to be very well organized. As the number of visitors was limited, you had to make all the necessary bookings a few months in advance, which would have cost us at least $500.

We were slowly walking on or by the railroad track, taking a short break every twenty minutes, whenever we saw a train approaching. We also tried to hitchhike this means of transport, but to no avail. We carefully passed through the first tunnel, on a constant look-out so as not to find ourselves facing a train in the middle of the dark and narrow tunnel. There was a small, unusual railroad vehicle that passed next to us, but we didn't even notice it at first, let alone try our luck by sticking out a thumb to try to stop it.

The nature was magnificent. A large and fast-flowing river was running on our left side, we saw a number of horses and donkeys while they were pasturing and also the peaks of the mountains in the distance. The peace of nature was a far cry from the noise of the big cities.

Kilometre 88

After more than an hour of walking, we took a lunch break. We met a local teacher who wasn't very optimistic about the progression of our little adventure.

"You've started your journey too late," she told us in a worried voice. "You don't have either a camping equipment or a lamp to help you walk through the dark."

"We know," we replied calmly. "We're planning on spending the night at the place of somebody we meet on the way."

"I think that's going to be mission impossible," she continued pessimistically. "People in this area aren't that welcoming to strangers. Also, a lot of people have died while walking on the railroad at night. It's pitch black, there are loads of tunnels and collapsed areas. All sorts. Listen to me, get back to Ollantaytambo or at least to Piscacucho, spend the night there, and start your journey at the break of dawn so that reach your destination before nightfall."

"Thanks for your advice," we smiled, and said goodbye to her.

She did shake our self-confidence a bit, but she didn't crush it. By now accustomed to Peruvian hospitality, we were convinced that we would find a place to spend the night on our journey.

Kilometre 90

We met two other groups of people who were on their way back from our planned destination and did nothing but bum us out even more. They seemed pretty surprised at how disorganized we were when they found out that we didn't have any camping equipment or even a single torch-light. They didn't have a single nice word to say about the people who lived beside the road. They hadn't even given them a glass of water when they asked them politely.

"And beware of the dogs", they warned us after we had already said goodbye. "Arm yourself with rocks. They usually scare them away."

By this time we had walked for two hours. We had to walk at least another five to get to our destination, and it would be getting dark in three hours. We didn't know what to do.

Kilometre 93

We saw a couple of houses, quite distant from each other. We got closer to them and tried to talk to the people who lived there. Some just shook their heads, while a pack of dogs barked at us from behind the fence, and others were nowhere to be found. We kept on searching. We could feel our hope at finding a place slowly fading. It was already too late to go back: it was getting darker and darker.

We came to a house on a beautiful estate. There was a small spring, ducks, a garden, and plants all around us. We yelled and shouted, but to no avail. We decided to go inside and snoop around a bit.

"Hola!" we shouted after taking a few steps, walking very cautiously. "Buenos dias!"

We passed next to a stable and behind a corner we noticed two women plucking chickens. Although they didn't notice us, the dogs that were right next to them did, jumping up suddenly and moving upon us, barking their lungs out. All six of them.

It only took them a few second to reach us and we were scared to death. Even though our guts were telling us to turn on our heels as quickly as possible and start running, our reason was suggesting that we stood our ground, not budging a single inch or giving the slightest hint that we might be terrified: if the dogs sensed our fear they would have attacked us in the blink of an eye.

The women finally noticed us and, without getting up, clasping half-plucked chickens in their hands, started to gesticulate something particularly rude to us, saying something that we couldn't hear given the deafening racket the mutts were making. They were foaming at the mouth and were obviously frustrated by the two strangers in their yard. The strangers, for their part, were scared by these hounds and, trying desperately to hide this from them, looked at each other and gradually edged back out of the yard, closing the gate behind them.

"We can't do this anymore," I said.

"I agree," she confirmed. "What are we going to do now?"

Our options weren't great. We could try at another house, assuming we came across house. But after the close encounter we'd just experienced, the dogs that were in front of every house didn't make us feel like taking a chance. We could return, retracing our steps, but it would have taken us at least three hours to get back. The sun was going to set down in two hours. We could spend the night out in the open, but we didn't have any camping equipment.

So, our final option was to continue for another 20 kilometres and night would overtake us during the last ten. We couldn't even count on the moon since it would only reveal itself after midnight. We had two mobile phones, but our batteries were low, so their lights were nearly dead.

"Let's hurry up and try to do as many miles as possible before it gets dark and then we'll take it slowly," I said after a few minutes of thinking about it. "We don't really have any other choice."

"Okay," Maria agreed, but I could tell that she was feeling down.

We upped our pace as much as possible given that we were walking over sharp rocks and all kinds of obstacles croped up every hundred yards.

Kilometre 96

We were approaching another house. We could tell it as soon as we heard the barking of the dogs that were guarding it. We armed ourselves with some stones. Although we passed without incident, they did come closer to us, snarling and barking.

"What's going to happen with the dogs when night falls?" Maria asked me, walking a few feet behind me.

I didn't say anything. I had kept asking myself the same question.

Kilometre 98

We were halfway there. We managed to cover 16 kilometres in four hours from a total of 32 kilometres. We'd need another four hours.
That fact bummed us out even more.

Kilometre 99

The dogs were barking again. We'd never seen dogs as mad as these over the last kilometre or so. The atmosphere of despair and desolation that had accumulated around us only added to the atmosphere. We were holding as many stones as we could fit in our hands. We were afraid of the dogs, we were afraid of the dark that was slowly, but surely, approaching. And above all, we were afraid of the combination of these two things.

Kilometre 101

Our pace was quite good, so in an hour we had probably covered a good five-six kilometres. We still didn't dare to look at our watches. The day was slowly fading away. We could hear some dogs barking, but they were on the other bank of the river.

Kilometre 102

That was it. Nighttime had arrived. Holding each other, we took out our mobile phones only to feel disappointed by the light they emitted. We continued slowly, one step at a time.
Another train passed by.
The trail was awful: we couldn't see more than few yards in front of us; there were holes we had to jump over and we had to cross over a bridge, stepping carefully on the worn railroad tracks, hoping that a train would not come. The forest surrounding us was so thick that, at one moment, we found ourselves in a tunnel without even noticing it at first. It was sheer luck that had saved us again from meeting a train head on.
There were loads of dogs in front of us. We had even stopped counting them. Our spirits were down and the situation seemed to

grow worse with every new bark we heard since the sounds they produced seemed even more dreadful in the dark.

"Hey!" Maria exclaimed. "We have your laptop!"

At first I didn't know what she was getting at, but then it hit me: the light emitted by my laptop screen was much stronger than that of our mobile phones. It was a great idea! I wanted to hug her and kiss her, but we didn't have time for that.

I took my laptop out of the bag, put away my phone, adjusted the screen brightness and went on.

I contemplated our situation. Two naive fools had started a 32 kilometre journey following a path that didn't actually exist, next to a railroad. Although they knew that it would take them seven or eight hours to get to their destination, they didn't start walking until after noon. Although they were fully aware that there weren't any "official" place to spend the night, they didn't bother to bring any sleeping bags or camping equipment: they were convinced that luck would be on their side and that they would experience the famed Peruvian hospitality. And, lastly, they barely managed to stay alive when faced with packs of threatening dogs that they encountered along the way. It was getting darker but they didn't even have a torch light to help them light the way.

So, there they were, more than ten kilometres from their destination with a laptop held in a free hand, while the other hands were clenched full of stones intended for the canines in case they got too close.

Great.

Kilometre 104

More dogs. Where were they coming from, for God's sake?

Maria took the laptop, she was walking beside me. I was very careful, ready to fight the dogs if necessary. They were barking and snarling. They were close, right behind us. The only thing we had in mind was moving forward.

We encouraged each other by talking, but it didn't help much. You could hear in our voices that we were exhausted, worried and depressed. As never before. The time was passing very slowly. Along with the miles that were passing even more slowly.

Kilometre 105

We were tired. We were cold. My feet were sore. By the sound of Maria's steps, I assumed she was limping, but she didn't want to say anything so I wouldn't get more worried. I didn't dare to ask her anything so as not to make the whole situation worse.

"Look, there's some kind of a light beyond that turn!" I said to her excitingly, and a glimmer of hope was born.

Kilometre 106

Our first impression was that we were approaching a village. There seemed to be lots of houses on our left. The only barrier that divided us from it was the raging river. We reached the bridge. We crossed it, but on the other side there was a fence. It was locked.

We noticed some people. They approached us. We explained to them our situation through the closed gate. We asked them where we were. We found out that it was some kind of a hydroelectric plant, and these were its workers: it wasn't possible for us to spend the night there. They wouldn't budge, no matter how hard we tried.

At the end of the complex we came across the workers who were loading that weird vehicle on the railroad that we'd seen when we started walking. We knew that this was our last chance.

"Good evening!" We approached them, smiling. "Are you by any chance going to Aguas Calientes?"

"Yes," one of the men replied coldly, with papers in his hands.

"Could you *por favor* give us a lift?" Maria asked. I would have asked the question myself, but I was convinced that she would have a little more luck.

"No," he replied curtly.

"Please," Maria said pleadingly. "We don't have a torch, we're exhausted and scared of all the barking dogs…"

"Sorry," repeated the man, continuing to do his job, all the time avoiding eye contact. "It's forbidden for us to drive tourists around."

Our hope was killed once again so we moved on.

"I don't think this guy has ever walked here during the night," I complained as we turned away. "If he had done it then he'd understand the situation we're in and would give us a ride without a moment's hesitation."

I had barely finished my sentence when we heard the sound of the engine starting up and the little thing started moving in our direction. We stopped, closed the laptop screen and, with our heads bowed, waited for them to pass us.

"Get in!" The locomotive engineer shouted, stopping the machine. "But crouch down so that nobody notices."

At that moment, we were the happiest people in the world. Finding it hard to believe, we held hands, and watched how easily we were gliding down the railroad. The light of the engine was lighting up the worn-out railroad that we tripped over so many times. The railroad that had provoked so many curses from our lips. And now we were leaving it behind in a blink of an eye.

It was wonderful. After all the sadness, frustration, helplessness, fear and other negative feelings over the past few hours, life surprised us in the most unexpected way. Once again, it confirmed to me something that I had long known. Ups and downs are, if not equally valuable, both essential. We wouldn't be able to appreciate the ups without experiencing the occasional down.

Kilometre 107

Kilometre 108

"Woof! Woof!" The biggest dog we had seen was running along and barking next to us. If we'd been on foot, it would have been the final test of our resolve.

Kilometre 109

We noticed some lights in the distance.

Kilometre 110

The vehicle was stopping.

"So here we are," the driver mumbled.

"Where are we?" We asked, taking our backpacks and getting off the vehicle. We expected that we would stop when we reached kilometre 114, so we were quite a little confused.

"Aguas Calientes," he said and disappeared into the darkness.

Feeling dead tired, but proud to have reached our destination in one piece after having walked through the whole night next to the railroad, accompanied by horrendous dogs, we were ambling around Aguas Calientes looking for a place to stay.

We knew we were probably in the most expensive town in Peru, which you had to visit if you wanted to go to Machu Picchu - the most popular tourist destination in this part of the world. It's the last stop before Machu Picchu so there are no other options for the tourists and the owners of the restaurants and hotels know exactly what to do - hike their prices. We browsed the shops and noticed that the prices were the double those in Cusco, which was itself very expensive anyway; the hotels were either fully booked or overpriced and by the looks of the restaurant we realized that we'd have to live off the most basic products or go hungry during our stay.

With our last ounce of strength, we found a hotel at a reasonable price. While trying to negotiate the deal, we made use of the fact that it was already very late and we also told them what we'd had to go through to even get there. We took a cold shower and went out to get something for dinner.

We stopped at the first restaurant we ran into to check the prices. Too expensive. Then we stopped at the second one - it was the same story. However, while we were looking at the menu, four people that were sitting at the table next to us got up and left. They had left seven slices of pizza on their plates: on each plate there was a fair portion. I looked at the price of the pizza and couldn't understand how they could leave so much of the expensive food. I looked around me and glanced over at Maria.

"Shall we?" I asked her.

"Let's," she briefly replied.

We grabbed the remaining untouched slices of pizza as quickly as possible, threw a smile at the surprised people who were sitting there, gawping at us, and took off.

Day 774

Dear Tom,

From all of us at Jauntaroo, we thank you for being an amazing part of our search for our very first Chief World Explorer. We were blown away by the attention this campaign has brought. We could never have imagined the level of creativity, engagement and enthusiasm for travel that candidates would demonstrate when we solicited applications. Narrowing the candidate pool has proven to be one of the most challenging endeavors we have ever undertaken.

After thoroughly reviewing all submissions from our Top 50, we have made the difficult decision to not have you participate in our Top 5. This decision was not made lightly and we cannot express how grateful we are for your efforts, both in your videos and in social media and other channels. As we looked at you as a candidate, we really were impressed by your abilities to gather support, especially with the Croatian media. People really rallied around your submission in a way we could ever have imagined. Your demeanor on camera was fun and easy to watch. You were definitely one of our top 10 choices. In an effort to provide some candid feedback on why you were not selected, we would say that mentioning Jauntaroo and how we function as a site would have helped. As great as this job will be, we want to make sure our Chief World Explorer can bring it back to Jauntaroo and our position within the travel space.

From the bottom of our hearts, thank you again for being part of this incredibly journey. May your love of travel never cease and may you continue to make this world a better place. We wish you well in all your future endeavors.

Sincerely,

Jauntaroo Executive Team

I reread the e-mail. I was sad. Disappointed. I'd put a lot of time and effort into this project, and it didn't yield the desired results. It was one of the few times in my life when I hadn't got what I'd wanted, despite my efforts.

Feeling down, I tried to regain my composure and further analyze the whole situation. I lay down on my back, staring at the ceiling fan that was slowly rotating. It was early morning, Maria was still asleep. What had this two-month project brought me?

First of all, it was such a great fun. Doing these two videos, giving interviews and making statements to the media, observing as I became the candidate with by far the largest number of votes in the first and second round, and holding on to this position. Also, receiving so many messages and emails of support from people who had previously never heard of me. I now had five thousand new fans from all over the world on my Facebook page.

On top of that, a few days ago, tired of constantly waiting for the results and news of whether or not I would get into the top 5 candidates, I started to write something I never thought I would: my first book.

A lot of positive things had come out of all this. And there was only one negative - I hadn't got *the best job around the world*.

On the other hand, what would have happened if I had got it? I would be working for a company, going where they sent me - writing, taking photographs, and making videos according to their demands. Most of the time I would be separated from Maria, and I wouldn't be free to make my own decisions. Who knows how it would have turned out? I'd have received a sum of one hundred thousand dollars, which would have been halved once you take all the different taxes and charges into consideration. People would start asking me to lend them money. I'd definitely lose plenty of friends among those to whom I lent money, and those whom I refused would call me a stingy bastard.

My disappointment and sadness practically vanished. But the eternal question still remained: what now?

"I didn't make it into the top 5," I whispered to her when she opened her eyes. She quietly approached and hugged me.

"What are we going to do now?" she asked after a while.

"I'm tired of buzzing around Peru," I said. "Let's go find some place where we will be based for a few months, where I can devote myself to writing my book."

"Santa Marianita?" she uttered.

"Santa Marianita," I confirmed.

There was the possibility of volunteering in a hotel on the coast of

Ecuador. Taking a break from traveling. There was the possibility of finding a base and dedicating myself to what I felt was my path and my biggest challenge.

I grabbed my laptop, opened my Facebook page and wrote a status.

Hey guys!

Unfortunately, I'm not one of the top 5 candidates for the "Best Job Around the World".
I just got an email from my would-be employer, thanking me for being a part of their competition and letting me know that I did great in doing the videos and getting likes, but that I wasn't what they were looking for. The reason for this was not mentioning their company in the video nor the way they function.
Either way, we gave it our best. The last two months were very interesting. I can't thank you enough for being here, liking, sharing, and crossing your fingers. Thanks to all the different media that covered the story more than I could have ever imagined, thanks to my friend Shale for catapulting me to the first place in the second round, and thanks to my aunt, who had so many sleepless nights from all the cheering.
Life goes on, this page goes on, our adventure goes on - a few days ago, Maria and I got an offer to work in a hotel on the coast of Ecuador. Who knows, maybe that will be our best job in the world!
This means that I'll also have time to work on my book...

Kisses to all of you from both of us!

Day 1000

"Huacachina was one of our last stops in Peru," I continued, changing the slide. The photo showed a beautiful oasis in the middle of the Peruvian desert. "Huacachina attracts many tourists with its appearance, but also because of all of the fun stuff you can try there, such as sandboarding, buggy driving, and relaxing in the healing waters and mud."

We actually didn't managed to do any of this in Huacachina, although we tried sandboarding. Unsuccessfully. Either we were naturally talentless or the problem was with the board that hadn't been properly waxed. On the other hand, we enjoyed the beautiful scenery of the desert, dunes, sunrise and sunset. After years of traveling, it was the first time that I was in a real desert.

"After four months in Peru, we visited Ecuador," I continued. "We came across a project at a small hotel on the coast on a web page offering all kinds of volunteering opportunities[9] and spend the next five months there. We only worked a few hours a day in exchange for bed and board, helping with breakfast and cleaning the rooms, walking the dogs on the beach and taking care of thirteen cats adopted by our landlady Linda. We got to know almost the whole town, and every night we would go to a small family run restaurant in which we took a fresh piece of fish, some sort of side dish and a salad for just two dollars."

"We didn't see much of Ecuador," I pointed out. "We visited Baños, a cute little town nestled in central Ecuador, and Quilotoa, a crater lake, but soon we were back in Santa Marianita because I had to get back to work and finish my book."

---
[9] www.workaway.info

Day 909

I closed my laptop's lid. A chapter in my life came to a close. My first child was born. I had finished writing my book.

I felt the same after passing the last exam in college. Pride and relief that came from working hard. Success that came after so much effort. I hated writing just as much as I hated revising for exams. The inspiration for writing the book lasted for a couple of days at most, at the very beginning, and the rest of it was a case of forcing myself to finish what I had started.

You're not a writer. This is a disaster. Your book is terribly boring. There's nothing special about your story. Your writing style resembles that of an average high-school student.

Those were the thoughts that were running through my head from one day to the next, from one page to the next. I was turning endlessly in my bed, feeling powerless in front of the blank laptop screen. I was changing the fonts, having fun editing the text, playing different music in the background, going on short walks on the beach, looking for inspiration. But to no avail. I didn't like my book in the making. I didn't like it at all. I found it dull. Nevertheless, I kept on writing.

Until one morning, when everything changed.

I was writing about day 794. The day when I had an interview with Croatian National Television, on a TV show called "Eighth Floor". I was face to face with presenter Daniela Trbović, talking about my travels on a budget of $10 a day.

I lay on my bed, playing the nine-and-a-half minute interview on YouTube. It took me more than three-quarters of an hour to play the whole video because the connection was so slow and I was taking notes of what we were saying. Daniela asked me about my previous job as a stockbroker. She kept asking me about Couchsurfing and my first trip. I was telling her about my first hitchhiking experience as I was heading for Sofia, traveling around Croatia, a two-month trip across Europe, about running out of money in Andalusia. I also mentioned the hitchhiking race to Istanbul, launching a Facebook page, Bangladesh and Portugal. Finally, I announced my longest trip - a thousand days of summer.

And then suddenly it hit me. I finally got it right. I skimmed through the book and realized that I had already covered all the topics. It looked as if I had been writing according to the interview script. It felt like Daniela knew exactly what she was supposed to ask me so that I could mention everything that happened to me from the moment I quit my job as a stockbroker to being there, opposite her, answering her questions and announcing the trip that lay ahead of me.

That was it. I decided that that interview would be the central point of my book. Everything would revolve around it. The chronology in the book would be disparate, with constant flashbacks to day 794 and the interview with Daniela. Just like *Slumdog Millionaire* with its flashbacks to the show and character's path to becoming a millionaire.

With this thought on my mind, a smile returned to my face as I finished off writing the book. I felt like a writer, it didn't sound boring, I didn't worry about my simple style of writing. With this idea in mind, I started to like my book.

"I'm done," I whispered to her when she opened her eyes.
"'Done' done?" She was a bit suspicious.
"'Done' done," I replied confidently.
We got up and started a day that was no different to any other day over the past five months.
Besides having two plane tickets to return to Europe by the end of the day in our pockets.

Our first day together in Lima

The view of Máncora from our volunteer cottage

Las Positas

A dead seahorse

Maria's striking a pose while hitch-hiking

Cajamarca

Ventanillas de Otuzco

Sweet little children

Means of transport over the Andes

A view of the road of death

Hammocks on the boat to Iquitos

Tamshiyacu

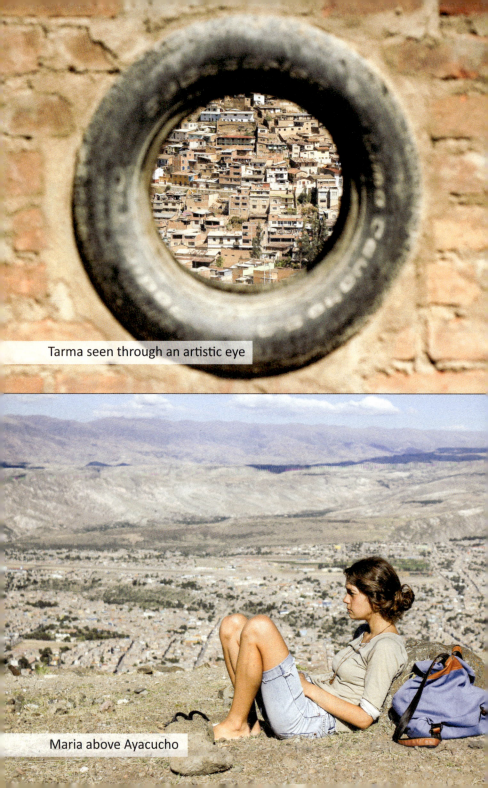

Tarma seen through an artistic eye

Maria above Ayacucho

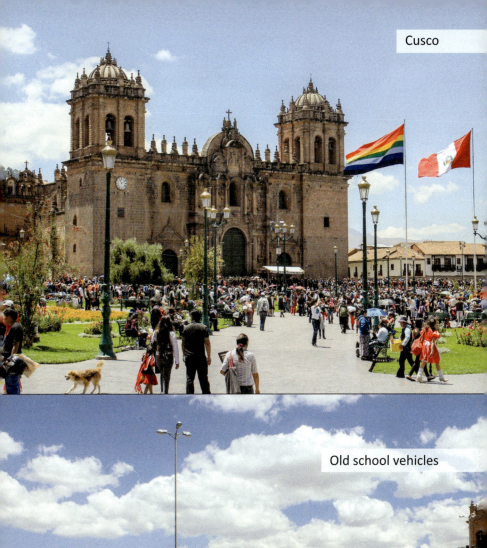
Cusco

Old school vehicles

The Saksaywaman ruins

Local competition

One of the tunnels on the way to Aguas Calientes

At our destination. Happy

The three of us at the summit

A magical place

My office

Two mums, my aunt and us in Venice, a couple of hours before returning to Zagreb

Day 1000

"After five months in Ecuador, we returned to Croatia, where I published my first book," I continued my lecture and changed the slide to the next photograph, showing my recently published book in Croatian and English. "*1000 Days of Spring*."

I could feel the audience's astonished gaze scorching into me.

"You must be wondering why I've been talking about my trip around the world that I called *1000 Days of Summer*, only to end it with a story about a book called *1000 Days of Spring*."

They nodded affirmatively.

"When I started writing the book, the plan was to call it 1000 days of summer and write about traveling around the world," I admitted. "But I didn't want to start from the moment I set off. I wanted to write about everything that came before it. I wanted to write about the years before traveling, about my student days, stockbroker business, hosting CSers in my rented apartment, my first hitchhiking, the first major trips, the hitchhiking race to Istanbul, the first sponsors, and traveling to Bangladesh. I believed that this story was even more interesting than the story about my trip around the world. After two hundred pages, realizing that I hadn't even started to write about my trip around the world, I decided to divide my story in two parts and two books: the book about my life before setting off on my trip around the world - 1000 days of spring, and the book about my life during my trip around the world - 1000 days of summer."

"Although I had several offers from Croatian publishers, I decided to self-publish my book," I continued. "I started a crowdfunding campaign through which I raised enough money for proofreading, design, an English translation and the printing of several thousand copies. At the moment, I'm traveling across Croatia and neighboring countries, holding lectures and promoting my book."

That was it. I had said all I had to say. The lecture was over. The funniest part, the Q&A session, was about to start.

"Does anyone have a question?" I asked, ending with a "thank you" slide.

Silence filled the hall. Just like in all previous lectures. It is always difficult to break the ice, but once that someone plucks up the courage and asks the first question, new questions keep coming.

"What is your favorite place that you've ever visited?" The first question came about.

Just as I expected. People usually tend to ask this question, especially when they do not have much time to talk, and want to learn as much as possible in the least amount of time.

I have long resisted answering this question at all. Such a simple question could cause such chaos in my mind. Since I have never been sloppy in answering the questions, every time I tried to make the effort to remember all the places where I'd been over the last couple of years and choose one. Most often it didn't work out, so I would give the answers such as:

- Oh, it's hard to say, I have visited so many places…
- It would be unfair to single out just one out of so many places…
- You know, a place's beauty depends on many different factors…
- It's not the places you go; it's the people you meet along the way…

One day I just stopped. I realized that people who asked simple questions also wanted simple answers. And that's just fine.

"Of all the places that I've visited," I started, "I think the Cocos Islands or Machu Picchu were the most visually beautiful. Maybe it was Uluru, too. Still, my favorite place in the world is a small town in the south of India."

Day 127

"Mmm, this is so good," Tanja said, eating fish with her hands. We were sitting in a restaurant on the southern cliff in Varkala. Several yards of sandy beach stretched out below us, ending where the waves started, the waves that were striking the shore at regular intervals.

It was her last day in India, the following morning she would be catching a flight to London. This was our last dinner together.

"Shall we call my parents on Skype?" I suggested when I had finished my meal. I hadn't seen them for a long time, and I knew that they would be delighted to hear from us, so that we could exchange a few words and show them where we were.

"Sure," she said, dabbing her lips with a napkin.

I took the laptop from the backpack, opened it, logged in to my emails and pressed the refresh button. One was waiting for me.

"Oops!" That was all I could say as I looked over in Tanja's direction. It wasn't any good. She looked down and fell silent.

"Go ahead, reply to her," she said quietly, looking out into the distance.

I closed the lid of my laptop and turned to her.

"I really don't know what to say..."

I knew that she had known all along. As soon as we had left the Taj Mahal, I had told her that Chloe was coming to Kuala Lumpur and that we would meet there. I told her that I had found out just a few hours before she had arrived to Delhi. I explained to her that it was the only unfinished story in my life, and that I had to finish it, one way or another.

I also knew that we had been successfully sweeping this subject under the rug, without looking back. The same had happened when I was leaving London to set off on my trip around the world. Until this moment, when, by chance, she noticed her name in my inbox.

"What are we going to do now?" She asked, with sadness in her voice.

"I don't know," I replied.

"But you do know that you still have feelings for her?" She looked me in the eye.

"Yes, I do," I said.

I didn't know how to define these feelings for a girl who, once upon a time, I'd only known for a few days before she broke my heart and who I had not seen for over two years. But I knew I felt *something*. Something big. Something strong. It had to be something like that if I couldn't get her out of my head for so long. I knew that there was only one way to finish this story - I had to see her again.

"If you know you still have feelings for her, why did you start whatever it is you have started with me in the first place?" she said, shedding her first tear.

"Because I had feelings for you too," I said. "I still do."

I had often asked myself that same question. I always reached the same justification. I was hoping that I would eventually be able to forget Chloe if I was with Tanja or some other girl who I liked. Staying single for as long as it took for me to forget her seemed impossible, but although the years were passing, my feelings weren't fading. I thought, or at least attempted to convince myself that one of the ways to forget her was to find someone new.

"You were up front with her and told her right from the start that there was this unfinished business," I explained, talking it through with myself from time to time. "It's not your fault if you both chose to ignore it and avoided talking about it."

However, a part of me knew that it was my fault, that I was a coward and that, by keeping quiet about it, I was contributing to the inevitable sadness that followed.

"Be honest, Tom," she said. "Be honest with me and with yourself. You never stopped loving her. But you couldn't have her, so you repressed your feelings. You came to terms with the fact that she might never be yours. So you took the first good thing that came your way all these years. To get over her. You've grown fond of me, to some extent, while you've been taking a break from those constant intense feelings. You loved me the best you could. But you didn't love me the way you loved her."

I didn't say anything. Every word she said pierced my heart like a knife, because it was all true. On top of that, I knew that the pain she felt was a thousand times stronger.

"I'm just sorry I didn't take up a few minutes of your time so that you could answer every question I had about her," she said, getting up from the table. "I'm sorry, because then I would have known you weren't ready..."

She picked up her things and ran down to the beach.

I sat alone for a few moments at the table since my thoughts were running wild. What could I have done differently, at the very beginning? Could I have avoided breaking this beautiful girl's heart? I definitely should have. I didn't have to start anything with her, I could have told her that I wasn't ready for a relationship or any kind of feelings. This would have certainly protected her from heartbreak. But then again, all those beautiful moments that we had experienced would never have happened.

Even being honest right from the start cannot always prevent such an outcome, because honesty can also get swept under the rug, overlooked, and ignored. All in the name of blind love.

We spent the whole night on the beach. We were talking, crying, and hugging.

"Have a safe trip, Tanja," I barely managed to say before dawn, putting her things in a taxi. "Take the guitar, you'll take better care of it."

"Goodbye, Tom," she barely managed to reply. "I hope you'll find what you're looking for."

She got in the taxi and left.

I stood motionless in the same place for a few moments, when someone touched me on my right shoulder. I turned around and saw a rickshaw driver who had obviously been there for a while, observing the sad parting scene.

He looked me in the eye, smiled sympathetically and gave me a silent hug.

I thanked him for the lovely gesture, thinking that I didn't really deserve that hug. I would have been happier if I could have given it to her, while she was heading to the airport all alone, at the break of dawn.

I walked back down to the beach to find some peace, before it was interrupted by the fishermen and the sunrise.

It was the middle of January, the sun was slowly rising and I could feel the sand around my feet here on the Varkala beach. I tried to think about the days to come. I tried to make a plan.

I could get myself a bike and start pedalling to Chennai from where I was supposed to fly to Kuala Lumpur in a month, or I could go to the very south of India, end up in a fishing village, and try to get to grips with one of the local crafts. Or maybe I could spend a month isolated from the outside world.

A couple more options crossed my mind, but at that moment I caught sight of a young white man sitting on the sand some twenty yards away who, with the sound of the waves as a backdrop, was waiting for the sunrise.

"Hi!" I got up and sat beside him.

This was the precise moment that changed all of the plans I thought I had.

Day 1000

"I spent one whole month in Varkala," I continued, still answering the first question, "feeling as though I was at home. I found a job, I went swimming at the beautiful sandy beaches, I played badminton, I learned some of the local language, Malayalam, and met some fabulous people."

All of this because of a single moment when I decided to approach an unknown young man on the beach. He was waiting for the fishermen, who had promised him that they would take him fishing, and then he took me up to the northern cliff that was full of restaurants, cafés and gift shops. It was completely different than the southern cliff, where I had spent a couple of nights. He showed me Shiva Garden, the place where he'd been staying for the last couple of days and that would soon become my home for the next thirty days.

I enjoyed serving food, observing the palm trees and the low-flying eagles as I lay in my *hammock*, listening to the same six songs by Krishna Das, and exchanged endless, deep stories with my new friends. I celebrated the first rains in the past few months.

I was scared when I heard coconuts hitting the ground around me, and even more so when I learned that more people were killed each year due to falling coconuts than in plane crashes. But I also thought that such a death would be beautiful. What would it be like to be lying in a hammock in such a wonderful place, in a beautiful garden in the south of India, as the sun fought its way through the branches of the coconut trees and to die in such a unique way? I'd definitely choose this as my way of dying.

"But do keep in mind, even though Varkala is my favorite place in the world, it doesn't mean that you would necessarily also like it," I said. "Whether you are going to like a place or not depends on many factors such as your current state of mind, your health, the weather conditions, food, the people you meet, accommodation, how long you stay, or even falling in love. Many beautiful places that I've visited might not have been so beautiful at some other time when I'll be different, the place will be different, the local population will be different, everything will be different - and so will be my impression."

"How much did your trip cost?" was the next question.

"I kept an accurate calculation of the costs until I returned from Africa to attend my brother's wedding," I replied. "Over that period I spent about five thousand euros, while at the same time I earned about three and a half thousand. So, in a little over 500 days I found myself one and a half thousand euros in the red."

"But you also had sponsors?" the same girl asked.

"That's right," I replied. But, the funds from the sponsorship deal went solely toward repaying my debts from my stockbroker days. I had a few exceptional cases though too, such as the occasion when I invited my dad to Africa or when I decided to jump out of a plane in Australia."

"Did you manage to pay off the whole debt?" Another girl asked me.

"I'm getting there," I said. "I hope I'll be able to get through it by selling this book."

I was very proud of myself because of that. Five and a half years or two thousand days ago, I found myself more than $30,000 in debt. I was only a couple of exams short of the requirements to graduate in a discipline I didn't like. I was losing sleep over these two things. I wanted to finish university and pay off my debt. At the same time, I wanted to travel. Eventually, I managed to finish college and travel, while still paying off my debts.

"What was the hardest part of your travel?" An elderly lady asked.

"Leaving was the hardest thing to do," I answered without hesitation. "It was hard to get going. I knew I was doing the right thing, but I still felt guilty about the pain that I caused my nearest and dearest when I left. However, once you get started, there's no looking back. The toughest challenges weren't challenging at all. Hitchhiking through all these countries, sleeping in complete strangers' homes or by the road, jumping out of a plane, sailing across the ocean. It felt normal, like it was just what I needed to do."

"Has anything bad happened to you on this trip?" Some guy asked.

I had to think about this a bit. Yes, nasty things happened. I was robbed in Lima, I was sick a few times, I was heartbroken, and I experienced that notorious ride on the back of a pickup truck in Australia that could have ended so badly...

Day 306

I took a look at the road map of Australia and weighed up the situation. I still had to cover nearly six thousand miles, which was also the distance I had traveled by then. My starting point was Townsville, a small town in the northeast of the country. My destination was Perth, a city in the South West region, from where I would fly to Kuala Lumpur, for the so-called *visa run*. My tourist visa lasted for a year, but every three months I had to leave and re-enter the country. Besides my starting point and the destination, the only place I wanted to visit was Uluru, the center of the continent.

It was early morning. Like many times before, I stuck my thumb out.

I had just completed a two-week job in Brisbane and was ready for my first real tour since I had arrived in Australia. It was also going to be my first proper solo tour since I'd set off on this adventure. Tanja had taken me by surprise in southern Turkey, where we started our two-week adventure hitchhiking across Turkey, Iraq and Iran. I'd crossed the rest of Iran and Pakistan on my own, in India I spent the first three weeks with Kev and Gina, and I crossed Nepal and a part of India with Caro. Tanja joined me again in Delhi, while I crossed Thailand and the first part of Australia with Chloe.

So much for me being a cool solo adventurer.

I was excited and nervous. I had only one host through Couchsurfing sorted out, but not before Mt Isa, which was about 450 miles away. Where would I be sleeping in the coming weeks? Would it be freezing during the desert nights, when the temperatures can drop below zero? Would I be bitten by a snake? Or eaten by a dingo? I had no idea. That is why I was so excited. Or was it because I had a feeling that something big was going to happen in the coming weeks?

It took me quite some time to cross the first sixty miles before I reached a gas station. There was another hitchhiker, a guy from Melbourne who was traveling the country during his winter break from college.

"How long have you been waiting?" I asked him, sitting on the sidewalk not far from him. I followed one of the unwritten rules of hitchhiking - if you happen to meet another hitchhiker, you had to let them go first. When they get a ride, then it's your turn to try. You can't join them, because in that case their chances of getting a ride become slimmer. So, since he had come first, he could also get the first ride.

"Three days," he replied with a wry smile.

"Ooh, shit!" That was my first reaction. I'd only covered 60 out of 5,500 miles and I was coming across another hitchhiker who had been waiting for a ride for three days. I did the math: if I managed sixty miles every three days, it would take me nine months to reach my destination. Great.

"I think it's because the road was closed for two days due to flooding," he said optimistically. "See, today I saw four cars heading to the west."

"That's just great!" I said ironically, stood up, took my backpack, wished him luck and started to walk along the road to the west.

I did not want to stay there and watch him hitchhike for hours, but to be fair and respectful to the hitchhiking rules, I moved away from him and headed west. If someone decided to pull over, they would notice him first anyway. Also, I counted on a car passing without pulling over, but when they see me, they could have mercy and change their mind.

There was also something romantic about hitchhiking while walking, with a large backpack. On the other hand, there was also something sad about it, too. Especially when you're carrying that backpack in +30°C.

It was still morning and the sun was beating down. White clouds were everywhere, and the sky looked like the biggest sky I'd ever seen. I can't really explain why - perhaps it was because there weren't any mountains around? The changing colors? Clean air and good visibility? I don't know, but I appreciated the grandeur.

But only for the first hour.

Then everything started getting on my nerves - the sky, the sun, the clouds, my backpack, and walking west. Five vehicles passed without pulling over, four of which were huge trucks that almost blew me off the road. I didn't have much water, and I had no idea how far I was from the next village. I began to lose hope again. My mind was the only thing that kept me alive. It kept reminding me that after the rain came sunshine and hope, without exception.

A few more hours went by with a few cars passing by. I kept walking west.

I heard another vehicle approaching. I turned around, smiled and stuck out my thumb. It was a car. A driver was honking, while the passenger was waving through the window. The car slowed down, but didn't pull over. The driver was smiling and the passenger shouted 'Good luck'! It was the fellow hitchhiker that I met earlier, who had finally managed to get a ride after three days of waiting.

Happy for him, I waved back. At the same time, I was also a bit sad because they might have picked me up, but I tried not to think about it that way. Think rose-tinted thoughts. At least there was a one less hitchhiker on the road. Maybe this fact would help me attract some good luck, just as I had been the lucky charm for my fellow hitchhiker.

I heard another car coming. The procedure was the same. I turned around, smiled and stuck out my thumb.

It started slowing down. I clenched my fist, full of excitement and hope. I pulled off a wider, more natural smile.

It pulled over. Two cheerful girls were inside the car. The car's interior was filled with smoke. That was a smell I knew quite well.

"We have less than an hour drive to our village," said the passenger, tidying up the mess on the back seat. "This is the time you have to tell an interesting story and give us something back for picking you up."

She winked at me and passed me the awkwardly rolled joint.

"I'm Tom from Croatia, twenty-seven years old, I'm hitchhiking around the world with a budget of ten dollars a day," I replied, a little too pleased with myself, as I exhaled the thick smoke. "Will this story be interesting enough?"

"Come on! You must be kidding!" The passenger said, turning around. "So tell us!"

I passed her the joint and started to tell my story. "You could say that I'm a travel writer," I added at the end. "Even if I really don't think so."

"What do you mean?" The passenger asked.

"Well, if a real writer read my texts, they probably wouldn't be too thrilled," I replied. "I'm not a qualified writer, I don't have my own style, and I don't think that what I write has any artistic value."

"There are different styles of writing," said the passenger. The driver, a girl with a dark complexion, didn't say a word the whole time. "I'd like to write novels and leave them to my children. But I'm never happy with what I write and I could never publish them. How do you manage to convey your thoughts, stories and feelings to people?"

"Honestly, I've no idea," I replied after a few seconds.

"So you see?" She said. "You're a writer. You don't know how you do it, but you're still doing it. You're a natural."

I smiled and thought about her words. I still didn't think of myself as a writer. That was probably because I didn't enjoy writing. While I was writing blogs, it always felt such a pain for me to take out my laptop and start typing letters onto that white background. I didn't have any inspiration, it was just work, work, and more work. And my attention was distracted by absolutely everything - the internet, games, people, and stories.

"Whether I'm a writer or not, one thing's for sure," I concluded. "I'll never write a book."

"Never say never," she smiled.

She was right. I had seen it myself so many times. For years I'd tried not to use the word never when talking about the future, along with the words *always and forever*. Especially because I had already done so many things that I'd previously said *I would never do*.

The driver still didn't say a word, but the passenger wouldn't stop talking. I enjoyed listening to her, the more so because it did me good to take a break from telling my own story. People found it interesting, I liked it very much, but exaggeration might become increasingly annoying. She touched upon many topics, traveling, education, family, but also her friend who was driving.

"She's Aboriginal," she said about the quiet driver. "Just as you can see for yourself. Their story isn't so great at all. She was kidnapped from her own family and community and put somewhere else so she could be *australized*. They took away her beliefs, culture, language, and also made it impossible for her to learn the truth. They believed they were all savages."

"I guess that today the situation is a little different," I asked, stunned by the fact that those things had happened in the recent past of Australia, a modern and advanced Western country.

"Partly, but it is still very bad," she said. "For example, the other day we were together in a movie theater, a lady asked me what I wanted to eat and drink, and didn't even look at her."

"You're shitting me!" I exclaimed.

"Unfortunately not," she replied. "Racism is still very much alive in Australia, I have cases like that in my own family."

"How come you don't think like that?" I asked curiously, wanting to hear her answer, her reason. I wanted to hear as many stories as possible from people who lived differently from their environment and try to draw some kind of conclusion, a recipe for treating prejudice.

"I was thirteen," she said without hesitation. "I'd just started going to high school, the kids I met there came from different parts of the world. There were the Whites, Chinese, people from Papua New Guinea, Aborigines. And when my two best friends hurt me, two Aboriginal girls were the first ones to approach me and made me feel loved and wanted. Since then, I felt like one of them, and once I had mastered the language and learned about the culture, they treated me as one of their own."

Experience may be the best cure for prejudice. Too bad it can't be purchased in a pharmacy without a prescription.

We arrived at the destination, I said goodbye to the girls and continued with the waiting game. There weren't so many cars and it was getting darker.

As I avoided hitchhiking at night, I was slowly getting ready for my second Australian night in the open. Just like in Sydney, that night wasn't going to be under the stars because the clouds had been following me for several days. One of the reasons why I was nervous before starting this long road trip across the continent was because I was afraid of sleeping in the desert due to the wildlife. Since I was currently in a semi-residential area, and still far from anything that would be annoyed by my presence in its territory, my mind was at ease.

"Here's the last car that I'll try to hitch," I said, talking to myself, just after the scarce road lighting had been turned on, noticing a slow truck in the distance.

It started slowing down. It pulled over.

"Where are you headed for?" The driver asked suspiciously, eyeing me from head to toe. There were two guys with cowboy hats inside.

"To the west," I replied and smiled.

"If you don't mind riding in the back part of the pick-up, get in!" He threw back his head and closed the window.

Without saying a word, I simply put my stuff on the truck and hopped on, gently tapping on the rear window to give the signal that I was ready to go, just like back then in Thailand.

I wasn't sure how far they were going, the closest city was at least sixty miles away, but it didn't matter. It was important to move in the right direction. For a while, I was sitting, leaned against the passenger's side of the cabin, but soon I got wrapped up in my sleeping bag to protect me from the wind. I was lying still, watching the sky.

Then the magic happened. The clouds that were following me for the past few days disappeared as if swept away by an invisible hand and the starry sky gradually became visible above me. The stars seemed so close, as if I could touch them, with the Southern Cross, the counterpart of the Great Bear in the southern hemisphere, shining over on my right.

The amazing beauty above me filled me with incredible happiness.

"I'm happy!" I said it out loud, looking at the stars.

I repeated once again, word by word. I. Am. Happy.

I waited a moment, just to see whether a *but* would sneak in after any of those sentences. It didn't happen.

I thought of Chloe and I realized why I was so madly in love with her all those years. From the first moment she arrived in Zagreb, I could see in her eyes something I didn't have, something I wanted, something I was striving for. She embodied everything I thought someone must have in order to be completely happy - she was free, independent, self-confident. Self-sufficient. She didn't need anyone else to be happy, smiling, or fulfilled. She was completely happy with her life. She didn't give a fuck about other people and their opinions.

I was never quite able to achieve that. Being alone and happy. This is exactly why I wanted her for the most part. I wanted her to give me a little of what she had, to teach me how to be like her. To teach me how to be alone and happy.

There was this one thing that didn't let me break away from her, from this brutally strong sense of attachment. The realization that she still had something that I didn't have. This ability to be happy with herself.

This is exactly what I experienced, perhaps for the first time in my life, in the back of the truck, under that starry sky in the Australian desert. I finally loved my life. There were no *buts*. I started to love myself. I felt worthy to be part of something big, something infinite. Most importantly, I was sure that nobody could do me any harm.

I was happy. Alone and happy.

I couldn't take the smile off my face, I was on top of the world. I was filled with an invisible energy that brought me where I was and that opened my eyes and allowed for this experience.

I realized that this was exactly what I was looking for from the beginning of the trip, perhaps even earlier. This sense of self-sufficiency. Empowered by this feeling, I realized that the chapter with Chloe was now finally closed. That I could move on in peace, without her in my mind. That I was free, after all these years.

I laughed out loud once again. I had to go thousands and thousands of miles away to find what had been there the whole time. Myself.

In this moment of sheer happiness, the truck started to slow down. I looked around me. There was no sign of civilization. We were out in the middle of nowhere. I remembered how I had thought that the two drivers had looked at me strangely. I remembered all the horror stories I had heard about hitchhikers disappearing all over Australia. I thought of my mother, who may not get another message from her prodigal son.

I reached for my pocket knife that was somewhere at the bottom of the backpack, but I didn't have enough time to grab it before the truck stopped. I could hear the driver opening his door, and a moment later, the passenger opened his door too.

Day 1000

Fortunately, the cowboys had only pulled over because they needed to take a piss.

"Yes, there were some negative moments," I briefly replied. "But I needed them because something nice would always follow. I was sick, but my joy after I got better was much more intense. I was robbed, but thanks to the little things that came after, I didn't sweat it too much. I was lonely, but then I would always meet someone who made having endured that loneliness worthwhile."

"Would you travel this way if you were a girl?" One girl asked.

"I find it hard to answer this question, for the obvious reason," I said. "But I know a lot of girls who travel solo, hitchhiking. And they wouldn't do it any other way. Being women, they wouldn't change their autonomy and freedom for anything in the world. Of course, a girl traveling solo will inevitably need to be a little more careful than a guy, but if they use common sense and logic, there shouldn't be a problem."

Many of my female friends said they found traveling alone more dangerous, but also much simpler. Drivers would rather pull over for a girl than for a guy, worried about their own safety. CS hosts are more open to hosting women than men, so they can find accommodation pretty quickly. However, they need to be more cautious.

"Which is the least expensive country in which to travel?" an elderly lady wanted to know.

"From my experience, in fact there's no difference between the budget for a trip in a very cheap destination, such as India, or a very expensive destination, such as Australia," I replied. "You only change your travel style."

"What do you mean?" she asked.

"It's very simple," I continued. "For starters, if you're traveling by classical methods, with a travel company, it will definitely be more expensive in more expensive countries, and cheaper in cheaper countries. That's obvious. But if you are using unconventional, alternative methods, the situation may be somewhat different."

"In more expensive places, including North America, Europe and Australia, public transport is so expensive that you are forced to avoid it, so you instead try alternative ways of traveling such as hitchhiking, walking, and cycling. You might possibly use public transport while traveling within major cities, although you can try fare dodging to save some money, instead of paying for the overpriced tram, bus and train tickets. In less expensive countries in South America, Africa and Asia, public transport is fairly cheap, so spending a few dollars to get to a remote destination doesn't seem like such a big expense. On top of this, alternative methods are really difficult to use if most people don't understand what hitchhiking is all about. If they, the poor locals, can pay for the transportation, why shouldn't you, as a rich white tourist, be able to pay for your ride? This is how they see it, of course. Furthermore, hitchhiking is quite common in some parts of the world, but then you are expected to share part of the cost with the driver. Walking and cycling are also less frequent, primarily due to the unsafe road conditions and drivers not paying attention to what's around them. So the conclusion is: in expensive countries you won't be spending on transportation, in less expensive countries you probably will. It won't be much, but the sum will grow over time."

"Now let me tell you something about the accommodation," I continued. "In expensive countries, the accommodation is generally so expensive that you really have to think whether to pay a few dozen dollars for a small room in a hostel, since this is the minimum for a relatively decent standard of accommodation. There are also other options, such as Couchsurfing. You'll find more potential hosts in more developed parts of the world. You can sleep where homeless people go, in night shelters, squats, and at different resorts, you can try house sitting, home exchange and stuff like that. In cheap countries, the accommodation will be inexpensive. You can find a place to sleep for just a couple of dollars. And let's not be stingy - from time to time, treat yourself and stay in a decent hotel or apartment. Couchsurfing is not so popular in inexpensive countries and the streets are often unsafe, so it wouldn't be too pleasant to sleep there. So my conclusion is that in expensive countries, you will have a greater choice of alternative ways of finding a place to sleep, while in cheaper countries paying for a hotel room might be the most convenient solution and not so expensive. It won't be much, but the sum will eventually grow.

As far as the cost of food is concerned, in expensive countries it's a good idea to avoid restaurants in all shapes and sizes. You can either go hungry, which isn't such a bad way to get in shape and lose a few pounds, or buy groceries and cook for yourself, either in your host's kitchen or using your own portable stove. In more extreme cases, you might opt for *dumpster diving*. In cheap countries you can eat in restaurants or on the street, even when you have a place to cook - you will come to realize that it's actually cheaper to eat out than buy ready-made food. Those meals won't be expensive and they'll be local, which will be an extra reason for you to start exploring the local cuisine. As for any leftovers, in poor countries there aren't many. Even if there are some, they'll find their way to people who are hungry. And a rich tourist definitely isn't at the top of the list for this. So my conclusion is that even though food is much cheaper in cheap countries, it is possible to spend less in expensive countries."

All in all, it's not that difficult to level up expenses in cheap and expensive countries, it all depends on how much effort you put in. In less expensive countries, you will definitely be much more relaxed when it comes to sticking to your budget. But in expensive countries you'll have the opportunity to earn some money, and this is something you can just forget when you're traveling through poor countries.

"What comes after all this? What are you going to do after your trip around the world? Are you going back to your job as a stockbroker?" A young man asked.

"I doubt it," I smiled. "My plan was to devote myself to promoting my first book and pay off the rest of my debt. At the same time, I'm trying not to plan too much in advance, because plans result in expectations, and expectations inevitably lead to disappointment."

"When is your second book coming out?" my friend Zvone asked from the front row. I would stay at his place whenever I was in Split and he was one of the first people to get a copy of my first book.

"Who knows," I replied. "I've just finished the first one, so hold fire for the time being. If everything goes according to plan, it should come out in a year or two."

I didn't even want to think about writing another book, even though my first book had ended at the most interesting point: setting off on a trip around the world. I knew that I would definitely write a sequel and that the title would be *1000 Days of Summer*, but I still didn't know the rest.

"We've got time for one more question," I said after the librarian pointed at her watch.

"After everything you've said here today, is there one thing that you would credit for everything you've experienced?" This question came from the back of the hall.

"That's a difficult one," I said, pausing for a moment. "Of course, many factors played a role - curiosity, light-headedness, different coincidences and stubbornness. So yeah, I think I have the answer, in the form of a question that I asked myself a long time ago, and that is: *What would you do if you knew you could not fail?* I think that everybody should ask themselves that question, answer it and then stick to it, accept it and be confident that you'll succeed, accept it in such a way that failure is never an option. I think that this way of thinking, along with being proactive, lead to all the situations I have experienced in recent years."

"Just to make it doubly clear," I said, "it doesn't have to be traveling. It could be a hundred things, but most importantly, you must believe in your plan. When I asked myself that question, my answer was traveling the world. Ask yourself this question and see where it takes you.

Thank you all for coming!" I said, taking a bow.

The hall erupted into loud applause. This was my moment. I was standing in front of them all, keeping quiet and enjoying the sound of their clapping.

I sat down, and people started to approach me to buy the book. We exchanged smiles, I wrote a few words, signed it and once again thanked them for coming.

"Let's go down to the waterfront!" Zvone said, after waiting patiently for the audience to go home.

"Sure, a cold beer is just what I need!" I replied.

We left the library and went to the harbor in a much-needed silence after nearly two hours of continuous talking.

We were passing by Diocletian's Palace, when I noticed a familiar face in the crowd. I immediately bowed my head, hoping that he wouldn't see me. It was no use. He caught my eye despite the crowds on the Split waterfront.

"Hey, Tom!" He approached me, surprised. "What are you doing here?"

"Well, I had a lecture here, in the library, promoting my book," I replied, looking him in the eye, but also looking around to see her. "And what are you doing here?"

"I'm getting married the day after tomorrow," he replied, with a big smile on his face.

"Congratulations!" I said sincerely. I knew he was getting married, but I didn't know when or where. "How is she?"

"She's fine," he said. "We're a little overcome by the wedding, but it's all fine. We're happy."

"I'm really glad to hear that," I said, patting him on the shoulder. "Say hi to you future wife. I wish you all the luck in the world, you both deserve it."

"Thanks! Good luck to you too!" he replied and went away.

"Who was that guy?" Zvone asked.

"Believe it or not, that was Tanja's fiancé," I replied. "I met him in London. He's a great guy, a Colombian, I heard from mutual friends that Tanja has been with him for a while now, but apparently they've decided to get married."

"Can you believe it?" Zvone replied. "And you bumped into him this very day, in Split."

"Yeah," I said. "This very day, exactly a thousand days since I set off on my trip around the world."

"Unbelievable," he concluded.

"But this isn't the biggest coincidence regarding Tanja," I remembered. "Besides ending up in Split, her hometown, on day 1000 of my trip around the world, and bumping into her fiancé two days before their wedding, there's another, even better story, an even more incredible coincidence. Just before I left London to set off on my trip around the world, she had told me that she would join me on day 500, exactly halfway through the journey, leaving her job, London, everything, to be with me. When that day came, I was somewhere in Tanzania. Although we'd broken up long before, of all the coincidences, I realized that day 500, when Tanja had wanted to join me fell exactly on her thirtieth birthday."

"You're shitting me!" Zvone said, shocked.

"Trust me, pal," I said. "I counted it more than once, I couldn't believe it either. But hey, it's just a coincidence. I have no idea how or why. The universe can play tricks on us sometimes."

We bought a couple of beers and sat down by the waterfront.

I took out my cell phone and started to read the e-mail that was waiting for me.

Hey T.

I arrived in Jindabyne a few hours ago. I live in an apartment next to the one where we were together. The bedroom is opposite my old bedroom. It's been two years. It's been so long since we last saw each other. Two meters, one wall and a lifetime away from where I'm lying right now.

I remember that moment when you were leaving, sad because I had said I wanted you to leave. You have to know that it wasn't because I didn't want to have you around, I wanted to be alone, for my own sake. It had nothing to do with you. Loneliness is a part of me, it refreshes me, it lifts me up. And I will always need it. I told you this so many times, but you never listened. Or you didn't understand. I understand how this could happen. I'm sorry if I caused you all this pain, but I was also hurt in the whole story. Don't think that I didn't feel the pain, that it was easy for me.

Do you know the TV series Sex and the City? It says that we all have three great loves in our lives. I pretty much agree with that, but I think that those three loves are quite different. I learned to accept that you were, remained, and that you always will be - the love of my life. For me it was love at first sight. The one that songs are written about. The one that time stands still for. Late nights and sore tummies and everything that the stories say. It was a fantasy. Which is exactly why it couldn't work out. Not in real life. I spent so much time waiting for your illusion of me to disappear. The illusion based on a girl that you briefly met a few years earlier, and which prevented you from loving my bad sides too. The girl you met a long ago didn't have any bad sides. But I have a bunch of them. I'm brutally honest. Independent. I long for solitude. I don't like to explain myself to others. I have spent my life assuming that people won't like me and it always comes as a surprise when they proved me wrong. I needed something real from you. I wanted to know that you would love me when I was shitty, when life got shitty, when everything around us was shitty. I wanted to be with someone who didn't need me, who was doing just fine without me, to realize that I did just fine without him.

When I was with you, I would often be at my worst, just to see if you could handle it. We both had so much more to learn, but I couldn't learn with you. I couldn't walk through life behind you, in your shadow, and I think you were expecting that. Someone who will follow you with gusto. But I can only follow myself.

Do you remember when we were driving across Thailand, along the border with Burma, in the car with that drunk driver? It was the moment at which I felt the most connected to you. I remember you said that you would drive because I told you I was afraid. That was the time you really listened to me. I never loved you more than then.

Did you write a book? Am I in it? I hope you wrote nice things about me. You'll have to send me a copy, so I can see what you wrote. When will it be translated? You have my address.

I'm so glad that our lives intertwined. I think we learned a lot from each other. I was one of the many who inspired you to search inside yourself and find your way. Or get lost looking for it. I showed you how to be alone, how to be silly, how to grab the world and make it your own. Do you know what I learned from you? That somebody can love me. That someone can love me so much that he was ready to turn the whole world upside down. That someone can look into my eyes and see the oceans, clouds, mountains and - himself. Thank you for that. It was amazing to learn that.

<3, Chloe.

I took another sip of beer and leaned on my elbows. The summer had come to an end, even if the astronomical summer had yet to start. It was June and a thousand days of spring and a thousand days of summer were behind me. The time has come for a thousand days of fall.

I inhaled deeply, exhaled, looked up at the sky and a few stars. And now what, I wondered?

I smiled in disbelief.

I just saw a shooting star.

POSTSCRIPT

So, you have reached the end of my book. I hope you liked it.

It was interesting to write these books about my life, to expose myself, knowing that many people would read them, and learn so much about me. But this was the only way to write these books. Although I have left some things out, or some people, insights, and feelings, I'm sure you'll understand - I need to keep something to myself. All the stories I share with all of you stop being mine in a way. They become yours, ours, everybody's. If I revealed everything - what would you have left to discover yourself?

These stories aren't so important, after all. Everyone can experience what I've experienced while traveling. The cool thing about this book and my travel writing in general is that there is nothing special in it. The hero is a guy who took his backpack and started to travel. There are literally millions of people who do the same thing. And their stories are wonderfully inspirational too. But the same goes for the stories of people who didn't travel, but who were just doing the same thing as me - following their dreams.

Finally, I'd like to thank some people.

My Mom and Dad, who bravely pulled through my wanderings, for their endless support. I would like to give special thanks to them for their life of dedication to my brother and me. For being the epitome of selflessness. Unfortunately, my Dad didn't live to see this book published. He passed away a few months ago, from lung cancer.

My brother Filip, who, together with my parents, made me the person I am today. Of course he didn't plan it - just in case he tries to beat me over the head with what I just wrote.

My aunts Crna and Nada, who have been my second mothers since I was born.

All my relatives - my grandmothers, my aunts and uncles, all my cousins. I only realized your importance while traveling the world.

My friends, my ex-roommate Marin, everyone mentioned in my two books - you know who you are.

Everyone whom I didn't mention in these two books, but who

played a role in my life - you know who you are.

My editor Maja, without whom my books wouldn't be what they are. If you don't like them, feel free to blame her.

My Maria, without whom these two books probably wouldn't exist. Thanks for being there.

All my faithful followers on Facebook, blog readers, those of you who come to my lectures. If it hadn't been for you, who knows what my travels would be like. You gave me so much, maybe more than I gave you.

If you ever want to ask me a question, feel free to contact me at tomislav@tomislavperko.com.

And so it goes. Thanks again. Live. Laugh. Love. And always ask yourself the question - what would you do if you knew you could not fail?

See you in the fall, T.

ABOUT THE AUTHOR

Born in Zagreb, Croatia, on 6 April 1985.

The rest can be read in the book 1000 Days of Spring and the book that you're holding in your hands right now.

Special thanks to those who generously supported the publication of this book:

- **PIVOVARA I PIVNICA MEDVEDGRAD** - a brewery and beer hall with the best beer and a relaxed atmosphere in the center of Zagreb

- **QATAR AIRWAYS** - the best companion to explore the world with

- **JUICE AND JUICE BAR, Masarykova 26** - the most delicious and healthiest juices in this part of the galaxy

- **HOMEEXCHANGE.COM** - the world's biggest home exchange community

- **GABRIJELA and FILIP PERKO**

- **MARKO MIŠULIĆ, Rentlio**

- **MATIJA BABIĆ, index.hr**

- **MARCELO KAWAMINAMI**

- **HERMAN DIERCKX**

- **and all of you who contributed to my crowdfunding campaign - you know who you are!**

Thank you, T.

Going places together

Every moment of your time together is precious. That's why we're dedicated to providing a premium service from the minute you check in, to the moment you land in any of the more than 150 places we fly to worldwide. Together, we can create experiences to cherish and memories that last a lifetime.

 qatarairways.com

QATAR AIRWAYS القطرية

GOING PLACES TOGETHER

Few reviews of "1000 Days of Spring":

Some genuine storytelling and emotions were put into writing this book and this is what every reader will be able to recognise. As soon as I saw this project on a crowdfunding platform, I instantly wanted to participate in publishing Tomislav's story; because I love to travel in such manner by myself (CS), and out of sheer curiosity. I was not disappointed with this title, I hope that it will reach as many people out there who want to be inspired to travel in such way, but are looking for that extra motivational push. Highly recommended!

Bojan

I've read a few travel-related books and ended up being disappointed, but this book is different. Tom wrote literally everything - good and bad part of his stories, his feelings, the lessons he got - and I love his honesty. I always believe that by telling the whole story we can get the most of it, and he proved it. And this book is also easy to read, I enjoyed reading it and I could have finished it in a day.

David K.

Excellent book!!!!!!! The author has given us an even greater desire to travel and and wider perspective what the world offers to us! :)

Tom G.

I can't recommend this book enough. The story was beautifully written and flows easily from one day (chapter) to the next. The authors glass half full perspective is also a refreshing addition to the story. His observations throughout his travels will have you questioning your own perspectives on life as well as peoples every day habits. He hits some tough topics and will force you to see perceive them in an unbiased view. All these things and more really make the book a good read

David

MIRKO PERKO (1956. - 2016.)